PRESENTED TO:

____

FROM:

____

DATE:

____

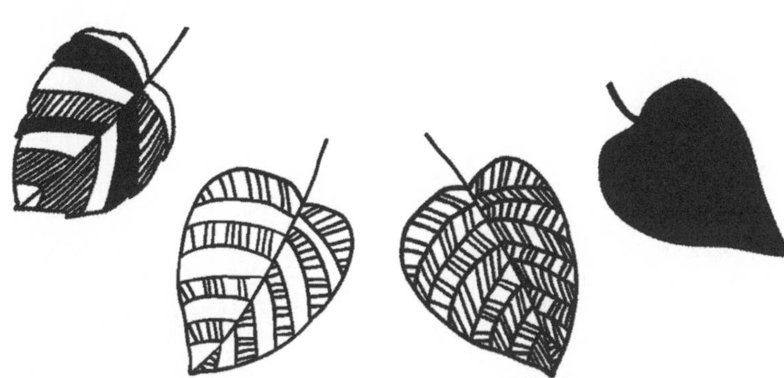

MAX LUCADO

GOD IS WITH YOU *every day*

365 - DAY DEVOTIONAL

THOMAS NELSON
Since 1798

God Is with You Every Day

Published in Nashville, Tennessee, by Thomas Nelson. Thomas Nelson is a registered trademark of HarperCollins Christian Publishing, Inc.

Thomas Nelson titles may be purchased in bulk for educational, business, fund-raising, or sales promotional use. For information, please e-mail *SpecialMarkets@ThomasNelson.com.*

Devotionals and prayers taken from previously published material in *Before Amen*; *God's Story, Your Story*; *Outlive Your Life*; *Grace*; *Glory Days*; *For the Tough Times*; *On the Anvil*; *In the Manger*; *Pocket Prayers*; and *On Calvary's Hill.*

ISBN-13: 978-1-4002-0996-5

Printed in China

19 20 21 22 23 GRI 6 5 4 3 2 1

JANUARY

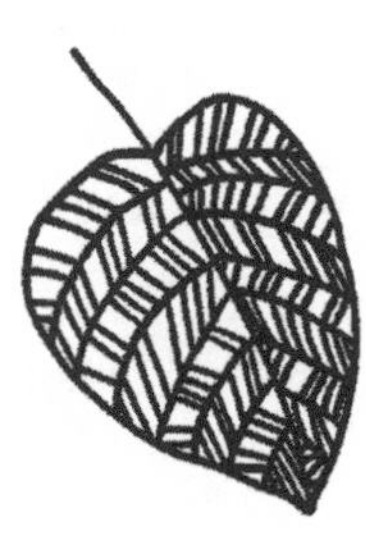

JANUARY 1

A Prayer . . . of Praise

Oh, give thanks to the Lord! Call upon His name; make known His deeds among the peoples! Sing to Him, sing psalms to Him; talk of all His wondrous works!

1 CHRONICLES 16:8–9

Father, you are so worthy of it all—my attention, praise, worship, and love. Your works are amazing, beyond anything I can even express.

Help me be a light that shines toward you today. It is often hard for me to stand out from the world and be different. Give me the courage to make your goodness known and to never be ashamed.

Please give peace to my friends who are standing up for you and as a result have found themselves friendless or with few who understand them.

I thank you for your wonderful works and all that you have done and will do.

In the glorious name of Jesus Christ, amen.

–*Pocket Prayers*

Today I Will . . .

Be very careful, then, how you live—not as unwise but as wise, making the most of every opportunity, because the days are evil.
EPHESIANS 5:15–16 NIV

Today I will make a difference. I will begin by controlling my thoughts. A person is the product of his thoughts. I want to be happy and hopeful. Therefore, I will have thoughts that are happy and hopeful. I refuse to be victimized by my circumstances. Optimism will be my companion, and victory will be my hallmark. Today I will make a difference.

I will be grateful for the twenty-four hours that are before me. Time is a precious commodity. I refuse to allow what little time I have to be contaminated by self-pity, anxiety, or boredom. I will face this day with the joy of a child and the courage of a giant. While it is here, I will use it for loving and giving. Today I will make a difference.

I will not let past failures haunt me. Even though my life is scarred with mistakes, I refuse to rummage through my trash heap of failures. I will admit them. I will correct them. I will press on. Victoriously. No failure is fatal. It's okay to stumble. . . . I will get up. It's okay to fail. . . . I will rise again. Today I will make a difference.

I will spend time with those I love. My spouse, my children, my family. Today I will spend at least five minutes with the significant people in my world. Five *quality* minutes of talking or hugging or thanking or listening.

Today I will make a difference.

–*On the Anvil*

JANUARY 3

Be About His Business

"Did you not know that I must be about My Father's business?"
LUKE 2:49

Time on God's anvil should clarify our mission and define our purpose. When a tool emerges from a blacksmith's anvil, there is no question as to what it is for. There is no question as to why it was made. One look at the tool and you instantly know its function.

As a human emerges from the anvil of God, the same should be true. Being tested by God reminds us that our function and task is to be about his business, that our purpose is to be an extension of his nature, an ambassador of his throne room, and a proclaimer of his message. We should exit the shop with no question as to why God made us. We know our purpose.

We are God's people, and we are to be about his business.

If we live our lives in this way, then we can enter our final years with the assurance of knowing that life was well spent and that heaven is but a wink away.

And is there any greater reward than this?

–*On the Anvil*

Stay in Your Own Lane

Stir up the gift of God which is in you.
2 TIMOTHY 1:6

A little boy named Adam wanted to be like his friend Bobby. Adam loved the way Bobby walked and talked. Bobby, however, wanted to be like Charlie. Something about Charlie's stride and accent intrigued him. Charlie, on the other hand, was impressed with Danny. Charlie wanted to look and sound like Danny. Danny, of all things, had a hero as well: Adam. He wanted to be just like Adam.

So Adam was imitating Bobby, who was imitating Charlie, who was imitating Danny, who was imitating Adam.

Turns out, all Adam had to do was be himself.[1]

Stay in your own lane. Run your own race. Nothing good happens when you compare and compete. God does not judge you according to the talents of others. He judges you according to yours. His yardstick for measuring faithfulness is how faithful you are with your own gifts. You are not responsible for the nature of your gift. But you are responsible for how you use it.

–*Glory Days*

JANUARY 5

Your Assignment

There are different kinds of gifts, but the same Spirit distributes them. There are different kinds of service, but the same Lord. There are different kinds of working, but in all of them and in everyone it is the same God at work.

1 CORINTHIANS 12:4–6 NIV

Stir up the gift of God which is *in you*" (2 Timothy 1:6, emphasis mine). You be you. Don't be your parents or grandparents. You can admire them, appreciate them, and learn from them. But you cannot be them. You aren't them. "Don't compare yourself with others. Each of you must take responsibility for doing the creative best you can with your own life" (Galatians 6:4–5 MSG).

Jesus was insistent on this. After the resurrection he appeared to some of his followers. He gave Peter a specific pastoral assignment that included great sacrifice. The apostle responded by pointing at John and saying, "'Lord, what about him?' Jesus answered, 'If I want him to live until I come back, that is not your business. You follow me'" (John 21:21–22 NCV).

In other words, don't occupy yourself with another person's assignment; stay focused on your own.

–Glory Days

Unimpeachable Authority

He sustains everything by the mighty power of his command.
HEBREWS 1:3 NLT

Jesus has unimpeachable authority.

The Roman government tried to intimidate him. False religion tried to silence him. The Devil tried to kill him. All failed. Even "death was no match for him" (Acts 2:24 MSG).

He was not kidding when he declared, "All authority in heaven and on earth has been given to me" (Matthew 28:18 NIV). Jesus is the command center of the galaxies. He occupies the Oval Office. He called a coin out of the mouth of a fish. He stopped the waves with a word. He spoke, and a tree withered. He spoke again, and a basket became a banquet. Economy. Meteorology. Botany. Food supply. "All things have been handed over to me by my Father" (Matthew 11:27 NRSV).

That includes Satan. The Devil was soundly defeated by Christ on the cross. Jesus outranks him in every situation. He must obey Jesus, and he knows it. Prayers offered in the name of Jesus have "divine power to demolish strongholds" (2 Corinthians 10:4 NIV). Demolish! Not damage or hamper but demolish.

Satan setting up a stronghold in your life? Lift up a prayer and unleash the demolition power of Jesus.

–Before Amen

JANUARY 7

God's Goal for You

Work hard to show the results of your salvation, obeying God with deep reverence and fear. For God is working in you, giving you the desire and the power to do what pleases him.

PHILIPPIANS 2:12–13 NLT

Envision the day you stand before Jesus and look back over your life. "God will give to each one whatever praise is due" (1 Corinthians 4:5 NLT). Your Savior will declare the final outcome of your life:

"With God's help John Doe took on the enemies of his Promised Land and drove them out.

"Greed!

"Explosive temper!

"Envy!

"Abused as a child yet stable as an adult.

"Tempted with drugs yet sober and steady.

"Strayed off course yet returned with vigor."

One by one the conquests will be read and celebrated.

Every witness will rejoice at the work God did. This is God's goal for you. This is your inheritance: more victory than defeat, more joy than sadness, more hope than despair.

–*Glory Days*

JANUARY 8 

A Prayer . . . to Shine

"Let your light so shine before men, that they may see your good works and glorify your Father in heaven."
MATTHEW 5:16

Heavenly Father, work in my life in such a way that people will see you shining forth. Help me to break free from the selfishness and sin that prevent me from being conformed to your image and expressing your holiness. In Jesus' name, amen.

–*On Calvary's Hill*

JANUARY 9

Live a Stirring Life

Do everything without grumbling or arguing, so that you may become blameless and pure, "children of God without fault in a warped and crooked generation." Then you will shine among them like stars in the sky as you hold firmly to the word of life.

PHILIPPIANS 2:14–16 NIV

Each of us should lead a life stirring enough to start a movement. We should yearn to change the world. We should love unquenchably, dream unfalteringly, and work unceasingly.

We should close our ears to the manifold voices of compromise and perch ourselves on the branch of truth. We should champion the value of people, proclaim the forgiveness of God, and claim the promise of heaven.

And we should lead a life stirring enough to cause a movement.

A movement comes of age when one life harvests the seeds planted by countless lives in previous generations. A movement occurs when one person, no greater or lesser than those who have gone before, lives a forceful life in the fullness of time.

Let's live lives stirring and forceful enough to cause a movement. A true mark of the visionary is his willingness to lay down his life for those whom he'll never see.

Will the movement come in our generation? I hope so. But even if it doesn't, even if we never see it, it will occur. And we'll be part of it.

–*On the Anvil*

Ask for Hebron

When doubts filled my mind, your comfort
gave me renewed hope and cheer.
PSALM 94:19 NLT

T*urn a deaf ear to doubters.* Ignore the naysayers. People have a right to say what they want. And you have a right to ignore them.

When the twelve spies reported back to Moses, all but Caleb and Joshua were spouting doubt (Numbers 13:26–33). They were outnumbered ten to two, but they still believed in God's power. Let's take our cue from Caleb. Disregard the lethal disbelief of cynics.

This is no sanction for rudeness or isolation. When people express their sincere struggles or questions, help them. But some folks do not want to be helped. They would rather pull you down than let you pull them up. Don't let them.

Caleb didn't. He filled his mind with faith and took on a God-size challenge.

When Moses sent Caleb to spy out the land, Caleb saw something that troubled him: the town of Hebron. Abraham had buried his wife there. He was buried there. So were Isaac, Rebekah, and Jacob.

Hebron was a sacred site, but it was inhabited by unholy people. So Caleb asked Moses for Hebron.

Moses took the request to God, and Caleb was given the land. Forty-five years later, at the age of eighty-five, the old soldier chased the enemy out and reclaimed the city.

Caleb wanted to do something great for God. He lived with a higher call. You can too. Ask for your Hebron.

–*Glory Days*

JANUARY 11

Wait for the Nudge

Since we are living by the Spirit, let us follow the Spirit's leading in every part of our lives.

GALATIANS 5:25 NLT

Is there anything in your life that needs to be removed? Any impediment to the impression of God's Spirit? We can grieve the Spirit with our angry words (Ephesians 4:29–30; Isaiah 63:10) and resist the Spirit in our disobedience (Acts 7:51). We can even quench the Spirit by having no regard for God's teachings.

Here is something that helps me stay in step with the Spirit. We know that the "fruit of the Spirit is love, joy, peace, patience, kindness, goodness, faithfulness, gentleness, self-control" (Galatians 5:22–23 NASB). God's Spirit creates and distributes these characteristics. They are indicators on my spiritual dashboard. So whenever I sense them, I know I am walking in the Spirit. Whenever I lack them, I know I am out of step with the Spirit.

To walk in the Spirit, respond to the promptings God gives you.

Don't sense any nudging? Just be patient and wait. Abraham waited for the promised son. Moses waited forty years in the wilderness. Jesus waited thirty years before he began his ministry. God instills seasons of silence in his plan. Winter is needed for the soil to bear fruit. Time is needed for the development of a crop. And disciples wait for the move of God. Wait for him to move, nudge, and direct you.

–*God's Story, Your Story*

JANUARY 12 

A SPIRITUAL BATTLE

For we do not wrestle against flesh and blood, but against principalities, against powers, against the rulers of the darkness of this age, against spiritual hosts of wickedness in the heavenly places.
EPHESIANS 6:12

For a book about conquests, the book of Joshua sure skimps on military details. What weapons did Joshua's army use? How many officers did his army have? The answer to these and other questions? We don't know.

We don't know because the emphasis is not on a physical battle but a spiritual one. The real conflict wasn't with Canaanites or Amorites; it was with Satan and his demons.

Canaan was the choicest real estate on earth. It was marked by fertile fields and valleys. Most important, the land was God's gift to Israel (Genesis 12:7).

God set this property apart for his people and his people apart to be a blessing for the world. God promised Abram, "I will make you a great nation" (v. 2). The Hebrews were the couriers of God's covenant to a galaxy of people. Israel was the parchment on which God's redemption story would be written.

Satan's counterstrategy was clear: contaminate the Promised Land and preempt the Promised Child. Destroy God's people and destroy God's work.

Joshua's battle, then, was a spiritual one.

So is ours.

–*Glory Days*

JANUARY 13

The Discovery That Changes Everything

"For I know the plans I have for you," declares the Lord, "plans to prosper you and not to harm you, plans to give you hope and a future."
JEREMIAH 29:11 NIV

You are in the hands of a living, loving God. Random collection of disconnected short stories? Far from it. Your life is a crafted narrative written by a good God, who is working toward your supreme good.

God is not slipshod or haphazard. He planned creation according to a calendar. He determined the details of salvation "before the foundation of the world" (1 Peter 1:20). The death of Jesus was not an afterthought, nor was it Plan B or an emergency operation. Jesus died "when the set time had fully come" (Galatians 4:4 NIV), according to God's "deliberate plan and foreknowledge" (Acts 2:23 NIV).

God isn't making up a plan as he goes along. Nor did he wind up the clock and walk away. "The Most High God rules the kingdom of mankind and sets over it whom he will" (Daniel 5:21 ESV). He "executes judgment, putting down one and lifting up another" (Psalm 75:7 ESV). "The Lord will not turn back until he has executed and accomplished the intentions of his mind" (Jeremiah 30:24 ESV). Look at those verbs: God *rules, sets, executes, accomplished.* These terms confirm the existence of heavenly blueprints and plans. Those plans include you. "In him we were also chosen, . . . according to the plan of him who works out everything in conformity with the purpose of his will" (Ephesians 1:11 NIV).

This discovery changes everything!

–*God's Story, Your Story*

A New Song

Oh, sing to the Lord a new song!
Sing to the Lord, all the earth.
Sing to the Lord, bless His name; . . .
For the Lord is great and greatly to be praised.
PSALM 96:1–4

God places a song in the hearts of his children. A song of hope and life. "He has put a new song in my mouth" (Psalm 40:3). Some saints sing this song loud and long every single day of their lives. In other cases the song falls silent. Life's hurts and happenings mute the music within. Long seasons pass in which God's song is not sung.

I want to be careful here. Truth is, we do not always know if someone has trusted God's grace.

A person may have feigned belief but not meant it. Judas is an example of one who seemed to have been saved but in truth was not. For three years he followed Christ. While the others were becoming apostles, he was becoming a tool of Satan. When Jesus said, "You are clean, though not every one of you" (John 13:10 NIV), he was referring to Judas, who possessed a fake faith.

Whether or not someone's faith is real isn't ours to know. But we know this: where there is genuine conversion, there is eternal salvation. Our task is to trust God's ability to call his children home.

We join God as he walks among his wayward and wounded children, singing.

Eventually his own will hear his voice, and something within them will awaken. And when it does, they will begin to sing again.

–Grace

JANUARY 15

A Prayer . . . to Live as Your Child

When the fullness of the time had come, God sent forth His Son, born of a woman, born under the law, to redeem those who were under the law, that we might receive the adoption as sons.

GALATIANS 4:4–5

Loving Father, your Son came into our broken world to redeem us from our sin and make a way for us to be adopted into your family. Thank you, Jesus, for paying the price, for I was helpless to pay it myself. Help me to live today as your child. In Jesus' name, amen.

–*In the Manger*

Who Are You?

Consider yourselves to be dead to the power of sin and alive to God.

ROMANS 6:11 NLT

Who are you?

I'm glad you asked.

You are:

- God's child (John 1:12),
- Christ's friend (John 15:15),
- a member of Christ's body (1 Corinthians 12:27),
- a saint (Ephesians 1:1),
- redeemed and forgiven of all your sins (Colossians 1:14),
- complete in Christ, lacking in nothing (Colossians 2:10),
- free from condemnation (Romans 8:1–2),
- God's coworker (2 Corinthians 6:1),
- seated with Christ in the heavenly realm (Ephesians 2:6),
- God's workmanship (Ephesians 2:10),
- a citizen of heaven (Philippians 3:20),
- adopted into God's family (Ephesians 1:5),
- born of God, and the evil one cannot touch you (1 John 5:18).

Get acquainted with your new self.

–*Glory Days*

JANUARY 17

What Will He Do with You?

"No man ever spoke like this Man!"
JOHN 7:46

Jesus claimed to be able to forgive sins—a privilege only God can exercise (Matthew 9:4–7). He claimed to be greater than Jonah, Solomon, Jacob, and even Abraham (Matthew 12:38–42; John 4:12–14; 8:53–56). Jesus commanded people to pray in his name (John 14:13–14). He claimed his words would outlive heaven and earth (Mark 13:31) and that all authority in heaven and on earth had been given to him (Matthew 28:18–20).

Does a decent fellow say things like this? No, but a demented fool does.

Maybe Jesus was a megalomaniac on par with Alexander the Great or Adolf Hitler. But, honestly, could a madman do what Jesus did?

Look at the devotion he inspired. People didn't just respect Jesus. They liked him; they left their homes and businesses and followed him. Men and women alike tethered their hope to his life. Impulsive people like Peter. Visionaries like Philip. Passionate men like John, careful men like Thomas, methodical men like Matthew the tax collector. When the men had left Jesus in the grave, it was the women who came to honor him—women from all walks of life, homemaking to philanthropy.

Jesus transformed common dockworkers and net casters into the authors of history's greatest book and founders of its greatest movement.

What will he do with you?

–*God's Story, Your Story*

Everyone Can Help Someone

"I was hungry and you gave Me food; I was thirsty and you gave Me drink; I was a stranger and you took Me in; I was naked and you clothed Me; I was sick and you visited Me; I was in prison and you came to Me."
MATTHEW 25:35–36

Many years ago I heard a woman discuss the work of Matthew 25:31–46. The event wasn't publicized. The audience was chatty and restless. Yet when she entered the room, all stirring stopped.

She wore her characteristic white Indian sari with a blue border that represented the Missionaries of Charity, the order she had founded in 1950. Her sixty-nine years had bent her already small frame. But there was nothing small about Mother Teresa's presence.

"Give me your unborn children," she offered. "Don't abort them. If you cannot raise them, I will. They are precious to God." Who would've ever pegged this slight Albanian woman as a change agent?

I wonder if God creates people like Mother Teresa so he can prove his point: "See, you can do something today that will outlive your life."

There are several billion reasons to consider his challenge. Some of them live in your neighborhood; others live in jungles you can't find and have names you can't pronounce. Some of them play in cardboard slums or sell sex on a busy street.

None of us can help everyone. But all of us can help someone. And when we help them, we serve Jesus.

Who would want to miss a chance to do that?

–*Outlive Your Life*

JANUARY 19

Voices of Failure

I waited patiently for the Lord to help me, and he turned to me and heard my cry. He lifted me out of the pit of despair, out of the mud and the mire. He set my feet on solid ground and steadied me as I walked along. He has given me a new song to sing, a hymn of praise to our God.

PSALM 40:1–3 NLT

Have you heard voices of failure? When you lost your job, flunked the exam, dropped out of school. When your marriage went south. When your business went broke. When you failed. The voices began to howl.

And you joined them!

Failure finds us all. Failure is so universal we have to wonder why more self-help gurus don't address it. Bookstores overflow with volumes on how to succeed. But you'll look a long time before you find a section called "How to Succeed at Failing."

Maybe no one knows what to say. But God does. His book is written for failures. It is full of folks who were foul-ups and flops. David was a moral failure, yet God used him. Elijah was an emotional train wreck after Mount Carmel, but God blessed him. Jonah was in the belly of a fish when he prayed his most honest prayer, and God heard it.

Perfect people? No. Perfect messes? You bet. Yet God used them. A surprising and welcome discovery of the Bible is this: God uses failures.

–*Glory Days*

The Final Word

"The Son of Man has power on earth to forgive sins."

MARK 2:10

If you are in Christ, your sin is gone. It was last seen on the back of your Sin Bearer as he headed out to Death Valley. When Jesus cried on the cross, "My God, my God, why have you forsaken me?" (Matthew 27:46 NIV), he entered the wilderness on your behalf. He carried your sin away.

He has the final word on your life. And his word is *grace.*

Jesus did his part. Now do yours.

Give God your guilt. Tell Jesus what you did. Hold nothing back. Be abundant in your confession, and . . .

Be concrete in your confession. Go into as much detail as you can. Healing happens when the wound is exposed to the atmosphere of grace.

Exactly what is it that you need forgiveness for? For being a bad person? That is too general. For losing your patience and calling your coworker a creep? There, you can confess that. Confession, you see, is not a punishment for sin; it is an isolation of sin so it can be exposed and extracted.

Be firm in this prayer. Satan traffics in guilt. So tell his guilt where to get off. Speak to it in the name of Jesus. "I left you at the foot of the cross, you evil spirit. Stay there!"

And, for heaven's sake, stop tormenting yourself. Jesus is strong enough to carry your sin. Did he not say he would do so? Believe him! He has the final word.

–*Before Amen*

JANUARY 21

Moved by Prayer

Now this is the confidence that we have in Him, that if we ask anything according to His will, He hears us.

1 JOHN 5:14

Let's pray, *first*. Traveling to help the hungry? Be sure to bathe your mission in prayer. Working to disentangle the knots of injustice? Pray. Weary of a world of racism and division? So is God. And he would love to talk to you about it.

Let's pray, *most*. Did God call us to preach without ceasing? Or teach without ceasing? Or have committee meetings without ceasing? Or sing without ceasing? No, but he did call us to "pray without ceasing" (1 Thessalonians 5:17).

Did Jesus declare: My house shall be called a house of study? Fellowship? Music? A house of exposition? A house of activities? No, but he did say, "My house will be called a house of prayer" (Mark 11:17 NIV).

No other spiritual activity is guaranteed such results. "When two of you get together on anything at all on earth and make a prayer of it, my Father in heaven goes into action" (Matthew 18:19 MSG). He is moved by the humble, prayerful heart.

He is moved by prayer.

—*Outlive Your Life*

A PRAYER . . . FOR STRENGTH

Be anxious for nothing, but in everything by prayer and supplication, with thanksgiving, let your requests be made known to God; and the peace of God, which surpasses all understanding, will guard your hearts and minds through Christ Jesus.

PHILIPPIANS 4:6–7

Dear Father, you are the Prince of Peace and the great I Am. You are my helper and my Redeemer.

I need your help today. I am weak and frail and tired. Give me the strength to get through just this day and the desire to work as if I am doing it all for your glory.

Help those who are carrying especially heavy burdens right now. They need your power and peace that goes beyond our understanding.

I am so grateful that I can come to you and present my requests at any time. Thank you for giving me peace and rest even in the hard times.

In the name of the Prince of Peace, I pray, amen.

–Pocket Prayers

JANUARY 23

Of Greater Worth than Gold

"I will refine them like silver
and test them like gold.
They will call on my name
and I will answer them;
I will say, 'They are my people,'
and they will say, 'The Lord is our God.'"
ZECHARIAH 13:9 NIV

With a strong forearm, the apron-clad blacksmith puts his tongs into the fire, grasps the heated metal, and places it on the anvil. His keen eye examines the glowing piece. He sees what the tool is now and envisions what he wants it to be. With a clear picture in his mind, he begins to pound.

On the solid anvil, the smoldering iron is remolded.

The smith knows the type of instrument he wants. He knows the size. He knows the shape. He knows the strength.

Whang! Whang! The hammer slams. The shop rings with noise, the air fills with smoke, and the softened metal responds.

But the response doesn't come easily. It doesn't come without discomfort. To melt down the old and recast it as new is a disrupting process. Yet the metal remains on the anvil, allowing the toolmaker to remove the scars, repair the cracks, refill the voids, and purge the impurities.

And with time, a change occurs: what was dull becomes sharpened, what was crooked becomes straight, what was weak becomes strong, and what was useless becomes valuable.

–*On the Anvil*

Your Best Weapon

God makes everything come out right;
he puts victims back on their feet.
PSALM 103:6 MSG

Satan has no recourse to your personal testimony. So your best weapon against his attacks is a good memory.

Don't forget a single one of God's blessings!
He forgives your sins—every one.
He heals your diseases—every one.
He redeems you from hell—saves your life!
He crowns you with love and mercy—a paradise crown.
He wraps you in goodness—beauty eternal.
He renews your youth—you're always young in his presence.

Create a trophy room in your heart. Each time you experience a victory, place a memory on the shelf. Before you face a challenge, take a quick tour of God's accomplishments. Look at all the paychecks he has provided, all the blessings he has given, all the prayers he has answered. Imitate the shepherd boy David. Before he fought Goliath, the giant, he remembered how God had helped him kill a lion and a bear (1 Samuel 17:34–36). He faced his future by revisiting the past.

Face your future by recalling God's past victories.

–*Glory Days*

JANUARY 25

A Plan for Grace

We can make our plans,
but the Lord determines our steps.
PROVERBS 16:9 NLT

Before we knew God's story, we made a mess of our own. Even afterward, we're prone to demand our own way, cut our own path, and hurt people in the process. Can God make good out of our bad?

He did with Paul.

"As I journeyed and came near Damascus . . . suddenly a great light from heaven shone around me. And I fell to the ground and heard a voice saying to me . . ." (Acts 22:6–7).

"I'm going to give you a taste of your own medicine."

"Back to the dust with you, you Christian-killer."

"Prepare to meet your Maker!"

Did Paul expect to hear words like these? Regardless, he didn't. Even before he requested mercy, he was offered mercy. Jesus told him, "I have a job for you. . . . I'm sending you off to open the eyes of the outsiders so they can see. . . . I'm sending you off to present my offer of sins forgiven, and a place in the family" (Acts 26:16–18 MSG).

Jesus transformed Paul, the card-carrying legalist, into a champion for mercy. Who would have thought? Yet who would be better qualified? Paul could write epistles of grace by dipping his pen into the inkwell of his own heart. He learned about love when Jesus paid him a personal visit on Damascus Highway.

–*God's Story, Your Story*

Sufficient, Sustaining Grace

I was given a thorn in my flesh, a messenger of Satan, to torment me. Three times I pleaded with the Lord to take it away from me. But he said to me, "My grace is sufficient for you, for my power is made perfect in weakness."

2 CORINTHIANS 12:7–9 NIV

A thorn in the flesh. Such vivid imagery. The sharp end of a thorn pierces the soft skin of life and lodges beneath the surface. Every step is a reminder of the thorn in the flesh.

The cancer in the body.

The child in the rehab center.

The red ink on the ledger.

The tears in the middle of the night.

"Take it away," you've pleaded. Not once, twice, or even three times. You've outprayed Paul. He prayed a sprint; you've prayed a marathon. But what you hear is this: "My grace is sufficient for you."

Grace takes on an added dimension here. Paul is referring to sustaining grace. Saving grace saves us from our sins. Sustaining grace meets us at our point of need and equips us with courage, wisdom, and strength. Sustaining grace promises not the absence of struggle but the presence of God.

And according to Paul, God has *sufficient* sustaining grace to meet every single challenge of our lives. Sufficient. We fear its antonym: *insufficient.* We've written checks only to see the words *insufficient funds.* Will we offer prayers only to discover insufficient strength? Never.

–*Grace*

JANUARY 27

UNSHEATHE THE PROMISE

The LORD your God is He who has fought for you.
JOSHUA 23:3

Not only does God desire that you live the Promised Land life, but he fights for you so you can. This was the main point of Joshua's victory speech (Joshua 23–24).

Joshua has seen every significant moment of the last half century. The Jordan River opened, and the Jericho walls fell. The sun stood still, and the enemies scattered. And Joshua in his final words wants to make sure they have gotten the message: "The LORD your God is He who has fought for you" (23:3).

Joshua summarized the victory by saying, "For the LORD has driven out from before you great and strong nations; . . . no one has been able to stand against you to this day. One man of you shall chase a thousand, for the LORD your God is He who fights for you" (vv. 9–10).

Don't you love that image? *One man of you shall chase a thousand.* I envision a single Hebrew soldier with drawn sword racing after an entire battalion of enemies. Since God fights for him, they scatter like scared pigeons.

I picture the same for you. The enemies of your life—fears, dread, hatred, and hurt—come at you like a legion of hoodlums. Yet rather than run away, you turn and face them. You unsheathe the promise of God's Word. You were not made to quake in fear. You are a living, breathing expression of God. He fights for you.

–*Glory Days*

JANUARY 28 

God's Unrivaled Goodness

Oh, taste and see that the LORD is good;
Blessed is the man who trusts in Him!
PSALM 34:8

The heart of God is unblemished. "There is nothing deceitful in God, nothing two-faced, nothing fickle" (James 1:17 MSG). He has no hidden agenda or selfish motive. He loves with a good love and forgives with a good forgiveness.

God's goodness is a major headline in the Bible. I think I know why. If God were only mighty, we would salute him. But since he is merciful and mighty, we can approach him. No wonder the psalmist invited, "Taste and see that the Lord is good" (Psalm 34:8). A glimpse of God's goodness changes us.

God's unrivaled goodness undergirds everything else we can say about prayer. If he is like us, only slightly stronger, then why pray? If he grows weary, then why pray? If he has limitations, questions, and hesitations, then you might as well pray to the Wizard of Oz.

However, if God is at once Father and Creator, holy—unlike us—and high above us, then we at any point are only a prayer away from help.

–*Before Amen*

JANUARY 29

A Prayer . . . for Boldness

We have this hope, so we are very bold.

2 CORINTHIANS 3:12 NCV

O God, you created all that exists, and you sustain all through your infinite wisdom and boundless power. Yet you invite me to come to you in prayer, boldly and with the expectation that you will hear and answer me. Teach me, Lord, to take full advantage of this privilege, especially in regard to reaching others with your love. Give me a heart for those who have yet to experience the fullness of your grace, and prompt me to pray for them and for their welfare, both in this world and in eternity. Lord, bring me to the front lines of this battle. In Jesus' name I pray, amen.

–*Outlive Your Life*

Find Your Lot

You saw me before I was born.
Every day of my life was recorded in your book.
Every moment was laid out
before a single day had passed.
PSALM 139:16 NLT

Uniqueness is a big message in the Bible. And—this may surprise you—it is a huge message of the book of Joshua. In fact, one could argue that the majority of its chapters advance one command: know your territory and possess it.

Joshua's first goal was to establish Israel in Canaan by taking the land, neutralizing the enemy armies, and eliminating the major seats of authority. Each tribe was given a distinct territory and/or assignment.

The inheritance was for everyone. All the Hebrews were welcomed to Canaan—the old, the young, the feeble, the forceful. The inheritance was universal.

But the assignments were individual. They are listed in detail in Joshua 13–21. If you can't fall asleep tonight, read these chapters. The book moves from an action novel to a land survey. The pages make for dull reading unless, of course, you stand to inherit something.

But the big message was this: No one gets everything. But everyone gets something. Drive out the remaining enemies. Build your farms. Cultivate your fields.

Find your lot in life and indwell it.

–*Glory Days*

JANUARY 31

Finding God's Will

Don't copy the behavior and customs of this world, but let God transform you into a new person by changing the way you think. Then you will learn to know God's will for you, which is good and pleasing and perfect.

ROMANS 12:2 NLT

Ever have trouble determining God's will for your future? You're not alone. The questions are endless. One follows another. Every new responsibility brings new decisions.

How in the world do we know what God wants?

To know God's will, we must totally surrender to God's will. Our tendency is to make God's decision for him.

Don't go to God with options and expect him to choose one of your preferences. Go to him with empty hands—no hidden agendas, no crossed fingers, nothing behind your back. Go to him with a willingness to do whatever he says. If you surrender your will, then he will "equip you with everything good for doing his will" (Hebrews 13:21 NIV).

It's a promise.

–On the Anvil

FEBRUARY

FEBRUARY 1

An Honest Look

A man who was lame from birth was being carried to the temple gate called Beautiful, where he was put every day to beg from those going into the temple courts. When he saw Peter and John about to enter, he asked them for money. Peter looked straight at him, as did John.

ACTS 3:2–4 NIV

Change begins with an honest look.

Just two years ago Bzuneh Tulema was the town drunk in Adama, South Africa. He and his wife were so consumed with alcohol that they farmed out their kids to neighbors and resigned themselves to a drunken demise.

But then someone *saw* them. Members of an area church began bringing the couple food and clothing. They invited them to worship services. Bzuneh was not interested. However, his wife, Bililie, was. She began to sober up and consider the story of Christ. The promise of a new life. The offer of a second chance. She believed.

Bzuneh was not so quick. He kept drinking until one night he fell so hard he knocked a dent in his face. Friends found him in a gully and took him to church and shared Jesus with him. He hasn't touched a drop since.

It all began with an honest look and a helping hand. Could this be God's strategy for human hurt? First, kind eyes meet desperate ones. Next, strong hands help weak ones. Then, the miracle of God. We do our small part, he does the big part, and life at the Beautiful Gate begins to be just that.

–Outlive Your Life

The Problem with Unprayed-for Problems

Cast your cares on the LORD and he will sustain you;
he will never let the righteous be shaken.
PSALM 55:22 NIV

Take your problems to Jesus. Don't take your problems to the bar. Jim Beam cannot solve them. Don't take your problems out on others. Temper tantrums never advance the cause. The moment you sense a problem, however large or small, take it to Christ.

"Max, if I take my problems to Jesus every time I have one, I am going to be talking to Jesus all day long." (Now you are getting the point.)

> Don't worry about anything; instead, pray about everything; tell God your needs, and don't forget to thank him for his answers. If you do this, you will experience God's peace, which is far more wonderful than the human mind can understand. His peace will keep your thoughts and your hearts quiet and at rest as you trust in Christ Jesus. (Philippians 4:6–7 TLB)

An unprayed-for problem is an embedded thorn. It festers and infects—first the finger, then the hand, then the entire arm. Best to go straight to the person who has the tweezers.

Let Jesus take care of you. He knows about thorns.

–*Before Amen*

FEBRUARY 3

Your Helper

The Lord is my light and my salvation;
Whom shall I fear?
The Lord is the strength of my life;
Of whom shall I be afraid?
PSALM 27:1

"I will not leave you nor forsake you" (Joshua 1:5).

That's the promise God gave Joshua. And he gives you the same promise. In fact, the writer of Hebrews quoted the words in his epistle: "For [God] has said, 'I will never leave you or forsake you.' So we can say with confidence, 'The Lord is my helper; I will not be afraid. What can anyone do to me?'" (13:5–6 NRSV).

That last question is a troubling one. *What can anyone do to me?* You know the answers. "Lie to me." "Deceive me." "Injure me." "Terrorize me." "Bully me."

But the Scripture asks a different question. If the Lord is your helper, what can anyone do to you?

The Greek word for "helper" in this passage is *boētheia*, from *boē*, which means "a shout," and *theō*, which means "to run."[1] When you need help, God runs with a shout, "I'm coming!" He never leaves you. Ever! He never takes a break, takes a nap, or takes time off for vacation. He never leaves your side.

Since God is strong, you will be strong. Since he is able, you will be able. Since he has no limits, you have no limits. With the apostle you can boldly say, "The Lord is my helper; I will not fear. What can man do to me?" (v. 6).

–*Glory Days*

A One-King Kingdom

"He will be King and sit on his great throne."
MATTHEW 25:31 NCV

Christ's coming will be a normal day. People will drink coffee, endure traffic snarls, laugh at jokes, and take note of the weather. Thousands of people will be born; thousands will die.

His coming will be unexpected. Most people will be oblivious.

His shout will get our attention. "For the Lord Himself will descend from heaven with a shout" (1 Thessalonians 4:16).

The shout of God will trigger the "voice of an archangel . . . with the trumpet of God" (1 Thessalonians 4:16). He will dispatch armies of angels to their greatest mission: to gather the children of God into one great assemblage.

Whether you are in Peoria or paradise, if you're a follower of Jesus, you can count on an angelic chaperone into the greatest gathering in history. The saved and lost alike will witness the assembly, for "all the nations will be gathered before him" (Matthew 25:32 NIV). At some point in this grand collection, our spirits will be reunited with our bodies, and the sky will stage a reunion of spirit and flesh.

By this point we will have seen and heard much: the shout of God and the angel, the trumpet blast, the ascension of the bodies, and the great gathering of the nations. But every sight and sound will seem a remote memory compared to what will happen next: "He will be King and sit on his great throne" (Matthew 25:31 NCV).

God's creation will return to its beginning: a one-King kingdom and all will be well with our souls.

–*God's Story, Your Story*

FEBRUARY 5

A PRAYER . . . FOR YOUR STORY

God created mankind in his own image, in the image of God
he created them; male and female he created them.
GENESIS 1:27 NIV

O Lord, Author of my life, thank you for creating me in your image and starting my story. Help me write it carefully and truly become like you. Come, O come, Immanuel, and help me complete my story well. In Jesus' name, amen.

–In the Manger

USE YOUR "YOU-NESS"

Do not neglect the gift that is in you.

1 TIMOTHY 4:14

No one else has your "you-ness." No one else in all history has your unique history. No one else in God's great design has your divine design. No one else shares your blend of personality, ability, and ancestry. When God made you, the angels stood in awe and declared, "We've never seen one like that before." And they never will again.

You are heaven's first and final attempt at you. You are matchless, unprecedented, and unequaled.

Consequently, you can do something no one else can do in a fashion no one else can.

Call it what you wish. A talent. A skill set. A gift. An anointing. A divine spark. An unction. A call. The terms are different, but the truth is the same: "The Spirit has given each of us a special way of serving others" (1 Corinthians 12:7 CEV).

Each of us—not some of us, a few of us, or the elite among us.

Many people stop short of their destiny. They settle for someone else's story. They fit in, settle in, and blend in. But they never find their call. Don't make the same mistake.

Your existence is not accidental. Your skills are not incidental. God "shaped each person in turn" (Psalm 33:15 MSG).

Find your "you-ness" and use it for the kingdom.

–*Glory Days*

FEBRUARY 7

Be Moved

"Anyone who has two shirts should share with the one who has none, and anyone who has food should do the same."

LUKE 3:11 NIV

Human hurt is not easy on the eyes. Yet there is something fundamentally good about taking time to see a person.

Simon the Pharisee once disdained Jesus' kindness toward a woman of questionable character. So Jesus tested him: "Do you *see* this woman?" (Luke 7:44, emphasis mine).

Simon didn't. He saw a hussy, a streetwalker, a scamp.

What do we see when we see . . .

- the figures beneath the overpass, encircling the fire in a fifty-five-gallon drum?
- the news clips of children in refugee camps?
- the reports of grueling poverty at home and abroad?

"When [Jesus] saw the multitudes, He was moved with compassion for them" (Matthew 9:36).

This word *compassion* is one of the oddest in Scripture. The New Testament Greek lexicon says this word means "to be moved as to one's bowel . . . (for the bowels were thought to be the seat of love and pity)."[2] Compassion, then, is a movement deep within—a kick in the gut.

Perhaps that is why we turn away. Why look suffering in the face if we can't make a difference? Yet what if by *seeing*, we were moved to compassion? Moved not just to *see*, but to *do*.

–*Outlive Your Life*

A Heart Transplant

"At that day you will know that I am in My
Father, and you in Me, and I in you."
JOHN 14:20

When grace happens, we receive not a nice compliment from God but a new heart. Give your heart to Christ, and he returns the favor. "I will give you a new heart and put a new spirit within you" (Ezekiel 36:26; see also John 14:20; Romans 8:10; Galatians 2:20).

You might call it a spiritual heart transplant.

Tara Storch understands this miracle as much as anyone can. In the spring of 2010, a skiing accident took the life of her thirteen-year-old daughter, Taylor. What followed was every parent's worst nightmare: a funeral, a burial, a flood of questions and tears. Tara and her husband, Todd, decided to donate their daughter's organs to needy patients. Few people needed a heart more than Patricia Winters. Her heart had begun to fail five years earlier, leaving her too weak to do much more than sleep. Taylor's heart gave Patricia a fresh start on life.

Tara had only one request: she wanted to hear the heart of her daughter. She and Todd flew from Dallas to Phoenix and went to Patricia's home to listen to Taylor's heart.

The two mothers embraced for a long time. Then Patricia offered Tara and Todd a stethoscope.[3]

When they listened to the healthy rhythm, whose heart did they hear? Did they not hear the still-beating heart of their daughter? And when God hears your heart, does he not hear the still-beating heart of his Son?

–*Grace*

FEBRUARY 9

Grace Seeps In

You were taught to be made new in your hearts, to become a new person. That new person is made to be like God—made to be truly good and holy.

EPHESIANS 4:23–24 NCV

Some years ago I underwent a heart procedure. My heartbeat had the regularity of a telegraph operator sending Morse code. Fast, fast, fast. Slooooow. After several failed attempts to restore healthy rhythm with medication, my doctor decided I should have a catheter ablation. The plan went like this: a cardiologist would insert two cables in my heart. One was a camera; the other was an ablation tool. To ablate is to burn. Yes, burn, cauterize, singe, brand. If all went well, the doctor, to use his coinage, would destroy the "misbehaving" parts of my heart.

As I was being wheeled into surgery, he asked if I had any final questions. (Not the best choice of words.) I tried to be witty.

"As long as you are in there, could you take your little blowtorch to some of my greed, selfishness, superiority, and guilt?"

He smiled and answered, "Sorry, that's out of my pay grade."

Indeed it was, but it's not out of God's. He is in the business of changing hearts.

We would be wrong to think this change happens overnight. But we would be equally wrong to assume change never happens at all. It may come in fits and spurts. But it comes. "The grace of God that brings salvation has appeared" (Titus 2:11). The floodgates are open, and the water is out. You just never know when grace will seep in.

–Grace

All Will Come to Pass

So the LORD gave to Israel all the land of which He had sworn to give to their fathers. . . . The LORD gave them rest all around, according to all that He had sworn to their fathers. And not a man of all their enemies stood against them. . . . Not a word failed of any good thing which the LORD had spoken to the house of Israel. All came to pass.

JOSHUA 21:43–45

Seven nations conquered. At least thirty-one kings defeated. Approximately ten thousand square miles of choice property claimed.

The Hebrew people were unstoppable.[4]

They hadn't always been. The Bible doesn't gloss over the checkered history of God's chosen people. Abraham had too many wives. Jacob told too many lies. Esau sold his birthright. Joseph's brothers sold Joseph. Four centuries of Egyptian bondage were followed by forty years of wilderness wandering. Then later, seventy years of Babylonian detention.

In the schoolroom of ancient societies, Israel was the kid with the black eye, bullied and beat-up.

Except for those seven years. The Glory Days of Israel. The Jordan River opened up. The Jericho walls fell down. The sun stood still, and the kings of Canaan were forced into early retirement. Evil was booted and hope rebooted.

What sweeping statements! "The LORD gave . . . all the land." "The LORD gave them rest." "Not a man of all their enemies stood against them." "All came to pass." Winter chill gave way to springtime thaw.

When you are wandering in the wintertime wilderness, remember spring is coming. A new season will be born.

–*Glory Days*

FEBRUARY 11

Our Redeemer

One day Ruth's mother-in-law Naomi said to her, . . . "Go down to the threshing floor. . . . When he lies down, note the place where he is lying. Then go and uncover his feet and lie down."

RUTH 3:1, 3–4 NIV

Uncover his feet and lie down. What was Naomi thinking?

Naomi was thinking about the law of the kinsman-redeemer. If a man died without children, his property was transferred to his brother. If the deceased husband had no brother, his nearest male relative was to provide for the widow.

But *this* was an audacious move. Boaz was under no obligation to marry Ruth. He was a relative, not a brother. Besides, she was a foreigner. He was a prominent landowner. She was a destitute alien. He was a local power broker. She, unknown. He, well known.

"Will you cover us?" Ruth asked him, and Boaz smiled.

Ruth's story is ours. We, too, are poor—spiritually, for sure; monetarily, perhaps. We wear robes of death. She buried her husband; we've buried our dreams, desires, and aspirations. Like the mother with lupus or the businessman in the unemployment line, we're out of options. But our Boaz has taken note of us. Christ, our Redeemer, came to us "while we were yet sinners" (Romans 5:8 NASB).

"Will you cover us?" we asked him, and Grace smiled.

–*Grace*

A Prayer . . . to Lead You

"Do not lead us into temptation,
But deliver us from the evil one."
LUKE 11:4

Dear Lord, help me see your hand in life's bewildering twists and knots. Speak to me so I'll understand your way when I find myself trapped in a hard place. Shine your light down upon me so I can follow you. In Jesus' name, amen.

–*In the Manger*

FEBRUARY 13

Everything You Need

I know the Lord is always with me.
I will not be shaken, for he is right beside me.
PSALM 16:8 NLT

You are fully equipped! Need more energy? You have it. More kindness? It's yours. Could you use some self-control, self-discipline, or self-confidence? God will "equip you with all you need for doing his will" (Hebrews 13:21 NLT). Just press the gas pedal. "God has given us everything we need for living a godly life" (2 Peter 1:3 NLT).

And that life begins with a paradigm shift.

Like Joshua and the Israelites marching into Canaan, you do not fight *for* victory. You fight *from* victory. In the wilderness you strive. In Canaan you trust. In the wilderness you seek God's attention. In Canaan you already have God's favor. In the wilderness you doubt your salvation. In Canaan you know you are saved. You move from wanting-to-have to believing you already do.

–*Glory Days*

WE NEVER TRAVEL ALONE

"I am with you always, even to the end of the age."
MATTHEW 28:20

Jesus loved people. He paid no heed to class or nationality, past sins or present accomplishments. The neediest and loneliest found a friend in Jesus:

- a woman scarcely clothed because of last night's affair. Christ befriended and defended her (John 8:3–11).
- an unscrupulous tax collector left friendless because of his misdealings. Christ became his mentor (Luke 19:2–10).
- a multiple divorcée who drew from the well in the heat of the day to avoid the stares of the villagers. Jesus gave her his attention (John 4:5–26).

Could a lying sham love this way? If his intent was to trick people out of their money or worship, he did a pitifully poor job, for he died utterly broke and virtually abandoned.

What if Peter was correct? "You are the Messiah" (Mark 8:29 NIV).

What if Jesus really was, and is, the Son of God? If so, then we can relish this wonderful truth: we never travel alone. True, we cannot see the path. We do not know what the future holds. But, no, we are not alone.

–*God's Story, Your Story*

FEBRUARY 15

Neglect or Rescue?

For he has rescued us from the dominion of darkness
and brought us into the kingdom of the Son he loves, in
whom we have redemption, the forgiveness of sins.
COLOSSIANS 1:13–14 NIV

God calls us to change the way we look at people. Not to see them as Gentiles or Jews, insiders or outsiders, liberals or conservatives. Not to label. To label is to libel. "We have stopped evaluating others from a human point of view" (2 Corinthians 5:16 NLT).

Let's view people differently; let's view them as we do ourselves. Blemished, perhaps. Unfinished, for certain. Yet once rescued and restored, we may shed light, like the two stained-glass windows in my office.

My brother found them on a junkyard heap. Some church had discarded them. Dee, a handy carpenter, reclaimed them. He repainted the chipped wood, repaired the worn frame. He sealed some of the cracks in the colored glass. The windows aren't perfect. But if suspended where the sun can pass through, they cascade multicolored light into the room.

In our lifetimes you and I are going to come across some discarded people. Tossed out. Sometimes tossed out by a church. And we get to choose. Neglect or rescue? Label them or love them? We know Jesus' choice. Just look at what he did with us.

–*Outlive Your Life*

Where Are You Empty?

Jesus fasted for forty days and nights. After this, he was very hungry. The devil came to Jesus to tempt him, saying, "If you are the Son of God, tell these rocks to become bread."

MATTHEW 4:2–3 NCV

God loves you too much to leave you undeveloped and immature. "God disciplines us for our good, in order that we may share in his holiness. No discipline seems pleasant at the time, but painful. Later on, however, it produces a harvest of righteousness and peace for those who have been trained by it" (Hebrews 12:10–11 NIV). Expect to be tested by the Devil.

And watch for his tricks. You can know what to expect. "We are not ignorant of his schemes" (2 Corinthians 2:11 NASB).

When General George Patton counterattacked Field Marshal Rommel in World War II, Patton is reported to have shouted in the thick of battle, "I read your book, Rommel! I read your book!" Patton had studied Rommel's *Infantry Attacks*. He knew the German leader's strategy and planned his moves accordingly.[5] We can know the same about the Devil.

We know Satan will *attack weak spots first*. Forty days of fasting left Jesus famished, so Satan began with the topic of bread. Jesus' stomach was empty, so to the stomach Satan turned.

Where are you empty? Are you hungry for attention, craving success, longing for intimacy? Be aware of your weaknesses. Bring them to God before Satan brings them to you.

–*God's Story, Your Story*

FEBRUARY 17

God Is Faithful

God has given both his promise and his oath. These two things are unchangeable because it is impossible for God to lie. Therefore, we . . . can have great confidence as we hold to the hope that lies before us. This hope is a strong and trustworthy anchor for our souls.

HEBREWS 6:18–19 NLT

Our God is a promise-keeping God. Others may make a promise and forget it. But if God makes a promise, he keeps it. "He who promised is faithful" (Hebrews 10:23 NIV).

Does this matter? Does God's integrity make a difference? Does his faithfulness come into play? When your daughter is on life support, it does. When you're pacing the ER floor, it does.

When you are wondering what to do with your worst nightmare, you have to choose. Faith or fear, God's purpose or random history, a God who knows and cares or a God who isn't there? We all choose.

Choose to trust God's promises. Choose to believe that God is up to something good even though all you see looks bad. Choose to believe because God is faithful.

–Glory Days

In Jesus' Name

You were washed, you were sanctified, you were justified in the name of the Lord Jesus Christ and by the Spirit of our God.

1 CORINTHIANS 6:11 NIV

The phrase "In Jesus' name" is not an empty motto or talisman. It is a declaration of truth: My cancer is not in charge; Jesus is. The economy is not in charge; Jesus is. The grumpy neighbor doesn't run the world; Jesus, you do! You, Jesus, are the Head Coach, CEO, President, King, Supreme Ruler, Absolute Monarch, High and Holy Baron, Czar, Overlord, and Rajah of all history.

Just speak the word, Jesus . . .

Pray! Since God works, prayer works. Since God is good, prayer is good. Since you matter to God, your prayers matter in heaven. You're never without hope, because you're never without prayer. And on the occasions you can't find the words to say, pull these out of your pocket:

Father,
You are good.
I need help. Heal me and forgive me.
They need help.
Thank you.
In Jesus' name, amen.

–*Before Amen*

FEBRUARY 19

A Prayer . . . to See

Jesus placed his hands on the man's eyes again, and his eyes were opened. His sight was completely restored, and he could see everything clearly.

MARK 8:25 NLT

My Lord and Savior, here I am. Just me. Help me to see you, really see you, even your eyes, and to hear your voice speaking words of peace. Ignite a fresh fire in my heart. In Jesus' name, amen.

–On Calvary's Hill

Believe That He Will!

All of us who have had that veil removed can see and reflect the glory of the Lord. And the Lord—who is the Spirit—makes us more and more like him as we are changed into his glorious image.
2 CORINTHIANS 3:18 NLT

You want your life to matter. You want to live in such a way that the world will be glad you did.

But how can you? How can I?

I have one hundred and twenty answers to that question. One hundred and twenty residents of ancient Israel. They were the charter members of the Jerusalem church (Acts 1:15). Fishermen, some. Revenue reps, others. A former streetwalker and a converted revolutionary or two. Truth be told, they had nothing more than this: a fire in the belly to change the world.

Thanks to Luke we know how they fared. He recorded their stories in the book of Acts. Let's listen to it. That's right—*listen* to the book of Acts.

Listen to the doors opening and walls collapsing. Doors into palaces, prisons, and Roman courts. And walls. The thick and spiked division between Jew and Gentile—*crash!* The partitions that quarantine male from female, landowner from pauper, master from slave, black African from Mediterranean Jew—God demolishes them all.

Acts announces, "God is afoot!"

Is he still? we wonder. *Would God do with us what he did with his first followers?*

You bet your sweet September he will!

–*Outlive Your Life*

FEBRUARY 21

ENTRUST THE PROBLEM TO JESUS

I asked the LORD for help, and he answered me.

PSALM 34:4 NCV

Life is a gift, albeit unassembled. It comes in pieces, and sometimes it falls to pieces. Inevitably, something seems to be missing. When the pieces of life don't fit, take your problem to Jesus.

Mary, the mother of Jesus, did. "On the third day there was a wedding in Cana of Galilee, and the mother of Jesus was there. Now both Jesus and His disciples were invited to the wedding" (John 2:1–2).

While they were there, the wedding party "ran out of wine." (v. 3). So "the mother of Jesus said to Him, 'They have no wine'" (v. 3).

Mary didn't whine about the wine. She just stated the problem.

Originally, Jesus had no intention of saving the wedding banquet. But then Mary entered the story—Mary, someone he loved—with a genuine need.

She has identified the problem, brought it to Jesus, and left it with him. She trusted him completely. She told the servants, "Whatever he says is okay with me."

In my imagination I see Jesus smile. I hear him chuckle. He looks at a cluster of six waterpots over in the corner.

At Jesus' command H_2O became abundant merlot. The master of the feast tasted the wine and licked his lips and said, "This is good stuff!" Problem presented. Prayer answered. Crisis avoided. All because Mary entrusted the problem to Jesus.

–Before Amen

That Kind of Faith

Faith is the substance of things hoped for,
the evidence of things not seen.
HEBREWS 11:1

You'll look a long time before you'll find a better man than Wes Bishop. He had a quick smile, warm handshake, and serious weakness for ice cream. He was a pillar in the small Texas town of Sweetwater. He raised three great sons, one of whom married my daughter Jenna. Wes never even missed a day of work until he was diagnosed with brain cancer.

We asked God to remove it. For a time it appeared that he had. But then the symptoms returned with a vengeance. In a matter of a few weeks, Wes was immobilized, at home, in hospice care.

The sons took turns keeping vigil so their mom could rest. They placed a baby monitor next to Wes's bed. Though he'd hardly spoken a word in days, they wanted to hear him if he called out.

One night he did. But he didn't call for help; he called for Christ. About one o'clock in the morning, the youngest son heard his father on the monitor. "Jesus, I want to thank you for my life. You have been good to me. And I want you to know, when you are ready to take me, I am ready to go." Those were the final words Wes spoke. Within a couple of days Jesus took him home.

I want that kind of faith. Don't you? The faith that turns to God in the darkest hour, praises God with the weakest body. The kind of faith that trusts in God's promises.

–*Glory Days*

FEBRUARY 23

Take That, Satan

Let us then approach God's throne of grace with confidence, so that we may receive mercy and find grace to help us in our time of need.

HEBREWS 4:16 NIV

Satan wants to take God's place, but God isn't moving. Satan covets the throne of heaven, but God isn't leaving. Satan wants to win you to his side, but God will never let you go.

You have his word. Even more, you have God's help.

You don't have to face Satan alone. You know his schemes. He will attack your weak spots first. He will tell you to meet your own needs. When you question your identity as a child of God, that is Satan speaking.

Even more, now you know what to do.

Pray. We cannot do battle with Satan on our own. He is a roaring lion, a fallen angel, an experienced fighter, and an equipped soldier. He is angry—angry because he knows that his time is short (Revelation 12:12 NIV) and that God's victory is secure. But there is wonderful news for the Christian: Christ reigns as our protector and provider. "We are more than conquerors through him" (Romans 8:37 NIV).

Arm yourself with God's Word. Load your pistol with scriptures and keep a finger on the trigger. And remember: "Our struggle is not against flesh and blood, but against the rulers, against the authorities, against the powers of this dark world and against the spiritual forces of evil in the heavenly realms" (Ephesians 6:12 NIV).

If I were the Devil, I wouldn't want you to know that. But I'm not the Devil, so good for you. And take that, Satan.

–God's Story, Your Story

What Just Happened?

In the past you were slaves to sin—sin controlled you. But thank God, you fully obeyed the things that you were taught. You were made free from sin, and now you are slaves to goodness.

ROMANS 6:17–18 NCV

All ships that land at the shore of grace weigh anchor from the port of sin. We must start where God starts. We won't appreciate what grace does until we understand who we are. We are rebels. We are Barabbas. Like him, we deserve to die. Four prison walls, thickened with fear, hurt, and hate, surround us. We are incarcerated by our past, our low-road choices, and our high-minded pride. We have been found guilty.

We sit on the floor of the dusty cell, awaiting the final moment. Our executioner's footsteps echo against stone walls. Head between knees, we don't look up as he opens the door; we don't lift our eyes as he begins to speak. We know what he is going to say. "Time to pay for your sins." But we hear something else.

"You're free to go. They took Jesus instead of you."

The door swings open, the guard barks, "Get out," and we find ourselves in the light of the morning sun, shackles gone, crimes pardoned, wondering, *What just happened?*

Grace happened.

–Grace

FEBRUARY 25

Thunderings and Lightnings

The smoke of the incense, with the prayers of the saints, ascended before God from the angel's hand. Then the angel took the censer, filled it with fire from the altar, and threw it to the earth. And there were noises, thunderings, lightnings, and an earthquake.

REVELATION 8:4–5

Ever wonder what prayers look like? What if you could actually see the prayers you pray? The prayers being prayed for you? The apostle John did. In his vision of heaven John saw the prayers of the saints ascending with incense into the presence of God. Then an angel took the censer, "filled it with fire from the altar, and threw it to the earth. And there were noises, thunderings, lightnings, and an earthquake" (Revelation 8:5).

Behold the power of prayer. You ask God for help, and *bam!* Fire falls to the earth. You lift your concerns to heaven, and turbulence happens! "Noises, thunderings, lightnings, and an earthquake."

Go ahead. Make the midnight knock. Stand up on behalf of those you love. And, yes, stand up on behalf of those you do not. "Pray for those who hurt you" (Matthew 5:44 NCV). The quickest way to douse the fire of anger is with a bucket of prayer. Rather than rant, rave, or seek revenge, pray. Jesus did this. While hanging on the cross, he interceded for his enemies (Luke 23:34). Jesus, even Jesus, left his enemies in God's hands.

Shouldn't we do the same? Pray for this hurting world. Pray—and then wait for the earth to quake.

–*Before Amen*

A Prayer . . . to Please Jesus

Therefore we make it our aim, whether present or absent, to be well pleasing to Him.

2 CORINTHIANS 5:9

Gracious Father, give me an understanding of what it means to truly have a relationship with your Son. Help me to stay so close to Jesus that I can see his face, even when I fail. Tune my heart into what brings him joy as well as pain. In Jesus' name, amen.

–*On Calvary's Hill*

FEBRUARY 27

Coheirs with Christ

The Spirit himself testifies with our spirit that we are God's children. Now if we are children, then we are heirs—heirs of God and co-heirs with Christ.
ROMANS 8:16–17 NIV

If we are coheirs with Christ, why do we struggle through life? Our inheritance is perfect peace, yet we feel like a perfect mess. We have access to the joy level of Jesus yet plod along like dyspeptic donkeys. God promises to meet every need, yet we still worry and fret. Why?

We don't know about our inheritance. No one ever told us about "the exceeding greatness of His power toward us who believe" (Ephesians 1:19). No one ever told us that we fight *from* victory, not *for* victory. No one told us that our Promised Land, our Canaan, is already conquered. Some Christians never live out of their inheritance because they don't know they have one.

But now you do. Now you know that you were made for more than wandering in the wilderness. God saved you from Egypt so that he could bless you in the Promised Land. Moses had to remind the people that "[God] brought us out from there, that He might bring us in [to Canaan]" (Deuteronomy 6:23). There is a reason for our redemption too. God brought us out so he could lead us in. He set us free so he could raise us up.

The gift has been given. Will you trust it?

–*Glory Days*

God Can

As for God, His way is perfect;
The word of the Lord is proven;
He is a shield to all who trust in Him.
2 SAMUEL 22:31

One reason we waste time worrying and fretting is because we don't really know about our inheritance in Christ. Yet another reason for our worrying ways is this:

We don't believe in our inheritance. That was the problem of Joshua's ancestors. They really didn't believe that God could give them the land of Canaan. The victories of the Hebrews could have begun four decades earlier, a point God alluded to in his promise to Joshua: "Every place that the sole of your foot will tread upon I have given you, as I said to Moses" (Joshua 1:3). The reminder? *I made this offer to the people of Moses' day, but they didn't take it. They chose the wilderness. Don't make the same mistake.*

Joshua didn't. Much to his credit he took God at his word and set about the task of inheriting the land.

Do the same. Receive yours. You are embedded with the presence of God. Don't measure your life by your ability; measure it by God's. Even though you can't forgive, God can. And since he can, you can. You can't break the habit, but God can. Since he can, you can. You can't control your tongue, temper, or sexual urges, but God can. And since you have access to every blessing of heaven, you, in time, will find strength.

Take God at his word and begin living your Promised Land life.

–*Glory Days*

MARCH

MARCH 1 

"Oh, Daddy"

Answer me when I call to you,
my righteous God.
Give me relief from my distress;
have mercy on me and hear my prayer.
PSALM 4:1 NIV

When my eldest daughter was thirteen years old, she flubbed her piano piece at a recital. Jenna went on to become a fine pianist and a wonderful singer. But everyone has an off day. She just happened to have hers in front of an auditorium crowded with family, friends, and onlookers.

The performance started well. But midway through the piece, her musical train jumped the track.

I can still see her staring straight ahead, fingers stuck as if in superglue. She backed up a few measures and took another run at it. No luck. For the life of her she couldn't remember the next part. The silence was broken only by the pounding of her parents' hearts.

Finally it did. Jenna's mental block broke, and she completed the piece. But the damage had been done. She stood up from the piano bench, chin quivering, and curtsied. The audience offered compassionate applause. Denalyn and I scurried out of our seats and met her at the side of the auditorium. She threw her arms around me and buried her face in my shirt.

"Oh, Daddy."

Prayer starts here. Prayer begins with an honest, heartfelt "Oh, Daddy."

–Before Amen

MARCH 2

Face Failures with Faith

Everyone has sinned; we all fall short of God's glorious standard. Yet God, in his grace, freely makes us right in his sight. He did this through Christ Jesus when he freed us from the penalty for our sins.

ROMANS 3:23–24 NLT

One stumble does not define or break a person. Though you failed, God's love does not. Face your failures with faith in God's goodness. He saw this collapse coming. When you stood on the eastern side of the Jordan, God could see the upcoming mishaps.

Still, he tells you what he told Joshua: "Arise, go . . . , you and all this people, to the land which I am giving" (Joshua 1:2). There is no condition in that covenant. No fine print. No performance language. God's Promised Land offer does not depend on your perfection. It depends on his.

In God's hands no defeat is a crushing defeat. "The steps of good men are directed by the Lord. He delights in each step they take. If they fall, it isn't fatal, for the Lord holds them with his hand" (Psalm 37:23–24 TLB).

To face your failures, put your faith in the One who is always faithful.

–*Glory Days*

God's Hold on You

The faithful love of the Lord never ends!
His mercies never cease.
LAMENTATIONS 3:22 NLT

On-and-off salvation never appears in the Bible. Salvation is not a repeated phenomenon. Scripture contains no example of a person who was saved, then lost, then resaved, then lost again.

Where there is no assurance of salvation, there is no peace. No peace means no joy. No joy results in fear-based lives. Is this the life God creates? No. Grace creates a confident soul who declares, "I know whom I have believed, and am convinced that he is able to guard what I have entrusted to him until that day" (2 Timothy 1:12 NIV).

Of all we don't know in life, we know this: "These things I have written to you who believe in the name of the Son of God, that you may know that you have eternal life" (1 John 5:13). Trust God's hold on you more than your hold on God. His faithfulness does not depend on yours. His performance is not predicated on yours. His love is not contingent on your own. Your candle may flicker, but it will not expire.

God's love for you does not—will not—end.

–*Grace*

MARCH 4

Linger in His Presence

"Remain in me, and I will remain in you."

JOHN 15:4 NCV

Could you use some high-octane boldness? If you want to outlive your life, you could. As long as you are stationary, no one will complain. Dogs don't bark at parked cars. But as soon as you accelerate—once you step out of drunkenness into sobriety, dishonesty into integrity, or lethargy into compassion—expect the yapping to begin. Expect to be criticized. Expect to be mocked. Expect to be persecuted.

So how can we prepare ourselves? Simple. Imitate the disciples. Linger long and often in the presence of Christ. Meditate on his grace. Ponder his love. Memorize his words. Gaze into his face. Talk to him. Courage comes as we live with Jesus.

Peter said it this way. "Don't give the opposition a second thought. Through thick and thin, keep your hearts at attention, in adoration before Christ, your Master" (1 Peter 3:14–15 MSG).

As we meditate on Christ's life, we find strength for our own.

Would you be bold tomorrow? Then be with Jesus today. Be in his Word. Be with his people. Be in his presence. And when persecution comes (and it will), be strong. Who knows? People may realize that you, like the disciples, have been with Christ.

–*Outlive Your Life*

A Prayer . . . for Grace and Mercy

For to You, O Lord, I lift up my soul.
For You, Lord, are good, and ready to forgive,
And abundant in mercy to all those who call upon You.
PSALM 86:5

God, you are abounding in forgiveness and mercy and goodness I cannot understand in this life. I worship you with my heart and soul.

As I sit in regret and guilt over past sin, remind me of your forgiveness. Please let me feel your mercy. Fill me with it so I can give it to others I encounter today.

Walk closely with those I love so they can know your grace. Lift their burdens and point their faces toward you.

I give you thanks for the grace I do not deserve and your mercies, which are new every morning. In Christ's name, amen.

–*Pocket Prayers*

MARCH 6

A Work in His Hands

Whenever I pray, I make my requests for all of you with joy, for you have been my partners in spreading the Good News about Christ from the time you first heard it until now. And I am certain that God, who began the good work within you, will continue his work until it is finally finished on the day when Christ Jesus returns.

PHILIPPIANS 1:4–6 NLT

The same work God did through Christ long ago on a cross is the work God does through Christ right now in you. Let him do his work. Let grace trump your arrest record, critics, and guilty conscience. See yourself for what you are—God's personal remodeling project. Not a world to yourself but a work in his hands. No longer defined by failures but refined by them. Trusting less in what you do and more in what Christ did. Graceless less, grace shaped more. Convinced down deep in the substrata of your soul that God is just warming up in this overture called life, that hope has its reasons and death has its due date.

Grace. Let it, let him, so seep into the crusty cracks of your life that everything softens. Then let it, let him, bubble to the surface, like a spring in the Sahara, in words of kindness and deeds of generosity. God will change you, my friend. You are a trophy of his kindness, a partaker of his mission. Not perfect by any means but closer to perfection than you've ever been.

Steadily stronger, gradually better, certainly closer.

This happens when grace happens. May it happen to you.

–Grace

Receive What God Gives

[They] could not drive out the inhabitants . . . the Canaanites were determined to dwell in that land.

JOSHUA 17:12

Do not be like the Hebrews. When God delivered the Promised Land into their hands and Joshua doled out the lots, they didn't hold up their end of the deal.

I wish I could report that each tribe moved quickly into its land, drove out the inhabitants, and put the acreage to good use. They didn't. In some cases the tribes did not drive out the enemies (Joshua 13:13; 16:10; 17:12). Your enemy, the Devil, is determined to linger in your land as well. You must drive him out. He will lure you with thoughts of greed, power, or jealousy. Be on your guard.

Other tribes fell victim not to Canaanites but to their own laziness. Long after Joshua had distributed the land, seven of the tribes were still in the military camp. Joshua had to scold them. "How long will you neglect to go and possess the land which the Lord God of your fathers has given you?" (Joshua 18:3).

Don't make the same mistake. You are an heir with Christ of God's estate. What God said to Joshua, he says to you: "Every place that the sole of your foot will tread upon I have given you" (Joshua 1:3).

But you must possess it. You must deliberately receive what God so graciously gives.

All that you need to enter your Promised Land is to walk by faith. So walk! Move forward! Find your lot in life and live in it.

–*Glory Days*

MARCH 8

How Will You Respond?

The apostles testified powerfully to the resurrection of the Lord Jesus, and God's great blessing was upon them all. There were no needy people among them.

ACTS 4:33–34 NLT

No one can do everything, but everyone can do something.

Some years back a reporter covering the conflict in Sarajevo saw a little girl shot by a sniper. The back of her head had been torn away by the bullet. The reporter threw down his pad and pencil and stopped being a reporter for a few minutes. He rushed to the man who was holding the child and helped them both into his car. As the reporter raced to the hospital, the man holding the bleeding child said, "Hurry, my friend. My child is still alive."

A moment later, "Hurry, my friend. My child is still warm."

Finally, "Hurry. Oh my God, my child is getting cold."

By the time they arrived at the hospital, the little girl had died. As the two men were washing the blood off their hands and their clothes, the man said, "This is a terrible task for me. I must go tell her father that his child is dead. He will be heartbroken."

The reporter was amazed. He looked at the grieving man and said, "I thought she was your child."

The man looked back and said, "No, but aren't they all our children?"[1]

Indeed. Those who suffer belong to all of us. And if all of us respond, there is hope.

–*Outlive Your Life*

THANK GOD FOR THUMPS!

My child, don't think the Lord's discipline is worth nothing. . . .
The Lord disciplines those he loves.
HEBREWS 12:5–6 NCV

When a potter bakes a pot, he checks its solidity by pulling it out of the oven and thumping it. If it "sings," it's ready. If it "thuds," it's placed back in the oven.

The character of a person is also checked by thumping. Thumps are those irritating inconveniences that trigger the worst in us. They catch us off guard. They aren't big enough to be crises, but if you get enough of them, watch out!

How do I respond? Do I sing, or do I thud?

Jesus said that out of the nature of the heart a man speaks (Luke 6:45). There's nothing like a good thump to reveal the true nature of a heart. If you have a tendency to thud more than you sing, take heart.

There is hope for us "thudders":

1. Begin by thanking God for thumps. Every thump is a reminder that God is molding you (Hebrews 12:5–8).
2. Learn from each thump. Look upon each inconvenience as an opportunity to develop patience and persistence.
3. Be aware of "thump-slump" times. Know your pressure periods. Bolster yourself with extra prayer, and don't give up.

Remember, no thump is disastrous. All thumps work for good if we are loving and obeying God.

–*On the Anvil*

MARCH 10

The Promised Land Life

The LORD your God is giving you a place of rest.
JOSHUA 1:13 NLT

Our Promised Land isn't a physical territory; it is a spiritual reality. It's not real estate, but a real state of the heart and mind.

It's a life in which "we are more than conquerors through [Christ] who loved us" (Romans 8:37).

A life in which "we do not lose heart" (2 Corinthians 4:16).

A life in which "[Christ's] love has the first and last word in everything we do" (2 Corinthians 5:14 MSG).

A life in which we are "exceedingly joyful in all our tribulation" (2 Corinthians 7:4).

A life in which we are "anxious for nothing" (Philippians 4:6), in which we are "praying always" (Ephesians 6:18), in which we "do all in the name of the Lord Jesus, giving thanks to God the Father through Him" (Colossians 3:17).

In God's plan, in God's *Promised Land*, we win more often than we lose, forgive as quickly as we are offended, and give as abundantly as we receive. We serve out of our giftedness and delight in our assignments. We may stumble, but we do not collapse. We may struggle, but we defy despair. We boast only in Christ, trust only in God, lean wholly on his power. We enjoy abundant fruit and increasing faith.

We live the Promised Land life.

–*Glory Days*

The Greatest of Treasures

God, who said, "Let light shine out of darkness," made his light shine in our hearts to give us the light of the knowledge of God's glory displayed in the face of Christ. But we have this treasure in jars of clay to show that this all-surpassing power is from God and not from us.

2 CORINTHIANS 4:6–7 NIV

Jesus himself is the treasure. Grace is precious because he is. Grace changes lives because he does. Grace secures us because he will. The gift is the Giver. To discover grace is to discover God's utter devotion to you, his stubborn resolve to give you a cleansing, healing, purging love that lifts the wounded back to their feet. Does he stand high on a hill and bid you climb out of the valley? No. He bungees down and carries you out. Does he build a bridge and command you to cross it? No. He crosses the bridge and shoulders you over. "You did not save yourselves; it was a gift from God" (Ephesians 2:8 NCV).

This is the gift that God gives. A grace that grants us first the power to receive love and then the power to give it. A grace that changes us, shapes us, and leads us to a life that is eternally altered. Do you know this grace? Do you trust this grace? If not, you can. All God wants from us is faith. Put your faith in God.

And grow in God's grace. More verb than noun, more present tense than past tense, grace didn't just happen; it happens. Grace happens here.

–*Grace*

A Prayer . . . to Reach Out to Others

"Love your neighbor as you love yourself."
LUKE 10:27 NCV

Gracious Father, you took the initiative to reach out to me—even in my sin and selfishness—in order to bring me into your eternal kingdom, through the work of Christ. I cannot fathom such love! And yet, Father, I try to hoard your grace! Put up walls of protection that I might keep hurt out and blessing in. I am like the clam that shuts itself up in its shell, afraid of threats from the outside. You call me to unshell myself and to partner with you in your mission of love. Unshell me, Lord, that I, too, may reach out to a lonely, discouraged, and even hopeless world. In Jesus' name, amen.

–*Outlive Your Life*

What the Master Wants

Each of you has your own gift from God;
one has this gift, another has that.
1 CORINTHIANS 7:7 NIV

Everybody gets a gift. And these gifts come in different doses and combinations. "Each person is given something to do that shows who God is" (1 Corinthians 12:7 MSG).

Our inheritance is grace based and equal. But our assignments are tailor-made. No two snowflakes are the same. No two fingerprints are the same. Why would two skill sets be the same? No wonder Paul said, "Make sure you understand what the Master wants" (Ephesians 5:17 MSG).

Do you understand what your Master wants? Do you know what makes you, you? Have you identified the features that distinguish you from every other human who has inhaled oxygen?

You have an "acreage" to develop, a lot in life. So "make a careful exploration of who you are and the work you have been given, and then sink yourself into that" (Galatians 6:4 MSG).

You be you.

–*Glory Days*

MARCH 14

Keep Sailing

Your real life is hidden with Christ in God. And when Christ, who is your life, is revealed to the whole world, you will share in all his glory.

COLOSSIANS 3:3–4 NLT

Myriad of mighty angels encircle us, the presence of our Maker engulfs us, the witness of a thousand galaxies and constellations calls to us, the flowing tide of God's history carries us, the crowning of Christ as King of the universe awaits us, but we can't get our eyes off the daily distractions of life: paychecks, gadgets, vacations, and weekends.

Open your eyes, Christ invites. *Lift up your gaze*. "Seek first the kingdom of God" (Matthew 6:33). Look down and focus on the small things of this life, and, mark it down, you will be disappointed. Limit your story to the days between your birth and death, and brace yourself for a sad ending. You were made for more than this life.

Five hundred years ago, sailors feared the horizon. Sail too far and risk falling off the edge, they reasoned.

But then came Christopher Columbus and the voyage of 1492. The discovery of the New World changed everything. Spain acknowledged this in its coins, which came to bear the slogan *plus ultra*—"more beyond."[2]

Why don't you chisel the *no* off your future? God has set your heart on home. Keep sailing until you reach it.

–*God's Story, Your Story*

Follow God's Strategy

"Arise, go up to Ai. See, I have given into your hand the king of Ai, his people, his city, and his land."
JOSHUA 8:1

A few miles north of Jericho sat Ai. Joshua circled the name of the city on his wall map and told his officers to attack. Flush with a Jericho victory, he assumed the small town would be easy pickins. But Joshua was in for a surprise. The town was a kennel of pit bulls. The people of Ai bit back. Joshua's division raced home, licking their wounds.

Joshua came undone, but God was not done.

God told Joshua to revisit the place of failure. In essence God told Joshua, "Let's do it again. This time my way."

Joshua didn't need to be told twice. He and his men made an early morning march to Ai.

The king of Ai, still strutting from victory number one, marched toward Joshua, leaving the town unprotected. Joshua's elite squad charged in and set fire to the city. Then Joshua reversed his course, catching the army of Ai in the middle. The victory was complete.

Contrast this attack with the first one. In the first, Joshua consulted spies; in the second, he listened to God. In the first, he stayed home. In the second, he led the way. The first attack involved a small unit. His second involved many more men. The first attack involved no tactics. His second was strategic and sophisticated.

The point? God gave Joshua a new plan: try again, my way. When he followed God's strategy, victory happened. A good lesson for us too.

–*Glory Days*

MARCH 16

Into the Wilderness

These trials will show that your faith is genuine. It is being tested as fire tests and purifies gold.
1 PETER 1:7 NLT

Satan is not absent from or peripheral to God's story. He is at its center. We can't understand God's narrative without understanding Satan's strategy. In fact, "the reason the Son of God appeared was to destroy the works of the devil" (1 John 3:8 ESV).

Nothing thrills Satan more than the current skepticism with which he is viewed. When people deny his existence or chalk up his works to the ills of society, he rubs his hands with glee. The more we doubt his very existence, the more he can work without hindrance.

Jesus didn't doubt the reality of the Devil. The Savior strode into the badlands with one goal, to unmask Satan, and made him the first stop on his itinerary. "Then Jesus was led by the Spirit into the wilderness to be tempted by the devil" (Matthew 4:1 NIV).

Might the Spirit of God lead us into the wilderness? If I were the Devil, I'd tell you no. I would want you to think that I, on occasion, sneak in when God isn't looking and snatch his children out of his hand.

But Scripture reveals otherwise. God uses Satan's temptation to strengthen us. Times of testing are actually times of training, purification, and strength building. You can even "consider it pure joy . . . whenever you face trials of many kinds, because you know that the testing of your faith produces perseverance" (James 1:2–3 NIV).

–*God's Story, Your Story*

He Prays for Us

"I have prayed for you, that your faith should not fail."

LUKE 22:32

On the night before his death, Jesus made this announcement: "All of you will be made to stumble because of Me this night, for it is written: 'I will strike the Shepherd, and the sheep of the flock will be scattered.' But after I have been raised, I will go before you to Galilee" (Matthew 26:31–32).

Translation? Your fall will be great, but my grace will be greater. You'll find me waiting for you in Galilee.

The promise was lost on Peter: "Even if all are made to stumble because of You, I will never be made to stumble" (v. 33).

Not one of Peter's finer moments. Arrogant. Self-sufficient. Peter's trust was in Peter's strength. Yet Peter's strength would peter out. Jesus knew it.

Satan would attack and test Peter. But Satan would never claim Peter. Why? Because Peter was strong? No, because Jesus was. "I have prayed for you" (Luke 22:32). Jesus' prayers hamstring Satan.

Jesus prays for you as well (John 17:11, 20 NLT).

Will God hear the intercessory pleas of his Son? Of course he will. Like Peter, our faith will wane, our resolve waver, but we will not fall away. We are "kept for Jesus" (Jude v. 1 NIV) and "shielded by God's power" (1 Peter 1:5 NIV). And that is no small power. It is the power of a living and ever-persistent Savior . . . who prays for us.

–Grace

MARCH 18

Angels Answer Him

If you make the Lord your refuge,
if you make the Most High your shelter,
no evil will conquer you;
no plague will come near your home.
For he will order his angels
to protect you wherever you go.
PSALM 91:9–11 NLT

When my daughters were small, they would occasionally cry out in the middle of the night. The wind would brush a branch against a window. They would hear a noise on the street. They would shout, "Daddy!"

I would do what all daddies do—tell their mother. Just kidding. I would walk down the hall and step into their room. When I did, the atmosphere changed. Strange noises? Odd sounds? Didn't matter. Daddy was here.

You need to know this: your Father is here. Here as the Commander. Here with his heavenly hosts.

This is the promise God gives to you. He is with you. "He is in charge of it all, has the final word on everything" (Ephesians 1:22 MSG). "He sustains everything by the mighty power of his command" (Hebrews 1:3 NLT).

All authority has been given to him. He needs only to lift a finger, and thousands upon thousands of mighty angels will respond to his call.

–*Glory Days*

MARCH 19

A PRAYER . . . FOR JESUS IS LORD!

Jesus said to him, "I am the way, the truth, and the life. No one comes to the Father except through Me."

JOHN 14:6

O Lord, conqueror over death, to hear you say "It is finished!" is glorious. I confess with my lips that there is nothing I can do or say that will add to what you did on the cross. You are my only hope of salvation. In Jesus' name, amen.

–On Calvary's Hill

MARCH 20

Your Attitude About You

Suppose I had wings
like the dawning day
and flew across the ocean.
Even then your powerful arm
would guide and protect me.
PSALM 139:9–10 CEV

To accept God's grace is to accept God's offer to be adopted into his family. Your identity is not in your possessions, talents, tattoos, kudos, or accomplishments. Nor are you defined by your divorce, deficiencies, debt, or dumb choices. You are God's child. You get to call him "Papa." You "may approach God with freedom and confidence" (Ephesians 3:12 NIV). You receive the blessings of his special love (1 John 4:9–11) and provision (Luke 11:11–13). And you will inherit the riches of Christ and reign with him forever (Romans 8:17).

The adoption is horizontal as well as vertical. You are included in the forever family. Dividing walls of hostility are broken down, and community is created on the basis of a common Father. Instant family worldwide!

Rather than conjure up reasons to feel good about yourself, trust God's verdict. If God loves you, you must be worth loving. If he wants to have you in his kingdom, then you must be worth having. God's grace invites you—no, *requires* you—to change your attitude about yourself and take sides with God against your feelings of rejection.

–*Grace*

What Kind of Man Was Judas?

"This is eternal life, that they may know You, the only true God, and Jesus Christ whom You have sent."
JOHN 17:3

I've wondered at times what kind of man this Judas was. What he looked like, how he acted, who his friends were. I've pictured him as estranged from the other apostles. Friendless. Distant.

Yet I wonder if that is true.

Perhaps he was just the opposite. Instead of sly and wiry, maybe he was robust and jovial.

But for all the things we don't know about Judas, there is one thing we know for sure: He had no relationship with the Master. He had seen Jesus, but he did not know him. He had a religion but no relationship.

As Satan worked his way around the table in the Upper Room, he needed a man who had seen Jesus but who did not know him.

We learn this timeless lesson from the betrayer. Satan's best tools of destruction are not from outside the church; they are within the church.

Judas bore the cloak of religion, but he never knew the heart of Christ. Let's make it our goal to know . . . deeply.

–*On the Anvil*

MARCH 22

Stay in His Shadow

"Whoever denies Me before men, him I will also deny before My Father who is in heaven."
MATTHEW 10:33

Peter was sharp. He kept his distance from Jesus. *I'll stay close enough to see him,* Peter reasoned. *But not too close, or I may get caught.*

Good thinking, Peter. Don't get too involved—it might hurt. Don't be too loyal—you might get branded. Don't show too much concern—they'll crucify you too.

We need more men like you, Peter. Men who keep religion in its place. Men who don't stir the water. Men who reek with mediocrity.

That's the kind of man God needs, yessir. One who knows how to keep his distance: *Now, I'll pay my dues and I'll come once a week, but . . . well . . . you can get carried away, you know.*

Yes, you can get carried away . . . up a hill . . . to a cross—*and killed.*

Peter learned a lesson that day—a hard lesson. It is better to have never followed Jesus than to have followed him and denied him.

Mark these words:

> *Follow at a distance and you'll deny the Master. Period.*
> *You won't die for a man you can't touch. Period.*
> *But stay near to him, in his shadow. . . .*
> *You'll die with him, gladly.*

–*On the Anvil*

Forsaken

About the ninth hour Jesus cried out with a loud voice, saying, "Eli, Eli, lama sabachthani?" that is, "My God, My God, why have You forsaken Me?"
MATTHEW 27:46

Jesus' death on the cross is not a secondary theme in Scripture; it is the core. The crucial accomplishment of Christ occurred on the cross. Lest we miss the message, God encased the climax of his story in high drama:

The garden: Jesus crying out, the disciples running out, the soldiers bursting in.

The trials: early morning mockery and deceit. Jews scoffing. Pilate washing.

The soldiers: weaving thorns, slashing whips, pounding nails.

Jesus: bloodied, beaten. More crimson than clean. Every sinew afire with pain.

And God: He ebonized the sky and shook the earth. He cleaved the rocks and ripped the temple curtain. He untombed the entombed and unveiled the Holy of Holies.

But first he heard the cry of his Son: "My God, my God, why have you forsaken me?" (Matthew 27:46 NIV).

This was the moment in which "God put the wrong on him who never did anything wrong" (2 Corinthians 5:21 MSG). "GOD . . . piled all our sins, everything we've done wrong, on him, on him. He was beaten, he was tortured, but he didn't say a word" (Isaiah 53:6–7 MSG).

He was forsaken for you and for me.

–*God's Story, Your Story*

MARCH 24

The Day Grace Happened to You

He personally carried our sins in his body on the cross so that we can be dead to sin and live for what is right. By his wounds you are healed.

1 PETER 2:24 NLT

Christ took away your sins. Where did he take them? To the top of a hill called Calvary, where he endured not just the nails of the Romans, the mockery of the crowd, and the spear of the soldier but the anger of God.

Saturate your heart in this, the finest summary of God's greatest accomplishment: "God in his gracious kindness declares us not guilty. He has done this through Christ Jesus, who has freed us by taking away our sins. *For God sent Jesus to take the punishment for our sins* and to satisfy God's anger against us. We are made right with God when we believe that Jesus shed his blood, sacrificing his life for us" (Romans 3:24–25 NLT, emphasis mine).

God didn't overlook your sins, lest he endorse them. He didn't punish you, lest he destroy you. He instead found a way to punish the sin and preserve the sinner. Jesus took your punishment, and God gave you credit for Jesus' perfection.

As long as the cross is God's gift to the world, it will touch you but not change you. Precious as it is to proclaim, "Christ died for the world," even sweeter it is to whisper, "Christ died for *me*."

Thank God for the day Jesus took your place, for the day grace happened to you.

–*Grace*

Remember the Bread

"I am the living bread which came down from heaven.
If anyone eats of this bread, he will live forever."
JOHN 6:51

Make sure you receive the bread.

And once you do, pass it on. After all, if we don't, who will? Governments don't feed the soul. The secular relief house can give a bed, a meal, and valuable counsel. But we can give much more. Not just help for this life but hope for the next.

"Turn back to God! Be baptized in the name of Jesus Christ, so that your sins will be forgiven. Then you will be given the Holy Spirit. This promise is for you and your children. It is for everyone our Lord God will choose, no matter where they live" (Acts 2:38–39 CEV).

So along with the cups of water and plates of food, let there be the message of sins forgiven and death defeated.

Remember the bread.

–*Outlive Your Life*

MARCH 26

A Prayer . . . at the Cross

Surely He has borne our griefs
And carried our sorrows;
Yet we esteemed Him stricken,
Smitten by God, and afflicted.
But He was wounded for our transgressions,
He was bruised for our iniquities.
ISAIAH 53:4–5

Man of sorrows, man of grief, it was for me that you stepped into the horror of bearing my sin. It is incomprehensible that you would take my place and plead for my life. I give you thanks and praise for your ultimate sacrifice. In Jesus' name, amen.

–*On Calvary's Hill*

MARCH 27 

The Offer

Therefore let all the house of Israel know assuredly that God has made this Jesus, whom you crucified, both Lord and Christ.

ACTS 2:36

The word was out that the Word was out.

People began to realize their mistake. The gravity of their crime settled over them like a funeral dirge. God came into their world, and they killed him. This was the thrust of Peter's sermon: "*You killed God*. You took him and had evil men put him to death." You. You. You.

The question of the hour became "Men and brethren, what shall we do?" (Acts 2:37).

They leaned in to hear Peter's reply. So much was at stake. What if he said, "It's too late"?

Peter, surely with outstretched arms and tear-filled eyes, gave this invitation: "Turn back to God! Be baptized in the name of Jesus Christ, so that your sins will be forgiven. Then you will be given the Holy Spirit" (Acts 2:38–39 CEV).

Peter would eventually speak about poverty. The church would soon address the issues of widows, disease, and bigotry. But not yet. The first order of the church's first sermon was this: pardon for all our sins. Peter delivered the bread.

Would you consider the same offer? Before you turn the page, before you carry on with the rest of your day, would you consider the offer of Jesus? "I am the bread of life. Whoever comes to me will never be hungry again" (John 6:35 NLT).

–*Outlive Your Life*

MARCH 28

Where Grace Abounds

Be kind to one another, tenderhearted, forgiving one another, even as God in Christ forgave you.

EPHESIANS 4:32

Give the grace you've been given.

You don't endorse the deeds of your offender when you do. Jesus didn't endorse your sins by forgiving you. Grace doesn't tell the daughter to like the father who molested her. It doesn't tell the oppressed to wink at injustice. The grace-defined person still sends thieves to jail and expects an ex to pay child support.

Grace is not blind. It sees the hurt full well. But grace chooses to see God's forgiveness even more. It refuses to let hurts poison the heart. "See to it that no one falls short of the grace of God and that no bitter root grows up to cause trouble and defile many" (Hebrews 12:15 NIV). Where grace is lacking, bitterness abounds. Where grace abounds, forgiveness grows.

–*Grace*

Let Grace Happen

I find rest in God;
only he can save me.
He is my rock and my salvation.
PSALM 62:1–2 NCV

Attempts at self-salvation guarantee nothing but exhaustion. We scamper and scurry, trying to please God, collecting merit badges and brownie points, and scowling at anyone who questions our accomplishments. Call us the church of hound-dog faces and slumped shoulders.

Stop it! Once and for all, enough of this frenzy. "Your hearts should be strengthened by God's grace, not by obeying rules" (Hebrews 13:9 NCV). Jesus does not say, "Come to me, all you who are perfect and sinless." Just the opposite. "Come to Me, all who are weary and heavy-laden, and I will give you rest" (Matthew 11:28 NASB).

There is no fine print. A second shoe is not going to drop. God's promise has no hidden language. Let grace happen, for heaven's sake. No more performing for God, no more clamoring after God. Of all the things you must earn in life, God's unending affection is not one of them. You have it. Stretch yourself out in the hammock of grace.

You can rest now.

–*Grace*

MARCH 30

Put the Devil Behind You

"Get behind Me, Satan!"
MATTHEW 16:23

I once had the opportunity to lead a group of five hundred people to Israel. One morning we had a Bible study on the southern steps of the Temple Mount.

For my lesson I chose a phrase out of John 3:16 (NIV)—"one and only." Since we were sitting where Jesus stood, it seemed only right to consider Jesus' claim that he was God's one and only Son.

A few minutes into the message a mysterious voice began to mock my words. It was high pitched and eerie. Each time I said, "one and only," it mimicked, "one and only." When I said the name "Jesus," the voice, heavy with an accent, scoffed, "Jesus."

The more I preached, the louder the voice parroted. For fear of conceding defeat to this odd force, I didn't stop. I prayed and proclaimed, "Jesus is the supreme authority of this place, any place, and every place, which, by the way, includes any demons, servants of hell, and Satan himself. You are not welcome in this gathering!"

The dissenting voice was suddenly silent. We completed the Bible lesson in peace. I later asked a tour guide if the culprit had been found. "We tried," he told me, "but we could not find him." The guide had no explanation.

I do.

When the authority of Christ is proclaimed, the work of Satan must stop. Call on God. Declare the name of Jesus and put the Devil behind you.

–*Glory Days*

The Bread of Life

"For the bread of God is He who comes down from heaven and gives life to the world."
JOHN 6:33

The grain-to-bread process is a demanding one. The seed must be planted before it can grow. When the grain is ripe, it must be cut down and ground into flour. Before it can become bread, it must pass through the oven. Bread is the end result of planting, harvesting, and heating.

Jesus endured an identical process. He was born into this world. He was cut down, bruised, and beaten on the threshing floor of Calvary. He passed through the fire of God's wrath, for our sake. He "suffered because of others' sins, the Righteous One for the unrighteous ones. He went through it all—was put to death and then made alive—to bring us to God" (1 Peter 3:18 MSG).

Bread of Life? Jesus lived up to the title. But an unopened loaf does a person no good. Have you received the bread? Have you received God's forgiveness?

–*Outlive Your Life*

APRIL

APRIL 1 

The King Is Risen!

The angel answered and said to the women, . . . "I know that you seek Jesus who was crucified. He is not here; for He is risen, as He said."
MATTHEW 28:5–6

"He has risen."

Three words in English. Just one in Greek: *Ēgerthē*. So much rests on the validity of this one word. If it is false, then the whole of Christianity collapses like a poorly told joke. Yet, if it is true, then God's story has turned your final chapter into a preface. If the angel was correct, then you can believe this: Jesus descended into the coldest cell of death's prison and allowed the warden to lock the door and smelt the keys in a furnace. And just when the demons began to dance and prance, Jesus pressed pierced hands against the inner walls of the cavern. From deep within he shook the cemetery. The ground rumbled, and the tombstones tumbled.

And out he marched, the cadaver turned king, with the mask of death in one hand and the keys of heaven in the other. He has risen!

Not risen from sleep. Not risen from confusion. Not spiritually raised from the dead; *physically* raised.

The bodily resurrection means everything. If Jesus lives on only in spirit and deeds, he is but one of a thousand dead heroes. But if he lives on in flesh and bone, he is the King who pressed his heel against the head of death. What he did with his own grave he promises to do with yours: empty it.

–*God's Story, Your Story*

APRIL 2

A Prayer . . . for Courage to Trust

Depend on the Lord;
trust him, and he will take care of you.
PSALM 37:5 NCV

Loving Father, I come to you as Jesus did, with all my fears and weaknesses out in the open. I lay down the masks that I hide behind and open my heart to you. Give me the courage to trust in you for all that I face. In Jesus' name, amen.

–*On Calvary's Hill*

Grace upon Grace

This is how God showed his love among us: He sent his one and only Son into the world that we might live through him. This is love: not that we loved God, but that he loved us and sent his Son as an atoning sacrifice for our sins.
1 JOHN 4:9–10 NIV

G*race* is simply another word for God's tumbling, rumbling reservoir of strength and protection. It comes at us not occasionally or miserly but constantly and aggressively, wave upon wave. We've barely regained our balance from one breaker, and then, *bam*, here comes another.

"Grace upon grace" (John 1:16 NASB). We dare to hang our hat and stake our hope on the gladdest news of all: if God permits the challenge, he will provide the grace to meet it.

We never exhaust his supply. God has enough grace to solve every dilemma you face, wipe every tear you cry, and answer every question you ask.

Would we expect anything less from God? Send his Son to die for us and not send his power to sustain us? Paul found such logic impossible: "He who did not spare his own Son, but gave him up for us all—how will he not also, along with him, graciously give us all things?" (Romans 8:32 NIV).

Stand in the shadow of God's crucified Son. Now pose your questions. *Is Jesus on my side?* Look at the wound in his. *Will he stay with me?* Having given the supreme and costliest gift, "how can he fail to lavish upon us all he has to give?" (Romans 8:32 NEB).

–*Grace*

APRIL 4

What Got into Peter?

"The Helper, the Holy Spirit, whom the Father will send in My name, He will teach you all things, and bring to your remembrance all things that I said to you."
JOHN 14:26

What got into Peter? Seven weeks ago he was hiding because of Jesus; today he is proclaiming the death of Jesus. On the eve of Good Friday, you couldn't get him to speak up. Today, you can't get him to shut up!

He was a coward at the crucifixion.

But look at him on the day of Pentecost, declaring to a throng of thousands, "God has made Jesus—the man you nailed to the cross—both Lord and Christ" (Acts 2:36 NCV). Gutsy language. The same crowd that shouted, "Crucify him!" could crucify Peter.

From wimp to warrior in fifty days.

What got into Peter?

God's Spirit did. Ten days after Jesus' ascension into heaven, "all of them were filled with the Holy Spirit" (Acts 2:4 NIV). The Holy Spirit, in his own time and according to his own way, filled the followers with supernatural strength.

Jesus promised this event. He said, "If I go, I will send him to you" (John 16:7 NIV).

The bad news: Jesus was going away. The wonderful news: Jesus was sending them the Spirit. During his earthly ministry, Jesus lived near the disciples. The Holy Spirit, however, would live *in* the disciples. What Jesus did with the followers, the Spirit would do through them and us. The Spirit continues the work of Christ . . . in and through us.

–*God's Story, Your Story*

Learning to Wait

He guides the humble in what is right
and teaches them his way.
PSALM 25:9 NIV

Wait on the Spirit. If Peter and the apostles needed the help of the Spirit, don't we? They walked with Jesus for three years, heard his preaching, and saw his miracles. They saw the body of Christ buried in the grave and raised from the dead. They witnessed his Upper Room appearance and heard his instruction. Had they not received the best possible training? Weren't they ready?

Yet Jesus told them to wait on the Spirit. "Do not leave Jerusalem, but wait for the gift my Father promised . . . the Holy Spirit" (Acts 1:4–5 NIV).

Learn to wait, to be silent, to listen for his voice. Cherish stillness; sensitize yourself to his touch. "Just think—you don't need a thing, you've got it all! All God's gifts are right in front of you as you *wait expectantly* for our Master Jesus to arrive on the scene" (1 Corinthians 1:7–8 MSG, emphasis mine). You needn't hurry or scurry. The Spirit-led life does not panic; it trusts.

Learn to wait on the Spirit.

–God's Story, Your Story

APRIL 6

Only the Beginning

Jesus said, . . . "I am the resurrection and the life. The one who believes in me will live, even though they die."
JOHN 11:25–27 NIV

This heart will feel a final pulse. These lungs will empty a final breath. The hand that directs this pen across the page will fall limp and still. Barring the return of Christ, I will die. So will you. As the psalmist asked, "Who can live and not see death, or who can escape the power of the grave?" (Psalm 89:48 NIV). Young and old, good and bad, rich and poor. Neither gender is spared; no class is exempt. "No one has power over the time of their death" (Ecclesiastes 8:8 NIV).

The geniuses, the rich, the poor—no one outruns it or outsmarts it. Julius Caesar died. Elvis died. John Kennedy died. Princess Diana died. We all die. We don't escape death.

The finest surgeon might enhance your life but can't eliminate your death. The Hebrew writer was blunt: "People are destined to die once" (Hebrews 9:27 NIV). Exercise all you want. Eat nothing but health food, and pop fistfuls of vitamins. Stay out of the sun, away from alcohol, and off drugs. Do your best to stay alive, and still, you die.

Death seems like such a dead end.

Until we read Jesus' resurrection story.

"He is not here. He has risen from the dead as he said he would" (Matthew 28:6 NCV).

–*God's Story, Your Story*

THE LAST WORD

Jesus said to him, "Away with you, Satan!"
MATTHEW 4:10

Satan never shuts up. The apostle John called him the Accuser: "For the Accuser has been thrown down to earth—the one who accused our brothers and sisters before our God day and night'" (Revelation 12:10 NLT).

Day after day, hour after hour. Relentless, tireless. The Accuser makes a career out of accusing. Unlike the conviction of the Holy Spirit, Satan's condemnation brings no repentance or resolve, just regret. He has one aim: "to steal, and to kill, and to destroy" (John 10:10). Steal your peace, kill your dreams, and destroy your future. But he will not have the last word. Jesus has acted on your behalf.

He stooped. Low enough to sleep in a manger, work in a carpentry shop, sleep in a fishing boat. Low enough to rub shoulders with crooks and lepers. Low enough to be spat upon, slapped, nailed, and speared. Low. Low enough to be buried.

And then he stood. Up from the slab of death. Upright in Joseph's tomb and right in Satan's face. Tall. High. He stood up to Satan . . . and he will stand up for you.

–*Grace*

APRIL 8

Finally Face-to-Face

Great is the LORD! He is most worthy of praise!

PSALM 145:3 NLT

On the great Day you'll hear billions of voices make the identical claim about Jesus Christ. "Every knee will bow to the name of Jesus—everyone in heaven, on earth, and under the earth. And everyone will confess that Jesus Christ is Lord" (Philippians 2:10–11 NCV).

Multitudes of people will bow low like a field of windblown wheat, each one saying, "Thou, O King, art the most worthy."

There will be one monumental difference. Some people will continue the confession they began on earth. They will crown Christ again, gladly. Others will crown him for the first time. They will do so sadly. They denied Christ on earth, so he will deny them in heaven.

But those who accepted him on earth will live with God forever. "I heard a voice thunder from the Throne: 'Look! Look! God has moved into the neighborhood, making his home with men and women! They're his people, he's their God'" (Revelation 21:3 MSG). The narrator makes the same point four times in four consecutive phrases:

"God has moved into the neighborhood"

"making his home with men and women"

"They're his people"

"he's their God"

The announcement comes with the energy of a six-year-old declaring the arrival of his father from a long trip. This is big news worthy of repetition.

We shall finally see God face-to-face.

–*God's Story, Your Story*

A Prayer . . . for the Journey

Then He said to them, "Follow Me, and I will make you fishers of men."
MATTHEW 4:19

My Lord and Savior, thank you for inviting me into the journey with you! It is my joy to follow you and to listen for your voice. You are the great and mighty King, and I choose you. In your precious name, Jesus, amen.

–*On Calvary's Hill*

APRIL 10

Triumphant in Christ

Thanks be to God, who gives us the victory
through our Lord Jesus Christ.
1 CORINTHIANS 15:57

Triumph is a precious thing. We honor the triumphant. The gallant soldier sitting astride his steed. The determined explorer, returning from his discovery. The winning athlete holding aloft the triumphant trophy of victory. Yes, we love triumph.

Triumph is fleeting, though. Hardly does one taste victory before it is gone.

The triumph of Christ is not temporary. "Triumphant in Christ" is not an event or an occasion. It's not fleeting. To be triumphant in Christ is a lifestyle . . . a state of being! To triumph in Christ is not something we do, it's something we are.

Here is the big difference between victory in Christ and victory in the world: A victor in the world rejoices over something he did. But the believer rejoices over who he is—a child of God, a forgiven sinner, an heir of eternity.

Nothing can separate us from our triumph in Christ. Nothing! Our triumph is based not upon our feelings but upon God's gift. Our triumph is based not upon our perfection but upon God's forgiveness. How precious is this triumph! For even though we are pressed on every side, the victory is still ours. Nothing can alter the loyalty of God.

"Triumphant in Christ." It is not something we do. It's something we are.

–On the Anvil

APRIL 11 

When God Closes a Door

Pray for us, too, that God may open a door for our message, so that we may proclaim the mystery of Christ, for which I am in chains.

COLOSSIANS 4:3 NIV

Do you know the frustration of a blocked door? If so, you have a friend in the apostle Paul.

He, Silas, and Timothy were on their second missionary journey. On his first one Paul enjoyed success at every stop. "They began to report all things that God had done with them and how He had opened a door of faith to the Gentiles" (Acts 14:27 NASB).

The missionaries felt the gusts at their backs, and then, all of a sudden, headwinds.

Paul and his companions traveled throughout the region of Phrygia and Galatia, having been kept by the Holy Spirit from preaching the word in the province of Asia. When they came to the border of Mysia, they tried to enter Bithynia, but the Spirit of Jesus would not allow them to (Acts 16:6–7).

Paul set his sights on Asia. Yet no doors opened. So the three turned north into Bithynia but encountered more blocked doors. They jiggled the knobs and pressed against the entrances but no access. We aren't told how or why God blocked the door. Just that he did.

He still does.

God owns the key to every door. He is "opening doors no one can lock, locking doors no one can open" (Revelation 3:7 MSG). Once God closes a door, no one can open it. When God closes a door, pray that he will show you the open door chosen for you.

–*God's Story, Your Story*

APRIL 12

Trust God's Story

The ways of the LORD are right;
the righteous walk in them.
HOSEA 14:9 NIV

As God's story becomes yours, closed doors take on a new meaning. You no longer see them as interruptions of your plan but as indications of God's plan.

This is what Paul learned. God blocked his missionary team from going north, south, or east. Only west remained. The closed doors in Asia led to an open-armed invitation to Philippi (Acts 16:11–12). Once there, Paul and his team got to work. Their efforts in Philippi were so effective that the pagan religious leaders were angered. So they conjured up a story against Paul and Silas.

"The multitude rose up together against them; and the magistrates tore off their clothes and commanded them to be beaten with rods. And when they had laid many stripes on them, they threw . . . them into the inner prison and fastened their feet in the stocks" (Acts 16:22–24).

Paul and Silas could have groaned, "Oh no. Not another locked door." But they didn't complain. From the bowels of the prison emerged the most unexpected of sounds: praise and prayer (Acts 16:25).

Their feet were in stocks, yet their minds were in heaven. How could they sing at a time like this? From whence came their song? There is only one answer: they trusted God and his story for them.

–*God's Story, Your Story*

Three Questions

Feed the hungry, and help those in trouble.
Then your light will shine out from the darkness.
ISAIAH 58:10 NLT

A few years back, three questions rocked my world. Question 1: Had you been a German Christian during World War II, would you have taken a stand against Hitler? Question 2: Had you lived in the South during the civil rights conflict, would you have taken a stand against racism? Question 3: When your grandchildren discover you lived during a day in which 1.75 billion people were poor and 1 billion were hungry, how will they judge your response?

I didn't mind the first two questions. They were hypothetical. I'd like to think I would have taken a stand against Hitler and fought against racism. But those days are gone, and those choices were not mine. But the third question has kept me awake at night. I do live today; so do you. We are given a choice . . . an opportunity to make a big difference during a difficult time.

What if we did? What if we rocked the world with hope? Infiltrated all corners with God's love and life? What if we followed the example of the Jerusalem church? This tiny sect expanded into a world-changing force. We still drink from their wells and eat from their trees of faith. What if we lived our lives by this prayer:

Do it again, Jesus. Do it again.

–*Outlive Your Life*

 APRIL 14

Leave the Devil No Choice

Put on the full armor of God, so that you can take
your stand against the devil's schemes.
EPHESIANS 6:11 NIV

Your battle—your real battle—is with your archenemy, the Devil. He has held this stronghold in your life for years. You've tried everything to overcome it: renewed discipline, self-help books, pop culture gurus . . . Nothing helps. But now you come in God's power with God center stage, Jesus in your heart, angels in front and back. You come, not with hope of a possible victory, but with assurance of complete victory.

March in like Joshua at the walls of Jericho. Blast your ram's horn. Sing songs of redemption, and declare scriptures of triumph. Marinate your mind with the declaration of Jesus, "It is finished!" (John 19:30), and the announcement of the angels, "He is not here; for He is risen" (Matthew 28:6). Personalize the proclamations of Paul: "We are more than conquerors through [Christ]" (Romans 8:37), and "I can do all things through Christ" (Philippians 4:13). As you do, the demons will begin to scatter. They have no choice but to leave.

Call upon God and leave the Devil no choice.

–*Glory Days*

God Works

We know that in all things God works for the good of those who love him, who have been called according to his purpose.

ROMANS 8:28 NIV

There are so many things we do not know. We do not know if the economy will dip or if our team will win. We do not know what our spouse is thinking or how our kids will turn out. We don't even know "what we ought to pray for" (Romans 8:26 NIV). But according to Paul, we can be absolutely certain about four things. We know:

1. *God works.* He is busy behind the scenes, above the fray, within the fury. He hasn't checked out or moved on. He is ceaseless and tireless. He never stops working.
2. *God works for the good.* Not for our comfort or pleasure or entertainment, but for our ultimate good. Since he is the ultimate good, would we expect anything less?
3. *God works for the good of those who love him.* Behold the benefit of loving God! Make his story your story, and your story takes on a happy ending. Guaranteed. Being the Author of our salvation, he writes a salvation theme into our biography.
4. *God works in all things.* God is all-inclusive. He works, not through a few things or through the good things, best things, or easy things. But in "all things" God works.

This we know.

—God's Story, Your Story

APRIL 16

A Prayer . . . to Shield You

You, O Lord, are a shield for me,
My glory and the One who lifts up my head.
I cried to the Lord with my voice,
And He heard me from His holy hill.
PSALM 3:3–4

Dear God, holy and mighty one. You are worthy of all praise, all honor. Your steadfast love amazes me each morning.

When I hear voices around me saying I am not good enough, help me hear your truth in my heart and give me strength.

Be with those who feel inadequate and doubt if anyone cares about them. When they question their value, give them a deeper sense of worth in Christ, and Christ alone.

Thank you that we don't have to fight for our worth because you have already called us your children. In Jesus' name, amen.

–*Pocket Prayers*

APRIL 17

Finding the Right Path

If anyone ministers, let him do it as with
the ability which God supplies.
1 PETER 4:11

How can you know what you should do with your life? What is your destiny? First, answer this question: *What is your ability?* Think about it. What do you do well? What do people ask you to do again? What task comes easily? What topic keeps your attention? That's your ability. And ability reveals destiny.

Your skill set—your ability—is your road map. It leads you to your destiny. Take note of your strengths. They are bread crumbs that will lead you to where God wants you to be, to the job and to the ministry that he wants you to do. Remember: God loves you too much to give you a job and not the skills to do it. Identify yours.

What you do for a living should conform to your design. Few situations are more miserable than a job misfit. Yet few maladies are more common. One study stated that only 13 percent of all workers find their work truly meaningful.[1] No wonder commuters look so grumpy. Nearly nine out of ten of them don't want to go to work. Imagine the impact this unhappiness has on health, family, and performance. If a person spends forty or more hours a week plodding through a job he or she does not like or care about, what happens?

Find something you like to do, and do it so well that people pay you to do it. That's not just good advice; it's godly design.

–*Glory Days*

APRIL 18

Take the Initiative

If it is possible, as much as depends on
you, live peaceably with all men.
ROMANS 12:18

You may find this hard to believe, but not everyone likes the preacher. There are times when I misstep or misspeak and incur the displeasure of a parishioner. In the early years of my ministry, when I got wind of someone's unhappiness, I dismissed the problem. "If he doesn't bring it to me, then I have no hand in the matter."

But then I read Jesus' words: "If you bring your gift to the altar, and there remember that your brother has something against you, leave your gift there before the altar, and go your way. First be reconciled to your brother, and then come and offer your gift" (Matthew 5:23–24). Jesus commands the offender, even if unintentional, to take the initiative. I find that passage to be quite unpleasant.

Even so, I have tried to apply it to my fragile friendships.

"Bob," I have inquired, "have I said something to upset you?"

"Mary," I have asked, "there seems to be tension between us. Are we okay?"

Without fail the step has resulted in restoration. Never in my four decades of ministry has this practical teaching failed to achieve its goal. When Scripture is mixed with obedience, a healing elixir results.

–*Glory Days*

APRIL 19

The Falling of a Wall

Then Philip went down to the city of Samaria
and preached Christ to them.
ACTS 8:5

Do any walls bisect your world? There you stand on one side. And on the other? The teen with the tats. The boss with the bucks. The immigrant with the hard-to-understand accent. Or the Samaritans outside Jerusalem.

Talk about a wall, ancient and tall. "Jews," as John wrote in his gospel, "refuse to have anything to do with Samaritans" (John 4:9 NLT).

Jesus, however, played by a different set of rules. He spent the better part of a day on the turf of a Samaritan woman (John 4:1–26). He stepped across the cultural taboo as if it were a sleeping dog in the doorway. Jesus loves to break down walls.

That's why he sent Philip to Samaria (Acts 8:5–7, 12). And when the city broke out into a revival, both men and women were baptized. Peter and John heard about the response and traveled to Samaria to confirm it. "Then they laid hands on them, and they received the Holy Spirit" (v. 17).

But why hadn't the Samaritans received the Holy Spirit when they were first baptized? Why delay the gift?

Simple. To celebrate the falling of a wall. The gospel, for the first time, was breaching an ancient bias. God marked the moment with a ticker-tape parade of sorts. He rolled out the welcome mat and sent his apostles to verify the revival and place hands on the Samaritans. Let any doubt be gone: God accepts all people.

–*Outlive Your Life*

APRIL 20

A Chance

Therefore, if anyone is in Christ, he is a new creation; old things have passed away; behold, all things have become new.

2 CORINTHIANS 5:17

Consider the Samaritan woman. By the time Jesus met her, she was on a first-century version of a downward spiral. Five ex-husbands and half a dozen kids, each looking like a different daddy. Decades of loose living had left her tattooed and tabooed and living with a boyfriend who thought a wedding was a waste of time.

Gossipers wagged their tongues about her. How else can we explain her mid-day appearance at the water well? Other women filled their buckets at sunrise, but this woman opted for noon, preferring, I suppose, the heat of the sun over the heat of their scorn.

Were it not for the appearance of a Stranger, her story would have been lost in the Samaritan sands. But he entered her life with a promise of endless water and quenched thirst. He wasn't put off by her past. Just the opposite. He offered her a chance, a fresh start, a clean slate. She accepted his offer. We know because of what happened next: "Many Samaritans from the village believed in Jesus because the woman had said, 'He told me everything I ever did!'" (John 4:39 NLT).

The woman on the margin became the woman with the message. No one else gave her a chance. Jesus gave her the chance of a lifetime. He came for people like her. He came for people like you and me.

–*Glory Days*

APRIL 21 

God Amid the Billows

Why are you cast down, O my soul?
And why are you disquieted within me?
PSALM 42:5

The writer of Psalm 42 was sad and discouraged. The struggles of life threatened to pull him under and take another victory. But at just the right time, the writer made this decision: "Hope in God, for I shall yet praise Him. . . . I will remember You from the land of Jordan, and from the heights of Hermon, from the Hill Mizar" (vv. 5–6).

There is resolve in those words. "I shall yet . . . I will remember You." The writer made a deliberate decision to treat his downcast soul with thoughts of God. *Everywhere I go, I will remember you.*

In your case the verse would read, "From the ICU to the cemetery, to the unemployment line, to the courtroom, I will remember you."

There is nothing easy about this. Troubles pounce on us like rain in a thunderstorm. Finding God amid the billows will demand every bit of discipline you can muster. But the result is worth the strain. Besides, do you really want to meditate on your misery? Will reciting your problems turn you into a better person? No. But changing your mind-set will.

"Stop allowing yourselves to be agitated and disturbed" (John 14:27 AMPC). Instead, *immerse your mind in God-thoughts.*

–*Glory Days*

APRIL 22

Making Satan Tremble

The effective, fervent prayer of a righteous man avails much.
JAMES 5:16

Most of us struggle with prayer. We forget to pray, and when we remember, we hurry through prayers with hollow words. Our minds drift; our thoughts scatter like a covey of quail. Why is this? Prayer requires minimal effort. No location is prescribed. No particular clothing is required. Yet you'd think we were wrestling a greased pig.

Speaking of pigs, Satan seeks to interrupt our prayers. Our battle with prayer is not entirely our fault. The Devil knows the stories; he witnessed the angel in Peter's cell and the revival in Jerusalem. He knows what happens when we pray. "Our weapons have power from God that can destroy the enemy's strong places" (2 Corinthians 10:4 NCV).

Satan is not troubled when Max writes books or prepares sermons, but his knobby knees tremble when Max prays. Satan does not stutter or stumble when you walk through church doors or attend committee meetings. But the walls of hell shake when one person with an honest heart and faithful confession says, "Oh, God, how great thou art."

Satan keeps you and me from prayer. He tries to position himself between us and God. But he scampers like a spooked dog when we move forward. So let's do.

–*Outlive Your Life*

A Prayer . . . to Draw Closer to Christ

For every child of God defeats this evil world, and we achieve this victory through our faith.

1 JOHN 5:4 NLT

Son of God, there's nothing I have faced or ever will face that you have not faced, endured, and conquered. And wonder of wonders, you run to me when I need your help. I come to you now. Draw close to me, Jesus. In your name, amen.

–*On Calvary's Hill*

APRIL 24

The Mountain Mover

Blessed is the man who trusts in the Lord,

And whose hope is the Lord.

JEREMIAH 17:7

When troubles come our way, we can be stressed and upset, or we can trust God.

"Set your minds and keep them set on what is above (the higher things)" (Colossians 3:2 AMP). When giants are in the land, when doubts swarm your mind, turn your thoughts to God. Your best thoughts are God-thoughts.

He is above all this mess! He is "the Most High over all the earth" (Psalm 83:18 ESV).

The psalmist asked, "Who in the skies is comparable to the Lord? Who among the sons of the mighty is like the Lord?" (Psalm 89:6 NASB).

Pain does not plague God.
The economy does not faze him.
The weather does not disturb him.
Elections do not define him.
Diseases do not infect him.
Death cannot claim him.

He is "able to do exceedingly abundantly above all that we ask or think" (Ephesians 3:20). Stare at the mountain less and at the Mountain Mover more. Ponder the holiness of God. Let his splendor stun you and inspire you.

–*Glory Days*

Tap or Two-by-Four?

My son, do not make light of the Lord's discipline,
and do not lose heart when he rebukes you,
because the Lord disciplines the one he loves,
and he chastens everyone he accepts as his son.
HEBREWS 12:5–6 NIV

Wake up! That's what God was really saying to Saul. Saul, the first king of Israel, was consumed with jealousy. He was upstaged by David, the youngest son of a shepherding family. David did everything better than Saul: he sang better, he impressed the women more, he even killed the giants Saul feared. But rather than celebrate David's God-given abilities, Saul grew insanely hostile. God, in an apparent effort to awaken Saul from this fog of jealousy, enlisted the help of his unwilling servant, Satan. "The next day an evil spirit from God rushed upon Saul, and he prophesied in his house" (1 Samuel 18:10 NCV).

Observe a solemn principle: there are times when hearts grow so hard and ears so dull that God turns us over to endure the consequences of our choices.

As drastic as it may appear, God will actually allow a person to experience hell on earth, in hopes of awakening his faith. A holy love makes the tough choice to release the child to the consequences of his rebellion.

Remember, discipline should result in mercy, not misery. Some saints are awakened by a tap on the shoulder, while others need a two-by-four to the head. And whenever God needs a two-by-four, Satan gets the call.

–*For the Tough Times*

APRIL 26

Testing

When He has tested me, I shall come forth as gold.

JOB 23:10

Satan likes to test the saints. Listen to the warning Jesus gives to Peter: "Simon, Simon, Satan has asked to test all of you as a farmer sifts his wheat. I have prayed that you will not lose your faith! Help your brothers be stronger when you come back to me" (Luke 22:31–32 NCV).

Satan may like to test the saints, but notice who is in control. Even though Satan had a plan, he had to get permission. "All authority in heaven and on earth has been given to me," Jesus explained (Matthew 28:18 NIV), and this is proof. The wolf cannot get to the sheep without the permission of the Shepherd, and the Shepherd will only permit the attack if, in the long term, the pain is worth the gain.

Jesus was allowing Peter to experience a trial so he could encourage his brothers. Perhaps God is doing the same with you. Your difficulty, your disease, your conflict are preparing you to be a voice of encouragement to your brothers. All you need to remember is:

No test or temptation that comes your way is beyond the course of what others have had to face. All you need to remember is that God will never let you down; he'll never let you be pushed past your limit; he'll always be there to help you come through it (1 Corinthians 10:13 MSG).

Turn to him.

–For the Tough Times

The Power of Confession

Search me, O God, and know my heart;
Try me, and know my anxieties;
And see if there is any wicked way in me,
And lead me in the way everlasting.
PSALM 139:23–24

Maybe your prayer needs to probe deeper than the simple transgressions of today. Beneath the epidermis of today's deeds are the unresolved actions of years past. Like King David, you made one stupid decision after another. You stayed when you should have gone, looked when you should have turned, seduced when you should have abstained, hurt when you should have helped, denied when you should have confessed.

Talk to God about these buried blades of sin and guilt. Go to him as you would go to a trusted physician. Explain the pain, and revisit the transgression together. Welcome his probing and healing touch. And, this is important, trust his ability to receive your confession more than your ability to make it. Oh, that unruly perfectionist who indwells us. He raises cankerous doubts: "Was my confession sincere? Sufficient? Did I forget any sin?"

Of course you did. Who among us knows all our violations? Who of us has felt sufficient remorse for our failings? If the cleansing of confession depends on the confessor, we are all sunk, for none of us have confessed accurately or adequately. The power of confession lies not with the person who makes it but with the God who hears it.

–*Grace*

APRIL 28

A Tool in the Hand of God

Pride leads to destruction; a proud attitude brings ruin.

PROVERBS 16:18 NCV

God uses Satan. That's right. The Ruler of All uses the ruler of evil for his own purposes. How? By refining the faithful.

Even the meekest among us have a tendency to think too highly of ourselves. Apparently the apostle Paul did. His résumé was impressive: a personal audience with Jesus, a participant in heavenly visions, an apostle chosen by God, an author of the Bible. Few could rival his achievements. And maybe he knew it. Perhaps Paul began to pat himself on the back. God, who loved Paul and hates pride, protected Paul from the sin. And he used Satan to do it.

"To keep me from becoming conceited, I was given me a thorn in my flesh, a messenger of Satan, to torment me" (2 Corinthians 12:7 NIV).

We aren't told the nature of the thorn, but we are told its purpose—to keep Paul humble. We are also told its origin—a messenger of Satan. The messenger could have been a pain, a problem, or a person who was a pain. We don't know, but please note what Paul says next: "Three times I pleaded with the Lord to take it away from me. But he said to me, 'My grace is sufficient for you, for my power is made perfect in weakness'" (vv. 8–9 NIV).

Satan and his forces were simply a tool in the hand of God to strengthen a servant.

–For the Tough Times

APRIL 29

Dressed in Goodness

I will greatly rejoice in the Lord,
My soul shall be joyful in my God;
For He has clothed me with the garments of salvation,
He has covered me with the robe of righteousness.
ISAIAH 61:10

At the cross Christ wrapped himself around us and felt the full force of the fall. He took the unrelaxed punishment of the guilty. He died, not like a sinner, but as a sinner—in our place. His sacrifice is a sufficient one. Our merits don't enhance it. Our stumbles don't diminish it. The sacrifice of Christ is a total and unceasing and accomplished work.

"It is finished," Jesus announced (John 19:30 NIV). His prayer of abandonment is followed by a cry of accomplishment. Not "It is begun" or "It is initiated" or "It is a work in progress." No, "It is finished."

Does better news exist? Actually, yes. There is more. He is "our righteousness" (1 Corinthians 1:30 NIV).

God does not simply remove our failures; he dresses us in the goodness of Christ! "For all of you who were baptized into Christ have clothed yourselves with Christ" (Galatians 3:27 NIV).

Now that's a wardrobe worth wearing.

–*God's Story, Your Story*

APRIL 30

A Prayer . . . to See God's Light

Your sun shall no longer go down, nor shall your moon withdraw itself; for the Lord will be your everlasting light, and the days of your mourning shall be ended.

ISAIAH 60:20

Father, you have the power to control the sun and the moon. You are the everlasting Light.

Help me to see a light at the end of my tunnel. Sometimes I can barely remember what light looks like or what it feels like to have simple joy. Help me to focus on you even in the darkness.

Support my friends as they struggle with losses and temptations. When these trials plague those I love, I feel so helpless. Would you show off your light in their lives?

Thank you, God, that you are our rock and healer and that you will bring our mourning to an end. In the name of the everlasting Light, amen.

–*Pocket Prayers*

MAY

MAY 1

This Isn't Home

"There is more than enough room in my Father's home. If this were not so, would I have told you that I am going to prepare a place for you? When everything is ready, I will come and get you, so that you will always be with me where I am."

JOHN 14:2–3 NLT

You were born heaven-equipped with a hunger for your heavenly home. Need proof?

Consider your questions. Questions about death and time, significance and relevance. Animals don't seem to ask the questions we do. Dogs howl at the moon, but we stare at it. How did we get here? What are we here for? Are we someone's idea or something's accident? Why on earth are we on this earth?

We ask questions about pain. The words *leukemia* and *child* shouldn't appear in the same sentence. And war. Can't conflict go the way of cassette tapes and telegrams? And the grave. Why is the dash between the dates on a tombstone so small? Something tells us this isn't right, good, fair. This isn't home.

From whence come these stirrings? Who put these thoughts in our heads? Why can't we, like rabbits, be happy with carrots and copulation? Because, according to Jesus, we aren't home yet.

–God's Story, Your Story

An Unmoving Target

All Scripture is given by inspiration of God, and is profitable for doctrine, for reproof, for correction, for instruction in righteousness, that the man of God may be complete, thoroughly equipped for every good work.

2 TIMOTHY 3:16–17

The key to spiritual growth is not increased church attendance or involvement in spiritual activities. People don't grow in Christ because they are busy at church. They grow in Christ when they read and trust their Bibles.

Desire some growth? Engage with the Bible. Meditate on it day and night. Think and rethink about God's Word. Let it be your guide. Make it the ultimate authority in your life.

Don't chart your course according to the opinions of people or suggestions of culture. If you do, you will make the mistake that the farmer's son made. The father sent the boy to prepare a field, reminding him to till straight lines. "Select an object on the far side of the field, and plow straight at it."

Later when the father checked on the boy's progress, there wasn't a straight furrow to be found. Every row was uneven and wavy.

"I thought I told you to select an object and plow toward it," the dad said.

"I did," the boy answered, "but the rabbit kept hopping."

A straight line, like a good life, requires an unmoving target. Set your sights on the unchanging principles of God. Let God's Word be the authoritative word in your world.

–*Glory Days*

MAY 3

Unexpected Majesty

"Truly I tell you, whatever you did for one of the least of these brothers and sisters of mine, you did for me."

MATTHEW 25:40 NIV

At 7:51 A.M., January 12, 2007, a young musician took his position against a wall in a Washington, DC, metro station. He opened a violin case, removed his instrument, threw a few dollars and pocket change into the case as seed money, and began to play.

He played for the next forty-three minutes. He performed six classical pieces. During that time 1,097 people passed by. They tossed in money to the total of $32.17. Of the 1,097 people, seven—only seven—paused longer than sixty seconds. And of the seven, one—only one—recognized the violinist Joshua Bell.

Three days prior to this metro appearance, Bell filled Boston's Symphony Hall. His talents can command $1,000 a minute. That day in the subway station, he barely earned enough to buy a cheap pair of shoes.

But no one expected majesty in such a context. Shoe-shine stand to one side, kiosk to the other. This was a workday. Who had time to notice beauty in the midst of busyness? Most did not.[1]

Most of us will someday realize that we didn't either. From the perspective of heaven, we'll look back on these days—these busy, cluttered days—and realize, *That was Jesus playing the violin. That was Jesus wearing the ragged clothes. That was Jesus in the orphanage . . . in the jail . . . in the cardboard shanty. The person needing my help was Jesus.*

What can we do for Jesus?

–*Outlive Your Life*

Your Sermon

I consider that our present sufferings are not worth comparing with the glory that will be revealed in us.

ROMANS 8:18 NIV

If Jesus heals you instantly, praise him.

If you are still waiting for healing, trust him. Your suffering is your sermon.

My friend Jim has battled a muscular condition for much of his adult life. The atrophy slurs his speech and impairs his walk. But it does not diminish his faith or erase his smile. On one particular Sunday we had asked members to park in the back of the parking lot and leave the closest spots for guests. As I arrived, I saw Jim. He had parked in the distant corner and was walking toward the sanctuary. *We didn't mean for you to park far away*, I wanted to say.

His life is an example. I pray that God will heal Jim's body. But until he does, God is using Jim to inspire people like me. God will do the same with you. He will use your struggle to change others.

God can use your suffering as your sermon.

–*Before Amen*

MAY 5

The Big News of the Bible

For the angel of the Lord is a guard;
he surrounds and defends all who fear him.
PSALM 34:7 NLT

Did you know that God is fighting for you? That "with us is the Lord our God, to help us and to fight our battles" (2 Chronicles 32:8)? That "Our God will fight for us" (Nehemiah 4:20)? That the Lord will fight against those who fight against you (Psalm 35:1)?

God fights for you. Let those four words sink in for a moment.

God. The CEO, President, King, Supreme Ruler, Absolute Monarch, Czar, Emperor, and Rajah of all history. He runs interference and provides cover. He is impeccably perfect, tirelessly strong, unquestionably capable. He is endlessly joyful, wise, and willing. And he . . .

Fights. He deploys angels and commands weather. He stands down Goliaths and vacates cemeteries. He fights . . .

For. For your health, family, faith, and restoration. Are the odds against you? Is the coach against you? Is the government against you? Difficult for sure. But God fights for . . .

You. Yes, you! You with the sordid past. You with the receding hairline. You with the absentee dad. You with the bad back, credit, or job. He fights not just for the rich, pretty, or religious. He fights for the yous of the world. Are you a *you*?

The big news of the Bible is not that you fight for God but that God fights for you. And to know this—to know that your Father fights for you—is an unparalleled source of empowerment.

–*Glory Days*

Risk Honesty

"Whenever you stand praying, if you have anything against anyone, forgive him, that your Father in heaven may also forgive you your trespasses."
MARK 11:25

Late evening. Bedtime. The pillow beckons. But so does your guilty conscience. An encounter with a coworker turned nasty earlier in the day. Words were exchanged. Accusations made. Lines drawn in the sand. Names called. Tacky, tacky, tacky behavior. You bear some, if not most, of the blame.

The old version of you would have suppressed the argument. Crammed it into an already-crowded cellar of unresolved conflicts. The quarrel would have festered into bitterness and poisoned another relationship. But you aren't the old version of you. Now you know better. You've been bought with blood, given grace, foot washed and indwelled by Christ. You can risk honesty with God. It's time to confess to the One who died to forgive you.

You tell the pillow to wait, and you step into the presence of Jesus. "Can we talk about today's argument? I am sorry that I reacted in the way I did. I was harsh, judgmental, and impatient. You have given me so much grace. I gave so little. Please forgive me."

There, doesn't that feel better? No special location required. No chant or candle needed. Just a prayer. The prayer will likely prompt an apology, and the apology will quite possibly preserve a friendship and protect a heart. You might even hang a sign on your office wall: "Grace happens here."

–*Grace*

MAY 7

A Prayer . . . Because the Lord Loves You

Though he was God, he did not think of equality with God as something to cling to. Instead, he gave up his divine privileges; he took the humble position of a slave and was born as a human being. When he appeared in human form, he humbled himself in obedience to God and died a criminal's death on a cross.

PHILIPPIANS 2:6–8 NLT

Gracious Lord, it's beyond my comprehension that nothing can separate me from your love . . . or that you love what you see when you see me. That you, my Maker and God, would die for me is a wonder. Thank you for opening the way back to you forever. In Jesus' name, amen.

–*In the Manger*

Chosen Children

But to all who believed him and accepted him, he gave the right to become children of God.

JOHN 1:12 NLT

Adopted children are chosen children.

That's not the case with biological children. When the doctor handed Max Lucado to Jack Lucado, my dad had no exit option. No loophole. No choice. He couldn't give me back to the doctor and ask for a better-looking or smarter son. The hospital made him take me home.

But if you were adopted, your parents chose you. Surprise pregnancies happen. But surprise adoptions? Never heard of one. Your parents could have picked a different gender, color, or ancestry. But they selected you. They wanted you in their family.

You object: "Oh, but if they could have seen the rest of my life, they might have changed their minds." My point exactly.

God saw our entire lives from beginning to end, birth to hearse, and in spite of what he saw, he was still convinced "to adopt us into his own family by bringing us to himself through Jesus Christ. This is what he wanted to do, and it gave him great pleasure" (Ephesians 1:5 NLT).

We can now live "like God's very own children, adopted into the bosom of his family, and calling to him, 'Father, Father.' . . . And since we are his children, we will share his treasures—for all God gives to his Son Jesus is now ours too" (Romans 8:15, 17 TLB).

It really is this simple.

–*Grace*

MAY 9

Who's Pushing Your Swing?

Suddenly a furious storm came up on the lake, so that the waves swept over the boat. But Jesus was sleeping.

MATTHEW 8:24 NIV

Children love to swing. There's nothing like it. Thrusting your feet toward the sky, leaning so far back that everything looks upside down. Spinning trees, a stomach that jumps into your throat.

Ahh, swinging. . . .

As a child, I only trusted certain people to push my swing. They could twist me, turn me, stop me. . . . I loved it! But let a stranger push my swing, and it was *hang on, baby!*

It's no fun when your swing is in the hands of a stranger.

Remember when Jesus stilled the storm in Matthew 8? This storm wasn't a gentle spring rain. It was frightening enough to scare the pants (or robes) off of a dozen disciples—even veteran fishermen like Peter. So they ran to wake up Jesus.

They ran to do what? Jesus was asleep? How in the world could he sleep through a storm?

Simple. He knew who was pushing the swing.

We live in a stormy world. Everywhere I look, private storms occur. Family deaths, strained marriages, broken hearts, lonely evenings. We must remember who is pushing the swing. We must put our trust in him. He won't let us tumble out.

Who pushes your swing? In the right hands, you can find peace . . . even in the storm.

–*On the Anvil*

Unlikely Witnesses

"You will be brought before governors and kings
as witnesses to them and to the Gentiles."
MATTHEW 10:18 NIV

They don't look like much. The tall one in the corner—that's Peter. Galilee thickened his accent. Fishing nets thickened his hands. Stubbornness thickened his skull.

And his cronies: Andrew, James, Nathanael. Never traveled farther than a week's walk from home. No formal education. In fact, what do they have? Humility? They jockeyed for cabinet positions. Sound theology? Peter told Jesus to forget the cross. Sensitivity? John wanted to torch the Gentiles. Loyalty? When Jesus was arrested, they ran.

Yet look at them six weeks later, crammed into the second floor of a Jerusalem house, wondering what in the world Jesus had in mind with his final commission: "You will be my witnesses."

You uneducated and simple folk will be my witnesses. *You*—who once shouted at me in the boat and doubted me in the Upper Room—will be my witnesses.

You will spearhead a movement that will explode out of Jerusalem and spill into the ends of the earth. You will be a part of something so mighty, controversial, and head spinning that two millennia from now a middle-aged, redheaded author will type this question on his laptop:

Does Jesus still do it? Does he still use ordinary folks as his witnesses?

You bet! The only real question is: Will you witness?

–*Outlive Your Life*

MAY 11

God Can Do Wonders

Now to him who is able to do immeasurably more than all we ask or imagine, according to his power that is at work within us, to him be glory in the church and in Christ Jesus throughout all generations, for ever and ever! Amen.

EPHESIANS 3:20–21 NIV

Grace is God walking into your world with a sparkle in his eye and an offer that's hard to resist. "Sit still for a bit. I can do wonders with this mess of yours."

Believe this promise. Trust it. Cling like a barnacle to every hope and covenant. Imitate Ruth and get busy. Go to your version of the grain field, and get to work. This is no time for inactivity or despair. Off with the mourning clothes. Take some chances; take the initiative. You never know what might happen. You might have a part in bringing Christ to the world.

–*Grace*

To Live as God's Child

We know how much God loves us, and we
have put our trust in his love.
1 JOHN 4:16 NLT

We never outgrow our need for a father's love. We were wired to receive it. May I tell you just a bit about that love? Listen closely. The words I give you are God's. Receive them slowly. Don't filter, resist, downplay, or deflect them. Just receive them.

My child, I want you in my new kingdom. I have swept away your offenses like the morning clouds, your sins like the morning mist. I have redeemed you. The transaction is sealed; the matter is settled. I, God, have made my choice. I choose you to be part of my forever family.

Let these words cement in your heart a deep, satisfying, fear-quenching confidence that God will never let you go. You belong to him.

To live as God's child is to know, at this very instant, that you are loved by your Maker not because you try to please him and succeed, or fail to please him and apologize, but because he wants to be your Father. Nothing more. All your efforts to win his affection are unnecessary. All your fears of losing his affection are needless. You can no more make him want you than you can convince him to abandon you. The adoption is irreversible. Accept your place as God's adopted child.

–*Grace*

MAY 13

Pure Genius

There is neither Jew nor Greek, there is neither slave nor free, there is neither male nor female; for you are all one in Christ Jesus.

GALATIANS 3:28

Consider the genius of God's plan. The first generation of Christians was a tinderbox of contrasting cultures and backgrounds. At least fifteen different nationalities heard Peter's sermon on the day of Pentecost. Jews stood next to Gentiles. Men worshipped with women. Slaves and masters alike sought after Christ. Can people of such varied backgrounds and cultures get along with each other?

We wonder the same thing today. Can Hispanics live in peace with Anglos? Can Democrats find common ground with Republicans? Can a Christian family carry on a civil friendship with the Muslim couple down the street? Can divergent people get along?

The early church did—without the aid of sanctuaries, church buildings, clergy, or seminaries. They did so through the clearest of messages (the cross) and the simplest of tools (the home).

God's plan of peace = pure genius.

–*Outlive Your Life*

A Prayer . . . for Being Rescued

Then I acknowledged my sin to you
and did not cover up my iniquity.
I said, "I will confess
my transgressions to the Lord."
And you forgave
the guilt of my sin.
PSALM 32:5 NIV

Father God, you redeem me from my sin. You have taken it far away from me. You are perfect love.

Help me as I search to find worth. I feel so unworthy of love at times, and I need your help to discover where my true worth is.

Be strength for those of your children who don't believe their sin is taken care of and are walking around with unnecessary weight on their shoulders.

How can I thank you for your sacrifice? How can I express my gratitude for my freedom? My words don't seem enough, but I thank you that you've healed and rescued me. It's in Jesus' name I pray, amen.

–*Pocket Prayers*

MAY 15

Unpack Your Bags

When the right time came, God sent his Son, born of a woman, subject to the law. God sent him to buy freedom for us who were slaves to the law, so that he could adopt us as his very own children.

GALATIANS 4:4–5 NLT

Do you question your place in God's family? Do you fear his impending rejection? What about wrestle with doubt-laced questions: Am I really in God's family? What if God changes his mind? Reverses his acceptance? Lord knows, he has reason to do so. We press forward only to fall back. We renew our resolve only to stumble again. We wonder, *Will God turn me out?*

Boyfriends do. Employers do. Coaches kick players off the team. Teachers expel students from school. Parents give birth to children and abandon them at a bus station. How do we know God won't do the same? What if he changes his mind about us? After all, he is holy and pure, and we are anything but. Is it safe to unpack our bags?

God answered this question at the cross. When Jesus died, the heavenly vote was forever cast in your favor and mine. He declared for all to hear, "This child is my child. My covenant will never change."

Unpack your bags.

–*Glory Days*

MAY 16

What Do You Think, God?

Pray about everything. Tell God what you need,
and thank him for all he has done.
PHILIPPIANS 4:6 NLT

Consult God in everything. Always. Immediately. Quickly. Live with one ear toward heaven. Keep the line open to God.

"Is this opportunity from you, God?"

"Are you in this venture, God?"

"Should I take this road, God?"

At every decision. At each crossroads. Acknowledge him, heed him, ask him, "Do I turn right or left?" "Trust in the LORD with all your heart, and lean not on your own understanding; in all your ways acknowledge Him, and He shall direct your paths" (Proverbs 3:5–6).

Our relationship with God is exactly that, a relationship. His invitation is clear and simple: "Come and talk with me, O my people" (Psalm 27:8 TLB). And our response? "Lord, I am coming" (v. 8 TLB). We abide with him, and he abides with us. He grants wisdom as we need it.

So don't be afraid to ask: *What do you think, God?*

–*Glory Days*

MAY 17

An Oasis of Grace

Accept one another, then, just as Christ accepted you, in order to bring praise to God.

ROMANS 15:7 NIV

The cross of Christ creates a new people, a people unhindered by skin color or family feud. A new citizenry, based not on common ancestry or geography but on a common Savior.

My friend Buckner Fanning experienced this firsthand. He was a marine in World War II, stationed in Nagasaki three weeks after the dropping of the atomic bomb. Can you imagine a young American soldier amid the rubble and wreckage of the demolished city? The conquering soldier, feeling not victory but grief for the suffering around him.

Instead of anger and revenge, Buckner found an oasis of grace. While patrolling the narrow streets, he came upon a Methodist church. The young marine stepped through the rubble, unsure how he would be received. Fifteen or so Japanese were setting up chairs and removing debris. When the uniformed American entered, they stopped and turned.

He knew only one word in Japanese. He heard it. *Brother.* "They welcomed me as a friend," Buckner relates. They offered him a seat. In that quiet moment the enmity of their nations and the hurt of the war was set aside as one Christian served another the body and blood of Christ.

One brother welcomed another. Accepted. Embraced.

We are a new people, a new family created in Christ.

–*Outlive Your Life*

Stack Some Stones

When your children ask their fathers in time to come, saying, "What are these stones?" then you shall let your children know, saying, "Israel crossed over this Jordan on dry land"; for the LORD your God dried up the waters of the Jordan before you until you had crossed over.

JOSHUA 4:21–23

The secret of survival in enemy territory? *Remember . . .*

Remember what God has done. Record his accomplishments in your memoirs. God knows we need to remember. That's why he had the Israelites stack some stones. So they would look back and see and remember.

Some years back my daughter Andrea reminded me of this truth. As I was driving her to middle school one morning, she noticed that I was anxious.

"Why are you so quiet, Dad?"

I told her that I was worried about meeting a book deadline.

"Haven't you written other books?"

"Yes."

"How many?"

At that point the answer was fifteen.

"Have you ever missed a deadline before?"

"No."

"So God has helped you fifteen times already?"

"Yes."

"If he has helped you fifteen different times, don't you think he will help you this time?"

Translation: Stack some stones, Dad.

– *Glory Days*

MAY 19

Unearned Salvation

If they could be made God's people by what they did,
God's gift of grace would not really be a gift.
ROMANS 11:6 NCV

Do.
Be.

Do. Be. Do.

Do-be-do-be-do.

Familiar with the tune? You might be. Most people embrace the assumption that God saves good people. So be good! Be moral. Be honest. Be decent. Pray the rosary. Keep the Sabbath. Keep your promises. Pray five times a day facing east. Stay sober. Pay taxes. Earn merit badges.

Yet for all the talk about being good, still no one can answer the fundamental question: What level of good is good enough? Bizarre. At stake is our eternal destination, yet we are more confident about lasagna recipes than the entrance requirements for heaven.

God has a better idea: "For by grace you have been saved through faith, and that not of yourselves; it is the gift of God" (Ephesians 2:8). We contribute nothing. Zilch. As opposed to the merit badge of the Scout, salvation of the soul is unearned. A gift. Our merits merit nothing. God's work merits everything.

–*Grace*

MAY 20 

God's Unending Story

I heard a loud voice from the throne, saying, "Now God's presence is with people, and he will live with them, and they will be his people. God himself will be with them and will be their God."

REVELATION 21:3 NCV

Who can understand what God is doing? These days on earth can seem so difficult: marred by conflict, saddened by separation. We fight, pollute, discriminate, and kill. Societies suffer from innumerable fiefdoms, small would-be dynasties. *What is this world coming to?* we wonder.

God's answer: a great Day.

On the great Day all of history will be consummated in Christ. He will assume his position "far above all rule and authority and power and dominion, . . . not only in this age but also in the one to come" (Ephesians 1:21 NASB). And he, the Author of it all, will close the book on this life and open the book to the next and begin to read to us from his unending story.

–God's Story, Your Story

MAY 21

A Prayer . . . to Stay on God's Path

Because we are his children, God has sent the Spirit of his Son into our hearts, prompting us to call out, "Abba, Father."
GALATIANS 4:6 NLT

Abba, thank you for sending a helper to direct my steps. You know everything and will guide me in your will.

Help me to know your will. Keep me on the path you have set for me. Give me the desire to stay true to that path, and forgive me for the times I have already strayed from you.

Be with my friends and family who are at a crossroads and don't know what to do next. May your spirit guide them and make the best decision clear.

Thank you for caring about the details of my life, for not believing any request is too small. I pray this in Jesus' name, amen.

–*Pocket Prayers*

Your Best Days

You know with all your heart and soul that not one of all the good promises the Lord your God gave you has failed. Every promise has been fulfilled; not one has failed.
JOSHUA 23:14 NIV

You don't need to cross the Jordan River or the Red Sea; you just need to get through the week. You aren't facing Jericho or a giant, but you are facing rejection or heartache. Enemies don't stalk you, but disease, discouragement, danger? Rampant. You wonder if you have what it takes to face tomorrow.

You can relate to the deflated little fellow I saw in the airport terminal. He and his family were beach-bound for a week of sand and sun. Everything about the dad's expression said, "Hurry up!" The concourse was his football field, and he was determined to score a touchdown.

Can the little fellow keep up? I wondered. Mom could. Big brothers could. But the little guy? He was five years old, six at most. He tried to match his parent's pace, he just couldn't.

Right in the middle of the mayhem, he gave up. He plopped his bag on the floor, took a seat on top of it, and shouted, "I can't keep up!"

Can you relate?

Sometimes the challenge is just too much. You want to keep up. You try. It's not that you don't. Life has a way of taking the life out of us.

When you run out of fight, remember that the promises of God are yours to claim. God's Word dares you to believe that your best days are ahead of you. God promises you a Promised Land.

–*Glory Days*

MAY 23

NEUTRALIZING SATAN

Draw near to God and He will draw near to you.

JAMES 4:8

Don't face Satan by facing Satan. Face Satan by facing God.

Don't obsess yourself with the Devil. No need to master in the hierarchy of hell. No need to disentangle the puzzle of principalities. Don't give Old Scratch the time of day. Glance at the Devil and gaze at Christ.

Yes, it is a war out there. But the war is already won. "God stripped the spiritual rulers and powers of their authority. With the cross, he won the victory and showed the world that they were powerless" (Colossians 2:15 NCV).

Satan is a fallen angel whose time is short.

Don't let him mess with your Glory Days. Neutralize him.

Remember what God has done. Face the future by remembering the past.

Remember whose you are. You are not who you used to be. You are God's child.

–*Glory Days*

The Definition of Sin

We do not want him to be our king.

LUKE 19:14 NLT

Jesus gave us a one-paragraph definition of sin:

> A nobleman was called away to a distant empire to be crowned king and then return. Before he left, he called together ten of his servants, saying, . . . "Invest this for me while I am gone." But his people hated him and sent a delegation after him to say, "We do not want him to be our king." (Luke 19:12–14 NLT)

To sin is to state, "God, I do not want you to be my king. I prefer a kingless kingdom. Or, better still, a kingdom in which I am king."

The Bible's word for this is *sin*. Sin is not a regrettable lapse or an occasional stumble. Sin storms the castle, lays claim to God's throne, and defies his authority. Sin shouts, "I want to run my own life, thank you very much!" Sin tells God to get out, get lost, and not come back. Sin is insurrection of the highest order, and you are an insurrectionist. So am I. So is every single person who has taken a breath.

But . . . oh, that wonderful word . . . *but*,

"God demonstrates His own love toward us, in that while we were still sinners, Christ died for us" (Romans 5:8).

Christ died to set the insurrectionist—you and me—free.

–*Grace*

MAY 25

What the Devil Fears

Pray in the Spirit on all occasions with all kinds of prayers and requests. With this in mind, be alert and always keep on praying for all the Lord's people.

EPHESIANS 6:18 NIV

The Devil fears prayer. Imagine this scene. He sat in the back of the room during a strategy session. A dozen demons had gathered to hear a report on the life of a particularly stalwart saint.

"He won't stumble," groused the imp responsible for his demise. "No matter what I do, he won't turn his back on God."

The council began to offer suggestions.

"Take his purity," one said.

"I tried," replied the fiend, "but he is too moral."

"Take his health," urged another.

"I did, but he refused to grumble or complain."

"Take his belongings."

"Are you kidding? I've stripped the man of every penny and possession. Yet he still rejoices."

For a few moments no one spoke. Finally, from the back of the room, came the low, measured voice of Satan himself. The entire council turned as the fallen angel rose to his feet. His pale face was all but hidden by the hood. A long cape covered his body. He raised his bony hand and made his point. "You must take what matters most."

"What is that?" asked the subordinate.

"You must take his prayer."

–*Before Amen*

MAY 26 

Hands Off!

Now it is God who makes both us and you stand firm in Christ. He anointed us, set his seal of ownership on us, and put his Spirit in our hearts as a deposit, guaranteeing what is to come.

2 CORINTHIANS 1:21–22 NIV

Jesus promised a new life that could not be forfeited or terminated. "Whoever hears my word and believes him who sent me has eternal life and will not be judged but has crossed over from death to life" (John 5:24 NIV). Bridges are burned, and the transfer is accomplished. Ebbs and flows continue, but they never disqualify. Ups and downs may mark our days, but they will never ban us from his kingdom. Jesus bottom-lines our lives with grace.

Even more, God stakes his claim on us. "By his Spirit he has stamped us with his eternal pledge—a sure beginning of what he is destined to complete" (2 Corinthians 1:22 MSG). You've done something similar: engraved your name on a valued ring, etched your identity on a tool or iPad. Cowboys brand cattle with the mark of the ranch. Stamping declares ownership. Through his Spirit, God stamps us. Would-be takers are repelled by the presence of his name. Satan is driven back by the declaration: *Hands off. This child is mine! Eternally, God.*

–*Grace*

MAY 27

When We Pray

The Lord is close to everyone who prays to him,
to all who truly pray to him.
PSALM 145:18 NCV

When the children of Israel went to battle against the Amalekites, Moses selected the mountain of prayer over the valley of battle (Exodus 17:8–13). The Israelites won.

When Abraham learned about the impending destruction of Sodom and Gomorrah, he "remained standing before the Lord" rather than rushing out to warn the cities (Genesis 18:22 NIV).

Advisers informed Nehemiah that Jerusalem was in ruins. He laid a foundation of prayer before he laid a foundation of stone (Nehemiah 1:4).

Paul's letters contain more requests for prayer than they do appeals for money, possessions, or comforts.

And Jesus. Our prayerful Jesus.

Awaking early to pray (Mark 1:35).

Dismissing people to pray (Matthew 14:23).

Ascending a mountain to pray (Luke 9:28).

Crafting a model prayer to teach us to pray (Matthew 6:9–13).

Cleansing the temple so others could pray (Matthew 21:12–13).

Stepping into a garden to pray (Luke 22:39–46).

Jesus immersed his words and work in prayer. Powerful things happen when we do the same.

–*Outlive Your Life*

A Prayer . . . to Hear God's Voice

A great and strong wind tore into the mountains and broke the rocks in pieces before the Lord, but the Lord was not in the wind; and after the wind an earthquake, but the Lord was not in the earthquake; and after the earthquake a fire, but the Lord was not in the fire; and after the fire a still small voice.

1 KINGS 19:11–12

Great God of the universe, King of the Jews, thank you that you are speaking to me in ways only I can understand. Help me learn to hear your voice in your Word and in all the other ways you speak. In Jesus' name, amen.

–On Calvary's Hill

MAY 29

Facing the Walls of Jericho

"Be strong and of good courage; do not be afraid, nor be dismayed, for the Lord your God is with you wherever you go."

JOSHUA 1:9

High walls. Protected sides. Joshua and his soldiers had never faced such a challenge. They had fought battles in the wilderness, but never, ever had they fought a fortified city. They had never passed this way before.

Perhaps you are facing a challenge unlike any you have ever faced before. It looms on the horizon like an angry Jericho. Imposing. Strong. It is ancient, thick walled, and impenetrable. It is the biggest challenge of your life.

Like Joshua, you can see it.

Like Joshua, you must face it.

And, like Joshua, you don't have to face your Jericho alone.

> Now when Joshua was near Jericho, he looked up and saw a man standing in front of him with a drawn sword in his hand. Joshua went up to him and asked, "Are you for us or for our enemies?"
>
> "Neither," he replied, "but as commander of the army of the Lord I have now come." (Joshua 5:13–14 NIV)

The message to Joshua is unmistakable. *Jericho may have its walls, but, Joshua, you have more. You have God. He is with you.*

Isn't that all any of us need? We need to know that God is near! We are never alone. In our darkest hour, in our deepest questions, the Lord of hosts never leaves us.

–*Glory Days*

God's Plans Are Better

"For My thoughts are not your thoughts,
Nor are your ways My ways," says the Lord.
"For as the heavens are higher than the earth,
So are My ways higher than your ways,
And My thoughts than your thoughts."
ISAIAH 55:8–9

God uses closed doors to advance his cause.

He closed the womb of a young Sarah so he could display his power to the elderly one.

He shut the palace door on Moses the prince so he could open shackles through Moses the liberator.

He marched Daniel out of Jerusalem so he could use Daniel in Babylon.

And Jesus. Yes, even Jesus knew the challenge of a blocked door. When he requested a path that bypassed the cross, God said no. He said no to Jesus in the garden of Gethsemane so he could say yes to us at the gates of heaven.

God's goal is people. He'll stir up a storm to display his power. He'll keep you out of Asia so you'll speak to Lydia. He'll place you in prison so you'll talk to the jailer. *It's not that our plans are bad but that God's plans are better.*

Your blocked door doesn't mean God doesn't love you. Quite the opposite. It's proof that he does.

–*God's Story, Your Story*

MAY 31

Your Pilot Has Spoken

Trust in the LORD forever,
for the LORD, the LORD himself, is the Rock eternal.
ISAIAH 26:4 NIV

My flight into Houston was delayed by storms. We landed at the exact time the final flight into San Antonio was scheduled to depart. As we taxied toward the gate, I was checking my watch, thinking about hotels, preparing to call and tell Denalyn of my delay, grumbling at the bad break.

Then over the loud speaker a promise. "This is the pilot. I know many of you have connections. Relax. You'll make them. We are holding your planes. We have a place for you."

Well, I thought, *he wouldn't say that if he didn't mean it.* So I decided to trust his promise.

I relaxed. I waited my turn to get off the plane and set my sights on my gate. I marched through the concourse with confidence. Hadn't the pilot given me a promise?

Other people in the airport weren't so fortunate. They were in a panic. Travelers were scrambling, white faced and worried.

Too bad their pilot hadn't spoken to them. Or perhaps he had and they hadn't listened.

Your pilot has spoken to you. Will you listen? No, I mean *really* listen? Let his promises settle over you like the warmth of a summer day. When everyone and everything around you says to panic, choose the path of peace. In this world of broken promises, do yourself a favor: take hold of the promises of God.

–*Glory Days*

JUNE

JUNE 1

The Tragedy of Old Wineskins

"No one puts new wine into old wineskins; or else the new wine bursts the wineskins, the wine is spilled, and the wineskins are ruined. But new wine must be put into new wineskins."

MARK 2:22

I'll never forget Steven. His twenty-three years had been hard on him, his arm scarred from the needle and his wrist scarred from the knife. His pride was his fist, and his weakness was his girl.

Steve's initial response to love was beautiful. As we unfolded the story of Jesus before him, his hardened face would soften and his dark eyes would dance.

But his girlfriend would have none of it. Any changes Steve made would be quickly muffled as she would craftily maneuver him back into his old habits. We begged him to leave her. He was trying to put new wine into an old wineskin.

He wrestled for days trying to decide what to do. Finally, he reached a conclusion. He couldn't leave her.

The last time I saw Steve, he wept . . . uncontrollably. The prophecy of Jesus was true. By putting his new wine into an old skin, it was lost.

Think for a minute. Do you have any wineskins that need to be thrown out? Maybe yours is an old indulgence—food, clothes, sex. Or an old habit, like gossip or profanity. Or possibly, like Steve, an old relationship. Repentance means change. And change means purging your heart of anything that can't coexist with Christ.

You can't put new life into an old lifestyle. The inevitable tragedy occurs. The new life is lost.

–*On the Anvil*

Ultimate Healing

Praise be to the God and Father of our Lord Jesus Christ,
the Father of compassion and the God of all comfort.
2 CORINTHIANS 1:3 NIV

If you are sick, cry out to Jesus!

He will heal you—instantly or gradually or ultimately.

He may heal you *instantly.* One word was enough for him to banish demons, heal epilepsy, and raise the dead. He may do this for you.

Or he may heal you *gradually.* In the case of a blind man from Bethsaida, Jesus healed him in stages (Mark 8:22–26).

And don't forget the story of Lazarus. By the time Jesus reached the cemetery, Lazarus had been in the tomb four days. But Jesus called him out. Did Jesus heal Lazarus? Yes, dramatically, but not immediately (John 11:1–44).

Our highest hope, however, is in our *ultimate* healing. In heaven God will restore our bodies to their intended splendor. "We know that when He is revealed, we shall be like Him" (1 John 3:2). God will turn your tomb into a womb out of which you will be born with a perfect body into a perfect world. In the meantime keep praying. *Father, you are good. I need help. Heal me.*

–*Before Amen*

JUNE 3

He Cares

The disciples woke him and said to him,
"Teacher, don't you care if we drown?"
MARK 4:38 NIV

Such an honest cry, a doggedly painful cry. I've asked that one before, haven't you? It's been screamed countless times. . . .

A mother weeps over a stillborn child. A husband is torn from his wife by a tragic accident. The tears of an eight-year-old fall on a daddy's casket. And the question wails.

"God, don't you care?" "Why *me*?" "Why *my* friend?" "Why *my* business?"

It's the timeless question. The question asked by literally every person who has stalked this globe.

As the winds howled and the sea raged, the impatient and frightened disciples screamed their fear at the sleeping Jesus.

"Teacher, don't you care that we are about to die?" He could have kept on sleeping. He could have told them to shut up. He could have pointed out their immaturity. . . . But he didn't.

With all the patience that only one who cares can have, he answered the question. He hushed the storm so the shivering disciples wouldn't miss his response. Jesus answered once and for all the aching dilemma of man: Where is God when I hurt?

Listening and healing. That's where he is. He cares.

–On the Anvil

A Prayer . . . Because Jesus Bridged the Gulf

"Between us and you there is a great gulf fixed, so that those who want to pass from here to you cannot, nor can those from there pass to us."
LUKE 16:26

Great God of heaven, thank you for finding a way through Jesus to bridge the gulf that separated me from you . . . forever. I was dead in my sins and mistakes. I will abide under the shadow of the cross where I have found safety. In Jesus' name, amen.

–On Calvary's Hill

JUNE 5

East from West, God Wants You

As far as the east is from the west,
so far has he removed our transgressions from us.
PSALM 103:12 NIV

How far is the east from the west? Farther and farther by the moment. Travel west and you can make laps around the globe and never go east. Journey east and, if you desire, maintain an easterly course indefinitely. Not so with the other two directions. If you go north or south, you'll eventually reach the North or South Pole and change directions. But east and west have no turning points.

Neither does God. When he sends your sins to the east and you to the west, you can be sure of this: he doesn't see you in your sins. His forgiveness is irreversible. "He does not treat us as our sins deserve or repay us according to our iniquities" (Psalm 103:10 NIV).

Headline this truth: when God sees you, he sees his Son, not your sin. God "blots out your transgressions" and "remembers your sins no more" (Isaiah 43:25 NIV). No probation. No exception. No reversals.

He did his due diligence. He saw your secret deeds and heard your unsaid thoughts. The lies, the lusts, the longings—he knows them all. God assessed your life from first day to last, from worst moment to best, and made his decision.

"I want that child in my kingdom."

You cannot convince him otherwise.

–*God's Story, Your Story*

Marinate Your Mind

It may be that the Lord will be with me, and I shall be able to drive them out as the Lord said.
JOSHUA 14:12

When Caleb was given his portion of the Promised Land, there was still work to be done, enemies to be driven out. In Joshua 14:6–12, Caleb spoke to Joshua about the struggles that lay ahead. Take a moment to read his words. What name appears and reappears in Caleb's words? The Lord. Nine references to the Lord! Who was on Caleb's mind? Who was in Caleb's heart? He centered his mind on the Lord.

What about you? What emphasis would a transcript of your thoughts reveal? The Lord? Or the problem, the problem, the problem, the problem? The economy, the economy? The jerk, the jerk?

God's people do not deny the presence of problems. Servants like Caleb aren't naive, but they immerse their minds in God-thoughts.

Imagine two cooking bowls. One contains fresh, clean water. The second contains battery acid. Take an apple and cut it in half. Place one half of the apple in the bowl of clean water. Place the other half in the bowl of battery acid. Leave each in its respective bowl for five minutes, and then pull out the two halves. Which one will you want to eat?

Your mind is the apple. God is good water. Problems are battery acid. If you marinate your mind in your problems, they will eventually corrode and corrupt your thoughts. But thoughts of God will preserve and refresh your attitudes. Caleb was different because he soaked his mind in God.

–*Glory Days*

JUNE 7

Ruler of Waves and Hearts

Then He arose and rebuked the wind, and said to the sea, "Peace, be still!" And the wind ceased and there was a great calm.

MARK 4:39

Incredible. Jesus doesn't chant a mantra or wave a wand. No angels are called; no help is needed. The raging water becomes a stilled sea, instantly. Immediate calm. Not a ripple. Not a drop. Not a gust. The reaction of the disciples? "They were in absolute awe, staggered. 'Who is this, anyway?' they asked. 'Wind and sea at his beck and call!'" (Mark 4:41 MSG).

They'd never met a man like this. The waves were his subjects, and the winds were his servants. And that was just the beginning of what his sea mates would witness. Before it was over, they would see fish jump into the boat, demons dive into pigs, cripples turn into dancers, and cadavers turn into living, breathing people.

Never had they seen such power, such glory. You wouldn't have needed to explain this verse to them: "For thine is the kingdom, and the power, and the glory, for ever" (Matthew 6:13 KJV).

In fact, it was two of these rescued fishermen who would declare his authority most clearly. Listen to John: "Greater is he that is in you, than he that is in the world" (1 John 4:4 KJV). Listen to Peter: "Jesus has gone into heaven and is at God's right side" (1 Peter 3:22 NCV).

It's only right that the disciples declare his authority. It's only right that we do the same. And when we do, we state without question: the ruler of the universe rules our hearts.

–*For the Tough Times*

JUNE 8 

The Strong Hold of Strongholds

Let us look only to Jesus, the One who began
our faith and who makes it perfect.
HEBREWS 12:2 NCV

We all have strongholds in our lives. The apostle Paul used the term to describe a mind-set or attitude. "The weapons of our warfare are . . . mighty in God for pulling down *strongholds*, casting down arguments and every high thing that exalts itself against the knowledge of God" (2 Corinthians 10:4–5, emphasis mine). A stronghold is a conviction, outlook, or belief that attempts to interfere with truth.

Does a stronghold have a strong hold on you?

God could never forgive me (the stronghold of guilt).

I could never forgive that person (the stronghold of resentment).

I don't deserve to be loved (the stronghold of rejection).

I'll never recover (the stronghold of defeat).

I must be good, or God will reject me (the stronghold of performance).

I'm only as good as I look (the stronghold of appearance).

My value equals my possessions (the stronghold of materialism).

But we don't have to live in the shadow of these joy-sucking strongholds. Our weapons are from God and have "divine power to demolish strongholds" (v. 4 NIV).

Isn't that what we want? We long to see our strongholds demolished, turned into rubble once and for all, forever and ever, *ka-boom!* How does this happen?

By keeping God in the center.

–*Glory Days*

JUNE 9

Traffic Signs and Pardons

For Your name's sake, O Lord, pardon my iniquity, for it is great.
PSALM 25:11

We cherish pardon, don't we? I was thinking about pardon a few afternoons ago on a south Texas country road. I know it well. I now know the highway patrolman who oversees it. And he now knows me. He looked at my driver's license. "Your name is familiar to me. Aren't you a minister here in San Antonio?"

"Yes, sir."

"On your way to a funeral?"

"No."

"An emergency?"

"No."

"You were going awfully fast."

"I know."

"Tell you what I'm going to do. I'm going to give you a second chance."

I sighed. "Thank you. And thanks for giving me a sermon illustration on pardon."

God has posted his traffic signs everywhere we look. In the universe, in Scripture, even within our own hearts. Yet we persist in disregarding his directions. But God does not give us what we deserve. He has drenched his world in grace. God offers second chances, like a soup kitchen offers meals to everyone who asks. And that includes you.

–*Outlive Your Life*

A Conversation

"Everyone who asks receives, and he who seeks finds,
and to him who knocks it will be opened."
MATTHEW 7:8

Prayer, for most of us, is not a matter of a monthlong retreat or even an hour of meditation. Prayer is conversation with God while driving to work or awaiting an appointment or before interacting with a client. Prayer can be the internal voice that directs the external action.

This much is sure: God will teach you to pray. Don't think for a minute that he is glaring at you from a distance with crossed arms and a scowl, waiting for you to get your prayer life together. Just the opposite. "Here I am! I stand at the door and knock. If you hear my voice and open the door, I will come in and eat with you, and you will eat with me" (Revelation 3:20 NCV).

Jesus waits on the porch. He stands on the threshold. He taps . . . and calls. He waits for you to open the door. To pray is to open it. Prayer is the hand of faith on the door handle of your heart. The willing pull. The happy welcome to Jesus: "Come in, O King. Come in."

We speak. He listens. He speaks. We listen. This is prayer in its purest form. God changes his people through such moments.

–Before Amen

JUNE 11

A Prayer . . . to Remember God's Power

With God's help we will do mighty things,
for he will trample down our foes.
PSALM 60:12 NLT

Father, you can wipe out the strongest army, move mountains, and create the earth out of nothing. Your strength and loving-kindness know no end.

Remind me of your power now. I am so quick to run to a friend for help and then feel let down. Be my strength in all situations.

My friends come to me for help sometimes, but you alone are the answer to their troubles. Help them to look to you first and always.

Thank you for being on our side and fighting for us. In Christ's name, amen.

–*Pocket Prayers*

Trust the Father

Trust in the LORD with all your heart,
And lean not on your own understanding;
In all your ways acknowledge Him,
And He shall direct your paths.
PROVERBS 3:5–6

In our house the game was called "Ladies and Gentlemen." Participants included three preschool-age daughters and one very-happy-to-ham-it-up father. The daughters were freshly bathed, pajama clad, and ready to fly from couch to recliner. The father was glad to serve as the chief ringmaster, spotter, and catapult.

"Ladies and gentlemen," I would announce to the audience of one—Denalyn, who was wondering why we needed to do acrobatics before bedtime. "Ladies and gentlemen, the Lucado girls will now fly through the air."

The living room became a carnival, and I was the human Tilt-A-Whirl. I held the girls upside down and swung them around as if they were rag dolls. They loved it. Never once did they question my judgment or strength. Their mom did. A pediatrician would have. But never in the cycle of a thousand flips and flops did my daughters say to me, "Are you sure you know how to do this?"

Never once did they think I would drop them. *Dad says he can, then he can. Dad says he will, then he will.* They trusted me completely. After all, I was their father.

Oh, that we would trust ours.

–*Glory Days*

JUNE 13

Radically Amazing Grace

If we say we have no sin, we are fooling ourselves, and the truth is not in us. But if we confess our sins, he will forgive our sins, because we can trust God to do what is right. He will cleanse us from all the wrongs we have done.

1 JOHN 1:8–9 NCV

C*onfession.* The word conjures up many images, not all of which are positive. Backroom interrogations. Chinese water torture. Admitting dalliances to a priest who sits on the other side of a black curtain. Walking down the church aisle and filling out a card. Is this what John had in mind?

Confession is not telling God what he doesn't know. Impossible.

Confession is not complaining. If I merely recite my problems and rehash my woes, I'm whining.

Confession is not blaming. Pointing fingers at others without pointing any at me feels good, but it doesn't promote healing.

Confession is so much more. Confession is a radical reliance on grace. A proclamation of our trust in God's goodness. "What I did was bad," we acknowledge, "but your grace is greater than my sin, so I confess it." If our understanding of grace is small, our confession will be small: reluctant, hesitant, hedged with excuses and qualifications, full of fear of punishment. But great grace creates an honest confession.

Honest confession clears the way for God's radically amazing grace.

–*Grace*

What God Will Do

We are hard-pressed on every side, yet not crushed; we are perplexed, but not in despair; persecuted, but not forsaken; struck down, but not destroyed.

2 CORINTHIANS 4:8–9

Maybe God and prayer are all you have. You face battles. Discouragement, deception, defeat, destruction, death. They roar into your world like a Hells Angels motorcycle gang. Their goal is to chase you back into the wilderness of sin.

Don't give an inch. Respond in prayer—honest, continual, and audacious prayer.

You are a member of God's family. You come to God not as a stranger but as an heir.

Confidently approach his throne. Earnestly make your requests known to him not because of what you have achieved but because of what Christ has done. Jesus spilled his blood for you. You can spill your heart before God.

Jesus said if you have faith, you can tell a mountain to go and jump into the sea (Mark 11:23). What is your mountain? What is the challenge of your life? Call out to God for help. Will he do what you want? I cannot say, but this I can. He will do what is best.

–*Glory Days*

JUNE 15

Blessing or Burden?

There is therefore now no condemnation to
those who are in Christ Jesus.
ROMANS 8:1

Is guilt having its way with you? If so, consider this promise: "No matter how deep the stain of your sins, I can take it out and make you as clean as freshly fallen snow" (Isaiah 1:18 TLB). God specializes in guilt removal. He can do what no one else can: extract every last mark from your soul.

When people come to God through faith in Jesus, they receive the greatest of blessings: grace for all their sins. Jesus issues a pardon for every act of rebellion. This grace is a gift. We don't earn it. We can't lose it. But we can forget it. If we're not careful, we can become guilt laden.

Understand: guilt is God's idea. He uses it the way highway engineers use rumble strips. When we swerve off track, they call us back. Guilt does the same. Guilt alerts us to the discrepancies between what we are and what God desires. It stirs repentance and renewal. In appropriate doses guilt is a blessing. In unmonitored dosages, however, guilt is an unbearable burden. We cannot carry it.

But God can. So, go ahead, give it to him.

–*Before Amen*

WRITTEN IN THE BOOK

She had a great and high wall with twelve gates . . .
and names written on them, which are the names of
the twelve tribes of the children of Israel. . . .
Now the wall of the city had twelve foundations, and on them
were the names of the twelve apostles of the Lamb.
REVELATION 21:12, 14

God engraved the names of the sons of Jacob on his gateposts. More ragamuffins than reverends. Their rap sheets include stories of mass murder (Genesis 34), incest (38:13–18), and brotherly betrayal (37:17–28). They behaved more like the 3:00 A.M. nightclub crowd than a Valhalla of faith. Yet God carved their names on the New Jerusalem gates.

And dare we mention the names on the foundations? Peter, the apostle who saved his own skin instead of his Savior's. James and John, who jockeyed for VIP seats in heaven. These were the disciples who told the children to leave Jesus alone (Luke 18:15), who told Jesus to leave the hungry on their own (Matthew 14:15), and who chose to leave Jesus alone to face his crucifixion (Matthew 26:36–45). Yet all their names appear on the foundations.

And yours? It's not engraved in the gate, but it is written in the Book of the Lamb. Not in pencil marks that can be erased, but with blood that will not be removed. No need to keep God happy; he is satisfied. No need to pay the price; Jesus paid it.

–God's Story, Your Story

JUNE 17

The Save Button

I will study your teachings
and follow your footsteps.
PSALM 119:15 CEV

We want to know if the Bible makes a difference. Does it work? Do the teachings of the Bible change us? There is only one way to find out. Click the Save button.

We all know what the Save button is. I do, and I am a remedial computer student. What great satisfaction occurs when, having created a document, we reach up and click the Save button.

The click reshapes the landscape of the hard drive. Words on the screen descend into the core of the machine. As long as the words are limited to the screen, they are vulnerable and exposed to the irascible cursor. It earns its name. We curse the little monster as it gobbles up our hard work. But once we save it, it is safe.

Are you clicking the button on Scripture? We save truth when we deliberately and consciously allow what we've heard to become a part of who we are. Jesus said, "You shall know the truth, and the truth shall make you free" (John 8:32). As we know (save) truth, the truth makes us free from guilt, fear, anger. Saved truth has a shaping, reconfiguring impact on a heart. Only when you allow the truth of Scripture to be the authority in your life can you know whether it works.

–*Glory Days*

A Prayer . . . as God's Child

For you did not receive the spirit of bondage again to fear, but you received the Spirit of adoption by whom we cry out, "Abba, Father."
ROMANS 8:15

Father, you have made me your child through your Spirit. In your kindness you adopted me and delivered me from sin and death.

Remind me today what it means to be your child and to be free from that law. It is so easy for me to live my day on my own terms. Help me to live it in light of your grace.

I pray for my friends and family. Help them experience your love as their Father and feel their inheritance in your Spirit.

Thank you for accepting me as I am but not leaving me the same. In Jesus' name, amen.

–*Pocket Prayers*

JUNE 19

As a Child Does

Jesus said, "Let the little children come to Me, and do not forbid them; for of such is the kingdom of heaven."

MATTHEW 19:14

Jesus invites us to approach God the way a child approaches his or her daddy. And how do children approach their daddies? I went to a school playground to find out.

I heard requests: "Daddy, can Tommy come home with me?" I heard questions: "Are we going home?" And I heard excitement: "Daddy! Look what I did!"

Here's what I didn't hear: "Father, it is most gracious of thee to drive thy car to my place of education and provide me with domestic transportation." I didn't hear formality or impressive vocabulary. I heard kids who were happy to see their dads and eager to speak.

God invites us to approach him in the same manner. What a relief! We prayer wimps fear "mis-praying." What are the expected etiquette and dress code of prayer? What if we kneel instead of stand? What if we say the wrong words or use the wrong tone?

Jesus' answer? "Unless you are converted and become as little children, you will by no means enter the kingdom of heaven" (Matthew 18:3). *Become as little children.* Carefree. Joy filled. Playful. Trusting. Curious. Excited. Forget greatness; seek littleness. Trust more; strut less. Make lots of requests, and accept all the gifts. Come to God the way a child comes to Daddy.

–*Before Amen*

Our Inheritance

Praise be to the God and Father of our Lord Jesus Christ, who has blessed us in the heavenly realms with every spiritual blessing in Christ.

EPHESIANS 1:3 NIV

When you were born into Christ, you were placed in God's royal family. "As many as received Him, to them He gave the right to become children of God" (John 1:12). Since you are a part of the family, you have access to the family blessings. All of them. "In Him also we have obtained an inheritance" (Ephesians 1:11).

Surprised? You ain't heard nuttin' yet. In another passage the apostle Paul described the value of your portfolio: "The Spirit Himself bears witness with our spirit that we are children of God, and if children, then heirs—heirs of God and joint heirs with Christ" (Romans 8:16–17).

We are joint heirs with Christ. We share the same inheritance as Christ! Our portion isn't a pittance. We don't inherit leftovers. We don't wear hand-me-downs. We aren't left out in the cold with the distant cousins. In the traditions of Paul's day, the firstborn son received a double portion while the rest of the siblings divvied up the remainder. Not so with Christ. "Our standing in the world is identical with Christ's" (1 John 4:17 MSG). Christ's portion is our portion!

Whatever he has, we have!

–Glory Days

JUNE 21

SIMPLE OIL CHANGES

Jesus looked at them and said, "With men it is impossible, but not with God; for with God all things are possible."
MARK 10:27

When I was fifteen years old, I inherited a Rambler station wagon from my big brother. It wasn't much to look at, but it was mine.

"You have to keep gas in the tank and air in the tires," Dad advised.

"I know."

"Can you change the oil and keep the car washed?"

"Of course I can," I lied. My ineptness surfaced the following Saturday. It was time to change the oil in the Rambler.

"You want me to help you?" Dad asked.

I should have said yes. Instead I spent an hour looking for the oil pan and another hour wrestling with the plug. I finally removed it, drained the oil, crawled out, and poured in five new quarts. Finished at last. Or so I thought. Dad was waiting for me in the garage.

"All done?"

"All done."

"Then what is that?"

He pointed to a river of oil running down the driveway—clean oil. I'd forgotten to replace the plug.

"Son, I fix things for a living. What is hard for you is simple to me. Let me help you. I'm a mechanic. And, besides, I'm your dad."

Here is what I think: our toughest challenges are simple oil changes to God.

–Before Amen

The One Who Hears the Prayer

"And when you pray, don't be like those people who don't know God. They continue saying things that mean nothing, thinking that God will hear them because of their many words."

MATTHEW 6:7 NCV

Jesus downplayed the importance of words in prayers. We tend to do the opposite. The more words the better. The *better* words the better.

Vocabulary might impress people but not God. There is no panel of angelic judges with numbered cards. "Wow, Lucado, that prayer was a ten. God will certainly hear you!" "Oh, Lucado, you scored a two this morning. Go home and practice." Prayers aren't graded according to style.

Just as a happy child cannot mis-hug, the sincere heart cannot mis-pray. Heaven knows, life has enough burdens without the burden of praying correctly. If prayer depends on how I pray, I'm sunk. But if the power of prayer depends on the One who hears the prayer, and if the One who hears the prayer is my Daddy, then I have hope.

Prayer really is that simple. Resist the urge to complicate it. Don't take pride in well-crafted prayers. Don't apologize for incoherent prayers. No games. No cover-ups. Just be honest to God. Climb into his lap. Tell him everything that is on your heart. Or tell him nothing at all. Just lift your heart to heaven and declare, *Father . . . Daddy . . .*

And sometimes "Daddy" is all we can muster. Stress. Fear. Guilt. Grief. Demands on all sides. All we can summon is a plaintive "Oh, Father." If so, that's enough.

–*Before Amen*

JUNE 23

Our Defender

Who then is the one who condemns? No one. Christ Jesus who died—more than that, who was raised to life—is at the right hand of God and is also interceding for us.

ROMANS 8:34 NIV

Many years ago, I preached my first sermon. No sermon is perfect. But a preacher's first sermon? I make no effort to defend mine. In an effort to say everything, I said very little.

But still, I didn't deserve the criticism from the pastor. He invited me into his study for a post-service postmortem. He pounced on the sermon like a hawk on a rat. By the end of the harangue, I felt like a scolded puppy.

I tucked my tail between my legs and slouched out to where my dad was waiting for me in his car. As I recounted the meeting, his face grew red, and his grip on the steering wheel tightened. He dropped me off at the house and said, "I'll be back soon."

The next day I learned the rest of the story. My dad had pulled into the pastor's driveway. He was soon in the preacher's face giving him "what for" and "how much" and demanding an explanation for the meeting.

The preacher called me the next day and asked my forgiveness.

Again, I am not defending the sermon. But it was a wonderful thing when my father defended me.

What's that? You wish you could say the same? You'd love for someone to rush to your defense?

Oh, dear child of heaven, God has!

—*Glory Days*

JUNE 24 

What a Father Does

They shall see His face.

REVELATION 22:4

You will see the face of God.

Let this sink in. *You will see the face of God.* You will look into the eyes of the One who has always seen; you will behold the mouth that commands history. And if there is anything more amazing than the moment you see his face, it's the moment he touches yours. "He will wipe every tear from their eyes" (Revelation 21:4 NIV).

God will touch your tears. Not flex his muscles or show off his power. Lesser kings would strut their stallions or give a victory speech. Not God. He prefers to rub a thumb across your cheek as if to say, "There, there . . . no more tears."

Isn't that what a father does?

–*God's Story, Your Story*

JUNE 25

A Prayer . . . to Listen and to Follow

"Follow me and be my disciple."

MATTHEW 9:9 NLT

Prince of Peace, the voice of the Enemy has been strong over my life, and I've been deceived into believing all sorts of lies. Speak to me now, Lord, and make your voice crystal clear. May it never be said of my life that I almost listened and almost followed you. I will follow! In Jesus' name, amen.

–*On Calvary's Hill*

JUNE 26

God Said It. Believe It.

"Blessed are those who hear the teaching of God and obey it."

LUKE 11:28 NCV

God promised Joshua, "You will make your way prosperous, and then you will have good success" (Joshua 1:8). This is the only place in the Old Testament where the two words *prosperous* and *success* are found together. This is an emphasized promise. Align yourself with God's Word and expect prosperity and success.

Don't cringe. Joshua 1:8 isn't a guarantee of early retirement. The Bible's promise of prosperity *occasionally* includes money, but it far more often refers to a wealthy spirit, mind, and body. God prospers the leader with new skills, the worker with good sleep, the teacher with added patience, the mother with deeper affection, the elderly with greater hope. Scriptural fluency leads to spiritual affluence.

God's command was enough for Joshua.

No hesitation. No reservation. Unlike Sarah, who said, "I am too old" (Genesis 18:12). Unlike Moses, who said, "I'm not a good speaker" (Exodus 4:10). Unlike the disciples who said, "We don't have enough food to feed the hungry" (Matthew 14:17). Others resisted God's call but not Joshua. God said it. He believed it.

Do likewise. Learn a lesson from Joshua.

–*Glory Days*

JUNE 27

The Wonder of a Second Chance

When the fishermen did as Jesus told them, they caught so many fish that the nets began to break.

LUKE 5:6 NCV

Out in a fishing boat, empty and exhausted, Peter discovered the wonder of God's second chance. One day Jesus used his boat as a platform. The crowd on the beach was so great that Jesus needed a buffer. So he preached from Peter's boat. Then he told Peter to take him fishing.

The apostle-to-be had no interest. He was tired; he had fished all night. He was discouraged; he had caught nothing. He was dubious. What did Jesus know about catching fish? Peter was self-conscious. People packed the beach. Who wants to fail in public?

But Jesus insisted. And Peter relented. "At Your word I will let down the net" (Luke 5:5).

This was a moment of truth for Peter. He was saying, "I will try again, your way." When he did, the catch of fish was so great the boat nearly sank. Sometimes we just need to try again with Christ in the boat.

Failures are fatal only if we fail to learn from them.

–*Glory Days*

Thank God for Everything

In everything give thanks; for this is the will
of God in Christ Jesus for you.
1 THESSALONIANS 5:18

I read about a lawyer who won a case for his client. The two men celebrated with a nice dinner. At the end of the meal, the client handed the lawyer a fine wallet made of Moroccan leather.

"Please accept this as my token of appreciation."

The lawyer resisted. "No, I can't settle for a wallet. My fee is $500."

The client looked at the lawyer and shrugged. "Whatever you say." He opened the wallet and extracted two $500 bills. He reinserted one and handed the lawyer the wallet.

Don't be too quick in your assessment of God's gifts to you. Thank him. Moment by moment. Day by day. Thank God for . . . everything.

–*Before Amen*

JUNE 29

No Future in the Past

Humble yourselves in the sight of the Lord, and He will lift you up.

JAMES 4:10

Everyone stumbles. The difference is in the response. Some stumble into the pit of guilt. Others tumble into the arms of God. Those who find grace do so because they "walk according . . . to the Spirit" (Romans 8:4 NASB). They hear God's voice. They make a deliberate decision to stand up and lean into God's grace.

The prodigal son did this. He resolved, "I will arise and go to my father" (Luke 15:18).

Remember his story? Just like you, he was a member of the family. Perhaps just like you, he squandered it on wild living and bad choices. His trail dead-ended in a pigpen.

One day he was so hungry that the slop smelled like sirloin. He leaned over the trough, took a sniff, and drooled. He was just about to dig in when something within him awoke. *Wait a second. What am I doing wallowing in the mud, rubbing shoulders with the swine?* Then he made a decision that changed his life forever. "I will arise and go to my father."

You can do that! Perhaps you can't solve all your problems or disentangle all your knots, but you can arise and go to your Father.

Rise up and step out. Even the apostle Paul had to make this choice. "Forgetting the past and looking forward to what lies ahead" (Philippians 3:13 NLT).

There ain't no future in the past. You can't change yesterday, but you can do something about tomorrow. *Put God's plan in place.*

–*Glory Days*

JUNE 30 

God Is Still on His Throne

"When the foundations for good collapse, what can good people do?"
The Lord is in his holy temple; the Lord sits on his throne in heaven.
PSALM 11:3–4 NCV

When all that is good falls apart, what can good people do? Isn't David's question ours? When illness invades, marriages fail, children suffer, and death strikes, what are we to do?

Curiously, David doesn't answer his question with an answer. He answers it with a declaration: "The Lord is in his holy temple; the Lord sits on his throne in heaven."

His point is unmistakable: God is unaltered by our storms. He is undeterred by our problems. He is unfrightened by these problems. He is in his holy temple. He is on his throne in heaven.

Buildings may fall, careers may crumble, but God does not. Wreckage and rubble have never discouraged him. God has always turned tragedy into triumph.

In our toughest times we may see what the followers of Christ saw on the cross. Innocence slaughtered. Goodness murdered. Heaven's tower of strength pierced. The apostles had to wonder, *When all that is good falls apart, what can good people do?*

God answered their question with a declaration. With the rumble of the earth and the rolling of the rock, he reminded them, "The Lord is in his holy temple; the Lord sits on his throne in heaven."

And, today, we must remember: He still is. He is still in his temple, still on his throne, still in control. What he did then, he will do still.

—*For the Tough Times*

JULY

JULY 1

Teach Us to Pray

Now it came to pass, as He was praying in a certain place, when He ceased, that one of His disciples said to Him, "Lord, teach us to pray."
LUKE 11:1

The first followers of Jesus requested, "Lord, teach us to pray."

Might their interest have had something to do with the jaw-dropping, eye-popping promises Jesus attached to prayer? "Ask and it will be given to you" (Matthew 7:7 NIV). "If you believe, you will get anything you ask for in prayer" (Matthew 21:22 NCV).

And he set a compelling prayer example. Jesus prayed before he ate. He prayed for children. He prayed for the sick. Jesus would even disappear for an entire night of prayer. I'm thinking of one occasion in particular. In the span of a few hours, he battled sorrow, stress, demands, and needs. He deserved a good night's rest. Yet "he went up into the hills by himself to pray" (Mark 6:46 NLT).

Apparently it was the correct choice. Because when a storm exploded over the Sea of Galilee, Jesus walked out upon the water as if it were a park lawn and the storm a spring breeze.

Do you think the disciples made the prayer-power connection? "Lord, teach us to pray *like that*. Teach us to find strength, to banish fear, to defy storms in prayer."

What about you? The disciples faced angry waves and a watery grave. You face angry clients, a turbulent economy, raging seas of stress and sorrow.

"Lord," we still request, "teach us to pray."

–Before Amen

JULY 2

A Prayer . . . for Christ to Love Through Your Heart

Let it be to me according to your word.

LUKE 1:38

O Lord, live in me. May your love beat in and through my heart. May you speak through my voice. Jesus, be the strength of my soul and the fire that purges wrongs from my desires. Fill me with your great abounding grace. In Jesus' name, amen.

–*In the Manger*

JULY 3 

CHRIST *IN* YOU

Whoever confesses that Jesus is the Son of God, God abides in him, and he in God.
1 JOHN 4:15

Paul said, "It is no longer I who live, but Christ lives in me" (Galatians 2:20). When grace happens, Christ enters. "Christ in you, the hope of glory" (Colossians 1:27).

For many years I missed this truth. I believed all the other prepositions: Christ *for* me, *with* me, *ahead of* me. And I knew I was working *beside* Christ, *under* Christ, *with* Christ. But I never imagined that Christ was *in* me.

No other religion or philosophy makes such a claim. No other movement implies the living presence of its founder *in* his followers. Influence? Instruct? Entice? Yes. But occupy? No.

Yet Christians embrace this inscrutable promise. "The mystery in a nutshell is just this: Christ is in you" (Colossians 1:27 MSG). The Christian is a person in whom Christ is happening.

We are Jesus Christ's; we belong to him. But even more, we are *increasingly* him. He moves in and commandeers our hands and feet, requisitions our minds and tongues. He repurposes bad decisions and squalid choices. Little by little a new image emerges. "He decided from the outset to shape the lives of those who love him along the same lines as the life of his Son" (Romans 8:29 MSG).

Christ lives and works and moves *in* you.

–*Grace*

JULY 4

Silence the Trumpets

"When you give to the needy, do not let your left hand know what your right hand is doing, so that your giving may be in secret. Then your Father, who sees what is done in secret, will reward you."

MATTHEW 6:3–4 NIV

Watch me! Watch me!" is a call used on the playground, not in God's kingdom. Silence the trumpets. Cancel the parade. Enough with the name-dropping. If accolades come, politely deflect them before you believe them. Slay the desire to be noticed. Stir the desire to serve God.

Heed the counsel of Christ: "First wash the inside of the cup and the dish, and then the outside will become clean, too" (Matthew 23:26 NLT). Focus on the inside, and the outside will take care of itself. Lay your motives before God daily, hourly. "Search me, O God, and know my heart; test me and know my anxious thoughts. Point out anything in me that offends you, and lead me along the path of everlasting life" (Psalm 139:23–24 NLT).

Do good things. Just don't do them to be noticed. You can be too good for your own good, you know.

–*Outlive Your Life*

Straight to the Top

Two blind men sitting by the road, when they heard
that Jesus was passing by, cried out, saying,
"Have mercy on us, O Lord, Son of David!"
MATTHEW 20:30

Three years of feeding, healing, and teaching had elevated Jesus to rock-star status. The people loved him. He stood up to the authorities. He commanded cadavers and called the shots. He was blue collared, big hearted, and a hometown hero.

The crowd was escorting him to Jerusalem to celebrate Passover. And then they heard this cry: "Have mercy on us, O Lord, Son of David!" The crowd turned and looked at the two blind men. Pitiful. This was a victory march, a day of triumph. Jesus was on an important mission. The people would have left the blind men on the side of the road.

Sound familiar? But the blind men brought their concern to Jesus. They didn't ask for Peter or John. They went straight to the top. They cried out to Jesus. Persistently, personally, passionately. *I need help. Heal me.*

Here is why you need to do the same. God's goal for you is wholeness. "Now may God himself, the God of peace, make you pure, belonging only to him. May your whole self—*spirit, soul, and body*—be kept safe and without fault when our Lord Jesus Christ comes" (1 Thessalonians 5:23 NCV, emphasis mine).

Two blind men were made whole because they took their troubles straight to the top. Shouldn't you do the same?

–Before Amen

JULY 6

It Was Worth It

"Greater love has no one than this, than to lay down one's life for his friends."
JOHN 15:13

Think for a minute about the people in your world. What do they think of your commitment to them? How would you rate your faithfulness? Does your loyalty ever waver? Do you have one person with whom your "contract" is nonnegotiable?

Once, two friends were fighting together in a war. The combat was ferocious, and many lives were being taken. When one of the two young soldiers was injured and could not get back to the trenches, the other went out to get him against his officer's orders. He returned mortally wounded, and his friend, whom he had carried back, was dead.

The officer looked at the dying soldier, shook his head, and said, "It wasn't worth it."

The young boy, overhearing the remark, smiled and said, "But it was worth it, sir, because when I got to him, he said, 'Jim, I knew you'd come.'"

Make the most of your relationships. Follow the advice of Benjamin Franklin: "Be slow in choosing friends and be even slower in leaving them."

–*On the Anvil*

Problems Happen

Who is he who overcomes the world, but he who believes that Jesus is the Son of God?
1 JOHN 5:5

You'll never have a problem-free life. Ever. You'll never drift off to sleep on the wings of this thought: *My, today came and went with no problems in the world.* This headline will never appear in the paper: "We have only good news to report."

You might be elected as president of Russia. You might discover a way to e-mail pizza and become a billionaire. You might be called out of the stands to pinch-hit when your team is down to its final out of the World Series, hit a home run, and have your face appear on the cover of *Sports Illustrated.*

It's not likely. But it's possible.

But a problem-free, no-hassle, blue-sky existence of smooth sailing? Don't hold your breath.

Problems happen. They happen to rich people, sexy people, educated people, sophisticated people. They happen to retired people, single people, spiritual people, and secular people.

But not all people see problems the same way. Some people are overcome by problems. Others overcome problems. Some people are left bitter. Others are left better. Some people face their challenges with fear. Others with faith.

You don't have a choice about having problems. But you do have a choice about what you do with them. Choose faith.

–*Glory Days*

JULY 8

God Guards You . . . Always

You have faith in God, whose power will protect you until the last day. Then he will save you, just as he has always planned to do.

1 PETER 1:5 CEV

When God became flesh, he fought for your soul. When Jesus faced the Devil in the wilderness, he fought for your peace. When he stood up for the neglected, was he not standing up for you? When he died on the cross for your sins, he fought for your salvation. When he left the Holy Spirit to guide, strengthen, and comfort you, he was fighting for your life.

Miss this truth and you might as well plant a mailbox in the wilderness. You will be there a long time. But believe this, and watch the clouds begin to clear.

Believe this:

> God guards you from every evil,
> he guards your very life.
> He guards you when you leave and when you return,
> he guards you now, he guards you always. (Psalm 121:7–8 MSG)

Always.

–*Glory Days*

A Prayer . . . to Serve

"For even the Son of Man did not come to be served, but to serve, and to give His life a ransom for many."

MARK 10:45

O Lord, what an amazing opportunity you have spread out before me—a chance to make a difference for you in a desperately hurting world. Help me to see the needs you want me to see, to react in a way that honors you, and to bless others by serving them gladly with practical expressions of your love. Help me be Jesus' hands and feet, and through your Spirit give me the strength and wisdom I need to fulfill your plan for me in my own generation. In Jesus' name I pray, amen.

–*Outlive Your Life*

JULY 10

Be Moses

First, I tell you to pray for all people, asking God for what they need and being thankful to him. Pray for rulers and for all who have authority so that we can have quiet and peaceful lives full of worship and respect for God.

1 TIMOTHY 2:1–2 NCV

You actually have a "seat with [Christ] in the heavens" (Ephesians 2:6 NCV). You don't have a seat at the Supreme Court or in the House of Representatives. You have one far more strategic; you have a seat in the government of God. Like a congressman you represent a district. You speak on behalf of your family, neighborhood, or softball team. Your sphere of influence is your region. As you grow in faith, your district expands. God burdens you with a concern for orphans, distant lands, or needy people. You respond to these promptings by prayer. *Father . . . they need help.*

You are Moses in your cul-de-sac. Moses in your workforce. Moses in your classroom. You plead with God on other people's behalf.

Intercessory prayer isn't rocket science. It acknowledges our inability and God's ability. We come with empty hands but high hopes. Why? God "is able to do exceedingly abundantly above all that we ask or think" (Ephesians 3:20). He "will supply all [our] needs according to His riches" (Philippians 4:19 NASB). When God gives, he gives a gift that is "pressed down, shaken together to make room for more, running over, and poured into your lap" (Luke 6:38 NLT).

Take your seat at the feet of Jesus. Lift up your world in prayer. Be Moses today.

–*Before Amen*

JULY 11 

The Missing Ingredient

Two are better than one,
Because they have a good reward for their labor.
For if they fall, one will lift up his companion.
But woe to him who is alone when he falls,
For he has no one to help him up.
ECCLESIASTES 4:9–10

What if the missing ingredient for changing the world is teamwork?

> When two of you get together on anything at all on earth and make a prayer of it, my Father in heaven goes into action. And when two or three of you are together because of me, you can be sure that I'll be there. (Matthew 18:19–20 MSG)

This is an astounding promise. When believers agree, Jesus takes notice, shows up, and hears our prayers.

And when believers disagree? When workers divide, it is the suffering who suffer most.

They've suffered enough, don't you think? The Jerusalem church found a way to work together. They found common ground in the death, burial, and resurrection of Christ. Because they did, lives were changed.

And as you and I do, the same will happen.

–*Outlive Your Life*

JULY 12

The Strategy

"If you abide in Me, and My words abide in you, you will ask what you desire, and it shall be done for you."

JOHN 15:7

My friend Greg Pruett is trained as an engineer, linguist, and Bible translator. But his most significant contribution might be in the area of "extreme prayer." In his book by that name, he relates how he returned from Guinea, West Africa, to assume the role as president of Pioneer Bible Translators. It was 2008. The great recession was sucking dollars out of the economy and confidence out of the public. The ministry's financial chart indicated a free fall toward insolvency. Greg had no experience in leading such an organization. He had no tangible place to cut expenses. Resources were few, and the donors were disappearing.

Greg knew of only one response: prayer. "That's when I began to learn not to pray about my strategies, but to make prayer *the* strategy."[1]

In July he wrote a half-page letter to his teammates worldwide, calling them to prayer. He urged them to stand before God's throne with specific and bold requests. They did. Greg described the result: "When I saw the end-of-the-year report, I knew God had heard our prayers. . . . I wanted to find trends to explain how it worked, so we could do it again. I never could . . . I just know [God] provided. All I had was God and prayer."[2]

Greg made prayer *the* strategy for his needs, and God answered. He'll do the same for you.

–*Glory Days*

KEEP WALKING

Let the mighty strength of the Lord make you strong.

EPHESIANS 6:10 CEV

"Yell a loud *no* to the Devil and watch him scamper" (James 4:7 MSG). He is not allowed where God is praised. Just keep praising and walking.

"But, Max, I've been walking a long time," you say.

Yes, it seems like it. It must have seemed that way to the Hebrews too. Joshua did not tell them how many trips they would have to make around the wall of Jericho. They just kept walking.

Our Joshua didn't tell us either. Through Paul, Jesus urges us to "be steadfast, immovable, always abounding in the work of the Lord, knowing that your labor is not in vain in the Lord" (1 Corinthians 15:58).

Keep walking. For all you know this may be the day the walls come down. You may be only steps from a moment like this.

> It happened when the people heard the sound of the trumpet, and the people shouted with a great shout, that the wall fell down flat. Then the people . . . took the city. (Joshua 6:20)

The very walls that kept them out became stepping-stones onto which they could climb.

By the way, a great shaking is coming for this world too. Our Joshua, Jesus, will give the signal, and a trumpet will blast. He will reclaim every spoil and repel, once and for all, each demon. Until he does, keep marching and believing. It's just a matter of time before your Jericho comes down.

–Glory Days

JULY 14

Unity Matters

You are joined together with peace through the Spirit, so make every effort to continue together in this way.
EPHESIANS 4:3 NCV

The body of Christ—his church—has been known to misbehave. The brain discounts the heart. (Academics discount worshippers.) The hands criticize the knees. (People of action criticize people of prayer.) The eyes refuse to partner with the feet. (Visionary thinkers won't work with steady laborers.)

A clear case of mutiny on the body.

> If the ear should say, "Because I am not an eye, I am not of the body," is it therefore not of the body? If the whole body were an eye, where would be the hearing? If the whole were hearing, where would be the smelling? But now God has set the members, each one of them, in the body just as He pleased. (1 Corinthians 12:15–18)

The early Christians surely chuckled at these word pictures. What if the whole body were an eye? If you were a collection of eyeballs, how would you function? "The eye cannot say to the hand, 'I have no need of you'" (v. 21).

We cannot say, "I have no need of you." The megachurch needs the smaller church. The liberal needs the conservative. The pastor needs the missionary. Cooperation is more than a good idea; it is a command (Ephesians 4:3 NIV). There is "one flock and one shepherd" (John 10:16 NIV). Unity matters to God.

–*Outlive Your Life*

God Is in Charge

Oh, magnify the Lord with me,
And let us exalt His name together.
PSALM 34:3

It does us twice as much good to think about God as it does to think about anyone or anything else. God wants us to begin and end our prayers thinking of him. The more we focus up there, the more inspired we are down here.

Magnify. When you magnify an object, you enlarge it so that you can understand it. When we magnify God, we do the same. We enlarge our awareness of him so we can understand him more. This is exactly what happens when we worship—we take our minds off ourselves and set them on God. The emphasis is on him.

I love the way the final phrase of the Lord's Prayer is translated in *The Message* (Matthew 6:13):

> *You're in charge!*
> *You can do anything you want!*
> *You're ablaze in beauty!*
> *Yes. Yes. Yes.*

Could it be any simpler? God is in charge!

–*For the Tough Times*

JULY 16

A Prayer . . . Because Jesus Wore Your Thorns

They clothed Him with purple; and they twisted a crown of thorns, put it on His head, and began to salute Him, "Hail, King of the Jews!"
MARK 15:17–18

O Lord, how can I ever thank you enough for giving your entire life that I might be kissed by forgiveness? You bore the thorns of my accusations and the piercing of my rejection. I rejoice that today I can follow in your steps. In Jesus' name, amen.

–*In the Manger*

JULY 17

A New You

God said to Abraham, "As for you, you must keep my covenant, you and your descendants after you for the generations to come. . . . You are to undergo circumcision, and it will be the sign of the covenant between me and you."

GENESIS 17:9–11 NIV

The circumcision of the Old Testament was a symbolic separation from the past. Eight days after birth every male child was to be symbolically set apart. The act declared a new identity. He was not like the pagans, who didn't know God. He was a child of the covenant. "You are no longer who you were. You are mine." No longer slaves but free. No longer in bondage but liberated.

God's message to the Hebrews? Remember whose you are.

God's message to us? Remember whose you are.

In a sense all believers have been circumcised. This may be news to you. "When you came to Christ, he set you free from your evil desires, not by a bodily operation of circumcision but by a spiritual operation, the baptism of your souls" (Colossians 2:11 TLB).

Christ cut away the old life. He severed from you the power of sin and death. The old temptations, lusts, and longings? He detached you from their power when you gave your heart to Christ. It cannot be stated too often or too clearly. You are not the person you used to be. Your former self no longer exists. The old life is disempowered. When Christ died, you died. When Christ was buried, you were buried. When Christ rose from the dead, you arose with him.

You are a new you.

–*Glory Days*

JULY 18

People of Hospitality

"For where two or three are gathered together in
My name, I am there in the midst of them."
MATTHEW 18:20

Call us a fast society, an efficient society, but don't call us a personal society. Our society is set up for isolation. We wear earbuds when we exercise. We communicate via e-mail and text messages. Our mantra: "I leave you alone. You leave me alone."

Yet God wants his people to be an exception. Let everyone else go the way of computers and keyboards. God's children will be people of hospitality.

Long before the church had pulpits and baptisteries, she had kitchens and dinner tables. "The believers met together in the Temple every day. They ate together *in their homes*, happy to share their food with joyful hearts" (Acts 2:46 NCV, emphasis mine). "Every day in the Temple and *in people's homes* they continued teaching the people and telling the Good News—that Jesus is the Christ" (Acts 5:42 NCV, emphasis mine).

Even a casual reading of the New Testament unveils the house as the primary tool of the church. "To Philemon our beloved friend and fellow laborer . . . and to the church in your house" (Philemon vv. 1–2). "Greet Priscilla and Aquila . . . the church that is in their house" (Romans 16:3, 5).

It's no wonder that the elders were to be "given to hospitality" (1 Timothy 3:2 KJV). The primary gathering place of the church was the home.

–*Outlive Your Life*

JULY 19 

Making Beautiful Music

My heart, O God, is steadfast;
I will sing and make music with all my soul.
PSALM 108:1 NIV

Some kids in Cateura, on the outskirts of Asunción, Paraguay, are making music with their trash. Other orchestras fine-tune their maple cellos or brass tubas. Not this band. They play Beethoven sonatas with plastic buckets, washtubs, and drainpipes.

On their side of Asunción, garbage is the only crop to harvest. Garbage pickers sort and sell refuse for pennies a pound. Many of them have met the same fate as the trash; they've been tossed out and discarded.

But now, thanks to Don Cola Gomez, they are making music.

Gomez is a trash worker and carpenter. He had never seen, heard, or held a violin in his life. Yet when someone described the instrument, this untutored craftsman took a paint can and an oven tray into his tiny workshop and made a violin. His next instrument was a cello. He fashioned the body out of an oil barrel and made tuning knobs from a hairbrush, the heel of a shoe, and a wooden spoon.

Thanks to this Stradivarius, the junk gets a mulligan, and so do the kids who live among it. Since the day their story hit the news, they've been tutored by maestros, featured on national television programs, and have gone on a world tour. They've been called the Landfill Harmonic and also the Recycled Orchestra of Cateura.[3]

We could also call them a picture of God's grace.

–*Glory Days*

JULY 20

The Opening Lines

Then they cried to the Lord in their trouble,
and he saved them from their distress.
He sent out his word and healed them;
he rescued them from the grave.
Let them give thanks to the Lord for his unfailing love.
PSALM 107:19–21 NIV

Some of you live in such road-weary bodies: knees ache, eyes dim, skin sags. Others exited the womb on an uphill ride. While I have no easy answers for your struggle, I implore you to see your challenge in the scope of God's story. View these days on earth as but the opening lines of his sweeping saga. Let's stand with Paul on the promise of eternity.

> So we're not giving up. How could we! Even though on the outside it often looks like things are falling apart on us, on the inside, where God is making new life, not a day goes by without his unfolding grace. These hard times are small potatoes compared to the coming good times, the lavish celebration prepared for us. There's far more here than meets the eye. The things we see now are here today, gone tomorrow. But the things we can't see now will last forever. (2 Corinthians 4:16–18 MSG)

Your suffering isn't the end of the story. It's the opening scene of God's saga.

—*God's Story, Your Story*

Enemy Territory

The Lord himself will fight for you.
EXODUS 14:14 NLT

The idea of an actual devil strikes many people as odd and outdated. The popular trend of our day is to blame problems on genetics, governments, and environments. Yet the Bible presents a real and present foe of our faith. His name is Satan. Some call him the Devil. Others call him Beelzebub, Belial, the obstructor, the tempter, the evil one, the accuser, the prince of demons, the ruler of this world, or the prince of the power of the air. Whatever name you choose, he is the enemy, and he is real.

He is not the cute and harmless character of the cartoons. He is not an imaginary, dark counterpart to the Easter Bunny. He is the invisible yet forceful fallen angel called Lucifer, who desired the high place only God could occupy. He rebelled and disobeyed and wants you and me to do the same. "The devil, your enemy, goes around like a roaring lion looking for someone to eat" (1 Peter 5:8 NCV).

Any person who has dared to draw near to God has felt Satan's attack.

Satan incites, sifts, persuades, binds, blinds, and rules.

He has one objective: "to steal, and to kill, and to destroy" (John 10:10).

Satan's got you in his sights. You are in enemy territory. But the battle is not yours alone. God fights for you.

–*Glory Days*

JULY 22

"Abba"

> The Spirit you received does not make you slaves, so that you live in fear again; rather, the Spirit you received brought about your adoption to sonship. And by him we cry, "Abba, Father."
>
> ROMANS 8:15 NIV

Jesus taught us to begin our prayers by saying, "Our Father in heaven" (Matthew 6:9). But more specifically, our "*Abba* in heaven." *Abba* is an intimate, tender, folksy, pedestrian term, the warmest of the Aramaic words for "father."[4]

Abba is *Daddy.* The term takes aim at our pride. Other salutations permit an air of sophistication. As a pastor I know this well. Deepen the tone of voice, and pause for dramatic effect. "O holy Lord . . ." I allow the words to reverberate throughout the universe as I, the pontiff of petition, pontificate my prayer.

"God, you are my King, and I am your prince."

"God, you are the Maestro, and I am your minstrel."

"God, you are the President, and I am your ambassador."

But God prefers this greeting: "God, you are my Daddy, and I am your child."

Here's why: it's hard to show off and call God "Daddy" at the same time.

–*Before Amen*

A PRAYER . . . FOR LIGHT AND JOY

Do not be afraid, for behold, I bring you good tidings
of great joy which will be to all people.
LUKE 2:10

Father, thank you that you have no problem walking through the walls that I sometimes hide behind. I welcome you to come with your forgiveness and shed your light and joy into my life. In Jesus' name, amen.

–On Calvary's Hill

JULY 24

Do I Matter?

For you are all children of God through faith in Christ Jesus.

GALATIANS 3:26 NLT

Out of the dark he pounced, the "Man" with a capital *M*, for this was no common man. Through the night the two fought, until the Man decided to settle the matter once and for all. With a deft jab to the hip, the Man left Jacob writhing. The jolt cleared Jacob's vision, and he realized, *I'm tangling with God.* He grabbed hold of the Man and held on for dear life. "I will not let You go unless You bless me!" he insisted (Genesis 32:26).

What are we to make of this? God in the mud. A tooth-and-nail fight to the finish. Bizarre. But the blessing request? I get that part. Jacob was asking, "God, do I matter to you?"

I would ask the same question. Given a face-to-face encounter with the Man, I'd venture, "Do you know who I am? In the great scheme of things, do I count for anything?"

So many messages tell us we don't. We get laid off at work, turned away by the school. Everything from acne to Alzheimer's leaves us feeling like the girl with no date to the prom.

We react. We validate our existence with a flurry of activity. We do more, buy more, achieve more. Like Jacob, we wrestle. All our wrestlings, I suppose, are merely asking this question: "Do I matter?"

All of grace, I believe, is God's definitive reply: "Be blessed, my child. I accept you. I have adopted you into my family."

You matter to God.

–Grace

Take God at His Word

What he says he will do, he does.
What he promises, he makes come true.
NUMBERS 23:19 NCV

We need to learn to take God at his word.

Sounds easy enough, especially when it's smooth sailing. But in the midst of a storm, even the disciples of Jesus needed a reminder. On one occasion he told them, "Let us go over to the other side" (Mark 4:35 NIV). They did. En route to the other side of the Sea of Galilee, however, their boat encountered "a furious squall" (v. 37 NIV). The sky opened, and buckets of water fell, and waves threatened to upend the boat. The disciples turned to Jesus and found him sound asleep! They screamed, "Don't you care if we drown?" (v. 38 NIV). Jesus woke up, stood up, commanded the storm to shut up, and then said to the disciples, "Do you still have no faith?" (v. 40 NIV).

What a stunning rebuke! The sea was raging; the water was churning. Why did Jesus scold them?

Simple. They didn't take him at his word. He said they were going to the other side. He didn't say, "We are going to the middle of the lake to drown." Jesus had declared the outcome. But when the storm came, the disciples heard the roar of the winds and forgot his word.

Storms are coming your way. Winds will howl, your boat will be tossed, and you will have a choice. Will you hear Christ or the crisis? Heed the promises of Scripture or the noise of the storm? Will you take God at his word?

–*Glory Days*

JULY 26

Blasting Through Walls

Let anyone who is thirsty come. Let anyone who desires drink freely from the water of life.
REVELATION 22:17 NLT

God sent Philip on a cross-cultural mission.

> Now an angel of the Lord spoke to Philip, saying, "Arise and go toward the south along the road which goes down from Jerusalem to Gaza." . . . So he arose and went. And behold, a man of Ethiopia . . . was returning. And sitting in his chariot, he was reading Isaiah the prophet. (Acts 8:26–29)

Walls separated Philip from the eunuch. The Ethiopian was dark skinned; Philip was light. The traveler was rich enough to travel. And who was Philip but a simple refugee, banished from Jerusalem?

But Philip didn't hesitate. He "preached Jesus to him. . . . And the eunuch said, 'See, here is water. What hinders me from being baptized?'" (vv. 35–36).

No small question.

What if Philip had said, "Sorry. We don't take your type"?

But Philip, charter member of the bigotry-demolition team, blasted through the wall and invited, "'If you believe with all your heart, you may.' And he answered and said, 'I believe that Jesus Christ is the Son of God'" (v. 37).

Next thing you know, the eunuch is stepping out of the baptism waters, whistling "Jesus Loves Me," Philip is on to his next assignment, and the church has her first non-Jewish convert.

–*Outlive Your Life*

The Heart Surgeon

God demonstrates His own love toward us, in that while we were still sinners, Christ died for us.
ROMANS 5:8

Grace is God as heart surgeon, cracking open your chest, removing your heart—poisoned as it is with pride and pain—and replacing it with his own. Rather than tell you to change, he creates the change. Do you clean up so he can accept you? No, he accepts you and begins cleaning you up. His dream isn't just to get you into heaven but to get heaven into you. What a difference this makes! Can't forgive your enemy? Can't face tomorrow? Can't forgive your past? Christ can, and he is on the move, aggressively budging you from graceless to grace-shaped living. The gift-given giving gifts. Forgiven people forgiving people. Deep sighs of relief. Stumbles aplenty but despair seldom.

Grace is everything Jesus. Grace lives because he does, works because he works, and matters because he matters. He placed a term limit on sin and danced a victory jig in a graveyard. To be saved by grace is to be saved by him—not by an idea, doctrine, creed, or church membership, but by Jesus himself, who will sweep into heaven anyone who so much as gives him the nod.

–Grace

JULY 28

Do It Again, Lord

"Our Father in heaven, hallowed be your name, your kingdom come, your will be done, on earth as it is in heaven."

MATTHEW 6:9–10 NIV

Dear Lord,

We're still hoping we'll wake up. We're still hoping we'll open a sleepy eye and think, What a horrible dream.

We are sad, Father. And so we come to you. We don't ask you for help; we beg you for it. We don't request; we implore. We've read the accounts. We've pondered the stories, and now we plead, "Do it again, Lord. Do it again."

Remember Joseph? You rescued him from the pit. And Sarah? Remember her prayers? You heard them. Joshua? Remember his fears? You inspired him. The women at the tomb? You resurrected their hope. The doubts of Thomas? You took them away. Do it again, Lord. Do it again.

Most of all, do again what you did at Calvary. After your Son lay three days in a dark hole, you turned the darkest Friday into the brightest Sunday. Do it again, Lord. Turn this Calvary into an Easter.

Let your mercy be upon all who suffer. Give us grace that we might forgive and faith that we might believe.

Do it again, Lord. Do it again.

Through Christ, amen.[5]

–*For the Tough Times*

Assurance

When you see the ark of the covenant of the Lord your God, . . .
then you shall set out from your place and go after it.
JOSHUA 3:2–3

When God said, "Follow the ark," he was saying, "Follow me."

As the Israelites prepared to cross the Jordan, God led the way. Not soldiers. Not Joshua. Not engineers and their plans or Special Forces and their equipment. When it came time to pass through the impassable waters, God's plan was simple: trust me.

The people did. A chosen band of priests walked toward the river. Carrying the ark, they inched their way down toward the Jordan.

Scripture does not veil their fear: the priests "dipped" their feet into the edge of the water (Joshua 3:15). They did not run, plunge, or dive into the river. It was the smallest of steps, but with God the smallest step of faith can activate the mightiest of miracles. As they touched the water, the flow stopped. And all of Israel crossed over on dry ground (v. 17).

If God could turn a raging river into a red carpet, then "Watch out, Jericho. Here we come!" As Joshua had told them, "By this [crossing] you shall know that the living God is among you" (v. 10). The Hebrews knew they couldn't lose! They had every right to celebrate.

So do we.

For Joshua's people, assurance came as they stood on dry land looking back at the Jordan.

For us, assurance comes as we stand on the finished work of Christ and look back at the cross.

–*Glory Days*

JULY 30

A Prayer . . . to Help

Pure and genuine religion in the sight of God the Father means caring for orphans and widows in their distress and refusing to let the world corrupt you.

JAMES 1:27 NLT

Dear Lord, you promised we would always have the poor among us. Help me to make sure that the reverse is also true: that I am always among the poor—helping, encouraging, and lending a hand wherever I can. Enable me to love the invisible God by serving the very visible poor in my corner of the world. Help me to be creative without being condescending, encouraging without being egotistical, and fearless without being foolish. May the poor bless you because of me, and may my efforts somehow reduce the number of the poor. In Jesus' name I pray, amen.

–*Outlive Your Life*

Do Something!

"The Spirit of the Lord is upon Me, because He has anointed Me to preach the gospel to the poor; He has sent Me to heal the brokenhearted."

LUKE 4:18

The day was special. Jesus was in town. The people asked him to read Scripture, and he accepted. Shuffling the scroll toward the end, he read, "The Spirit of the Lord is upon Me, because He has anointed Me to preach the gospel to the poor; He has sent Me to heal the brokenhearted."

Jesus had a target audience. The poor. The brokenhearted. "This is my mission statement," Jesus declared. The Nazareth Manifesto.

Shouldn't it be ours too? Shouldn't our manifesto look something like this:

> *Let the church act on behalf of the poor.* The ultimate solution to poverty is found in the compassion of God's people.
>
> *Let the brightest among us direct us.* "Poverty," as Rich Stearns, president of World Vision in the United States, told me, "*is* rocket science." Simple solutions simply don't exist. We need our brightest and best to tackle it.
>
> *Get ticked off.* Riled up enough to respond. Poverty is not the lack of charity but the lack of justice. Righteous anger would do a world of good.

No one can do everything, but everyone can do something. So get out of your comfort zone for Christ's sake. Get ticked off. Do something!

–*Outlive Your Life*

AUGUST

Decide Now

The good man does not escape all troubles—he has them too. But the Lord helps him in each and every one.

PSALM 34:19 TLB

Voices await you today. At work, in your cul-de-sac, at school, on the Internet. They're waiting for you. They stand on the intersections of your social life and family. You can't eliminate their presence. But you can prepare for their invitation.

Remember who you are; you are God's child. You've been bought by the most precious commodity in the history of the universe: the blood of Christ. You are indwelled by the Spirit of the living God. You are being equipped for an eternal assignment that will empower you to live in the very presence of God. You have been set apart for a holy calling. You are his.

The Devil has no jurisdiction over you. He acts as if he does. He walks with a swagger and brings temptation, but as you resist him and turn to God, he must flee (James 4:7).

Decide now what you will say when the voices speak.

Choose obedience. And, as you do, you can expect blessings: the blessing of a clean conscience, the blessing of a good night's sleep, the blessing of God's fellowship, the blessing of God's favor. This is no guarantee of an easy life. It is the assurance of God's help. And it is yours to claim.

–*Glory Days*

AUGUST 2

SIN'S REALITY

Lord, do not forsake me;
do not be far from me, my God.
Come quickly to help me,
my Lord and my Savior.
PSALM 38:21–22 NIV

The best-known prayer of confession came from King David, even though he took an interminably long time to offer it. This Old Testament hero dedicated a season of his life to making stupid, idiotic, godless decisions.

Yes, David. The man after God's own heart allowed his own to calcify. He suppressed his wrongdoing and paid a steep price for doing so. He later described it this way: "When I refused to confess my sin, my body wasted away, and I groaned all day long. Day and night your hand of discipline was heavy on me. My strength evaporated like water in the summer heat" (Psalm 32:3–4 NLT).

Sin's reality replaced sin's euphoria. David knew his secret sin was no secret at all.

Bury misbehavior and expect pain, period. Unconfessed sin is a knife blade lodged in the soul. You cannot escape the misery it creates, unless you pray as David did:

"Come quickly to help me, my Lord and my Savior."

Then Grace will come.

–Grace

Why Sickness?

Heal me, Lord, and I will be healed;
save me and I will be saved,
for you are the one I praise.
JEREMIAH 17:14 NIV

Why do we get sick? For the same reason we still sin. This is a fallen world, and the kingdom is a coming kingdom. Sickness and sin stalk our planet. But neither sin nor sickness will have dominion over God's people. Sin cannot condemn us. Disease cannot destroy us. Guilt is defanged, and death has lost its sting. In fact, the very sin and sickness that Satan intends for evil, God redeems for good. Sin becomes a showcase of his grace. Sickness becomes a demonstration of God's ability to heal.

We aren't victims of rogue molecules or rebellious cells. We do not live beneath the specter of uncontrollable plagues or emotions. Every fiber, molecule, and brain wave answers to his command.

God is in charge!

–Before Amen

AUGUST 4

Look Up

I will lift up my eyes to the hills—from whence comes my help?
My help comes from the Lord, who made heaven and earth.
PSALM 121:1–2

God will come to you. In the form of a hospital companion or Holy Commander? Perhaps. Or he may come through the word of a scripture or the kindness of a friend. Why, he may even speak to you through a book like this one.

But this much is certain: God comes to his people. "The Commander of the armies of heaven is here among us" (Psalm 46:7 TLB). You are no exception to this promise. His love includes all people.

And he is for you. "If God is for us, who can be against us?" (Romans 8:31 NIV).

Are you facing a Jericho-level challenge? Do you face walls that are too high to breach and too thick to crack? Do you face a diagnosis, difficulty, or defeat that keeps you from knocking down the walls? If so, do what Joshua did.

"When Joshua was by Jericho . . . *he lifted his eyes* and looked, and behold, a Man stood opposite him" (Joshua 5:13, emphasis mine). After Joshua lifted his eyes, he saw Jesus. As long as our eyes are only on our Jericho, we won't see Jesus. Look up. The Lord, your Help, is coming.

–*Glory Days*

AUGUST 5 

NO OTHER GOD

"Heaven is my throne,
and the earth is my footstool. . . .
My hand made all things.
All things are here because I made them,"
says the LORD.
ISAIAH 66:1–2 NCV

Most people suffer from small thoughts about God. In an effort to see him as our friend, we have lost his immensity. In our desire to understand him, we have sought to contain him. The God of the Bible cannot be contained. He brought order out of chaos and created creation. With a word he called Adam out of dust and Eve out of a bone. He consulted no committee. He sought no counsel.

He has no peer. "I am God, and there is no other; I am God, and there is none like me" (Isaiah 46:9 NIV). The greatest kings have surrendered their crowns. Alexander the Great is a mound of dust in a tomb. The queen of England is called Her Majesty, yet she must eat and bathe and rest. The True Majesty, on the other hand, is never hungry. He never sleeps. He has never needed attention or assistance.

From the tiniest microbe to the mightiest mountain, "he sustains everything by the mighty power of his command" (Hebrews 1:3 NLT).

He has authority over the world and . . .

He has authority over *your* world. He's never surprised. And he has never, ever uttered the phrase "How did that happen?"

—*Before Amen*

AUGUST 6

A Prayer . . . to Follow God

Good and upright is the Lord;
Therefore He teaches sinners in the way.
The humble He guides in justice,
And the humble He teaches His way.
PSALM 25:8–9

Dear Father, you are good. Your ways are perfect and above my own. You deserve my full obedience and my worship. You are my teacher and authority because of your goodness.

Humble me today when I choose my way over yours. Use my prideful moments as an opportunity to teach me and redirect me.

Show my friends that your goodness is more important than their desires. Provide them with encouragement to seek your good and upright way.

Thank you for your constant instruction and concern for each step of my life.

In the name of Jesus I pray these things, amen.

–*Pocket Prayers*

The Journey Isn't Our Destination

We set our eyes not on what we see but on what we cannot see. What we see will last only a short time, but what we cannot see will last forever.

2 CORINTHIANS 4:18 NCV

Jesus tells us to "seek first the kingdom of God" (Matthew 6:33). This is his invitation to us. Set your hearts on your home.

In his plan it's all about the King and his kingdom. He wrote the script, built the sets, directs the actors, and knows the final act—an everlasting kingdom. "And this is [God's] plan: At the right time he will bring everything together under the authority of Christ—everything in heaven and on earth" (Ephesians 1:10 NLT).

Reach for it!

The journey home is nice, but the journey is not the destination. Those who are content with nothing more than joy in the journey are settling for too little satisfaction. Our hearts tell us there is more to this life than this life. We, like E.T., lift bent fingers to the sky. We may not know where to point, but we know not to call this world our home.

"God . . . has planted eternity in the human heart" (Ecclesiastes 3:11 NLT).

In God's narrative, life on earth is but the beginning: the first letter of the first sentence in the first chapter of the great story God is writing with your life.

–*God's Story, Your Story*

AUGUST 8

When the Devil Draws Near

Resist the devil and he will flee from you.

JAMES 4:7

When the Devil draws near, stand against him. "What are you doing here? I am dead to you!" Give him no quarter. Don't take his lies. Don't stand for his accusations. Don't cower at his attacks. When he dredges up your past mistakes, tell him whose you are. He has no recourse to this truth. He knows who you are. He just hopes that you don't or that you will forget. So prove to him that you know and remember. Tell him:

"I have been bought with a price. I belong to God" (1 Corinthians 6:20).

"I have not been given a spirit of fear but of power, love, and a sound mind" (2 Timothy 1:7).

"I cannot be separated from the love of God" (Romans 8:35).

"I can find grace and mercy in the time of need" (Hebrews 4:16).

"I can do all things through Christ who strengthens me" (Philippians 4:13).

God's people think like this. They walk with a reverent swagger. They live out of their inheritance. They show the Devil the new name on their spiritual passport.

The secret of survival when the Devil draws near? Remember. Remember what God has done. Remember whose you are.

–*Glory Days*

Holy Anger

Once he was approached by a leper, who knelt before him begging his help. "If only you will," said the man, "you can cleanse me." In warm indignation Jesus stretched out his hand, [and] touched him.

MARK 1:40–41 NEB

I was in an emergency room late one night last week.

Victims of Satan filled the halls. A child—puffy, swollen eyes. Beaten by her father. A woman—bruised cheeks, bloody nose. "My boyfriend got drunk and hit me," she said, weeping. An old man—unconscious and drunk on a stretcher. He drooled blood in his sleep.

Jesus saw the victims of Satan too. He saw a leper one day . . . fingers gnarled . . . skin ulcerated . . . face disfigured. And he got indignant . . . angry. Not a selfish, violent anger. A holy anger . . . a controlled frustration . . . a compassionate disgust. And it moved him. It moved him to action.

I'm convinced that the same Satan stalks today, causing the hunger in Somalia . . . the confusion in the Mideast . . . the egotism on the movie screen . . . the apathy in Christ's church.

And Satan giggles among the dying.

Dear Father,

May we never grow so "holy," may we never be so "mature," may we never become so "religious," that we can see the footprints of Satan and stay calm.

–*On the Anvil*

AUGUST 10

Protection

So do not fear, for I am with you;
do not be dismayed, for I am your God.
I will strengthen you and help you;
I will uphold you with my righteous right hand.
ISAIAH 41:10 NIV

Nadin Khoury was thirteen years old, five foot two, and weighed, soaking wet, probably a hundred pounds. His attackers were larger and outnumbered him seven to one. For thirty minutes they hit, kicked, and beat him. He never stood a chance. They dragged him through the snow, stuffed him into a tree, and suspended him on a seven-foot wrought-iron fence.

Khoury survived the attack and would have likely faced a few more except for the folly of one of the bullies. He filmed the pile-on and posted it on YouTube. The troublemakers landed in jail, and the story reached the papers.

A staffer at the nationwide morning show *The View* read the account and invited Khoury to appear on the broadcast. As the video of the assault played, his lower lip quivered. As the video ended, the curtain opened, and three huge men walked out, members of the Philadelphia Eagles football team.

Khoury, a rabid fan, turned and smiled. One was All-Pro receiver DeSean Jackson. Jackson took a seat close to the boy and promised him, "Anytime you need us, I got two linemen right here." Then, in full view of every bully in America, he gave the boy his cell phone number.[1] Who wouldn't want that type of protection?

You've got it . . . from the Son of God himself.

–*Glory Days*

AUGUST 11 

He Washes Your Feet Too

Jesus . . . rose from supper and laid aside His garments, took a towel and girded Himself. After that, He poured water into a basin and began to wash the disciples' feet.

JOHN 13:3–5

Jesus touched the stinky, ugly parts of his disciples. Knowing he came from God. Knowing he was going to God. Knowing he could arch an eyebrow or clear his throat, and every angel in the universe would snap to attention. Knowing that all authority was his, he exchanged his robe for the servant's wrap, lowered himself to knee level, and began to rub away the grime, the grit, and the grunge their feet had collected on the journey.

Jesus didn't exclude a single follower, though we wouldn't have faulted him had he bypassed Philip. When Jesus told the disciples to feed the throng of five thousand hungry people, Philip, in effect, had retorted, "It's impossible!" (John 6:7). So what does Jesus do with someone who questions his commands? Apparently, he washes the doubter's feet.

James and John lobbied for cabinet-level positions in Christ's kingdom. So what does Jesus do when people use his kingdom for personal advancement? He slides a basin in their direction.

Within hours Peter would curse the very name of Jesus and hightail his way into hiding. In fact, all twenty-four of Jesus' followers' feet would soon scoot, leaving Jesus to face his accusers alone. Do you ever wonder what God does with promise breakers? He washes their feet.

–*Grace*

AUGUST 12

Welcome God In

Here I am! I stand at the door and knock. If anyone hears my voice and opens the door, I will come in and eat with that person, and they with me.

REVELATION 3:20 NIV

When we invite God into our world, he walks in. He brings a host of gifts: joy, patience, resilience. Anxieties come, but they don't stick. Fears surface and then depart. Regrets land on the windshield, but then comes the wiper of prayer. The Devil still hands me stones of guilt, but I turn and give them to Christ. I'm completing my sixth decade, yet I'm wired with energy. I am happier, healthier, and more hopeful than I have ever been. Struggles come, for sure. But so does God.

Prayer is not a privilege for the pious, not the art of a chosen few. Prayer is simply a heartfelt conversation between God and his child. My friend, he wants to talk with you. Even now, as you read these words, he taps at the door. Open it. Welcome him in. Let the conversation begin.

–*Before Amen*

A Prayer . . . to Cover Me

I bow my knees to the Father . . . that Christ may dwell in your hearts through faith; that you, being rooted and grounded in love, may be able to comprehend with all the saints what is the width and length and depth and height—to know the love of Christ which passes knowledge; that you may be filled with all the fullness of God.

EPHESIANS 3:14–19

O Lord, you are divine love come down, and from you we have received grace and truth. Pour your love and mercy over me and cover all things in my life—my hurts and evil and secrets. I drink in your love for my every need. In Jesus' name, amen.

–*In the Manger*

AUGUST 14

Grace Gives More

No eye has seen, no ear has heard,
and no mind has imagined
what God has prepared
for those who love him.
1 CORINTHIANS 2:9 NLT

Grace goes beyond mercy. Mercy gave Ruth some food. Grace gave her a husband and a home. Mercy gave the prodigal son a second chance. Grace threw him a party. Mercy prompted the Samaritan to bandage the wounds of the victim. Grace prompted him to leave his credit card as payment for the victim's care. Mercy forgave the thief on the cross. Grace escorted him into paradise. Mercy pardons us. Grace woos and weds us.

Let me spell it out. Ruth's story is a picture of how grace happens in hard times. Jesus is your kinsman-redeemer.

He spotted you in the wheat field, ramshackled by hurt. And he has resolved to romance your heart. Through sunsets. The kindness of a Boaz. Providence. Whispers of Scripture. The book of Ruth. Even a book by Max. Marginalized and discarded? Others may think so. You may think so. But God sees in you a masterpiece about to happen.

–*Grace*

Together

"You will receive power when the Holy Spirit comes on you; and you will be my witnesses in Jerusalem, and in all Judea and Samaria, and to the ends of the earth."

ACTS 1:8 NIV

Jesus didn't issue individual assignments. He didn't move one by one down the line and knight each individual. "You [all of you collectively] will be my witnesses" (Acts 1:8 NIV).

Jesus works in community. For that reason you find no personal pronouns in the earliest description of the church:

> All the *believers* devoted *themselves* to the apostles' teaching, and to fellowship, and to sharing in meals . . . and to prayer. . . .
>
> And all the *believers* met together in one place and shared everything *they* had. *They* sold *their* property and possessions and shared the money with those in need. *They* worshiped together at the Temple each day, met in homes for the Lord's Supper, and shared *their* meals with great joy. (Acts 2:42–46 NLT, emphasis mine)

The cameo contains only plural nouns and pronouns.

No *I* or *my* or *you*. We are in this together. We are more than followers of Christ, disciples of Christ. "We are parts of his body" (Ephesians 5:30 NCV). "He is the head of the body, which is the church" (Colossians 1:18 NCV). I am not his body; you are not his body. We—together—are his body.

–*Outlive Your Life*

The Promotion

Whatever you do in word or deed, do all in the name of the Lord Jesus, giving thanks to God the Father through Him.

COLOSSIANS 3:17

For twenty years I was the senior minister of our church. I was in the thick of it all. I was happy to fill the role. But I was happiest preaching and writing. My mind was always gravitating toward the next sermon, the next series.

As the church increased in number, so did the staff. More staff meant more people to manage. More people to manage meant spending more time doing what I didn't feel called to do.

I was gradually becoming grumpy.

I was blessed to have options. I was equally blessed to have a church that provided flexibility. I transitioned from senior minister to teaching minister.

When I became teaching minister, a few people were puzzled.

"Don't you miss being the senior minister?"

Translation: Weren't you demoted?

Earlier in my life I would have thought so. But I have come to see God's definition of promotion: a promotion is not a move up the ladder; it is a move toward your call. Don't let someone "promote" you out of your call.

Look for ways to align your job with your skills. This may take time. This may take trial and error . . . but don't give up. Not every tuba player has the skills to direct the orchestra. If you can, then do. If you can't, blast away on your tuba with delight.

–*Glory Days*

AUGUST 17

Open Manholes

I don't really understand myself, for I want to do what is right, but I don't do it. Instead, I do what I hate.

ROMANS 7:15 NLT

It happens in an instant. One minute you are walking and whistling, the next you are wide-eyed and falling. Satan yanks back the manhole cover, and an innocent afternoon stroll becomes a horror story. Helplessly you tumble, unable to gain control.

Such is the pattern of sudden sin. Can you relate to it?

No one who is reading these words is free from the treachery of sudden sin. This demon of hell can scale the highest monastery wall, penetrate the deepest faith, and desecrate the purest home.

Want to sharpen your defenses a bit?

First, *recognize Satan.* Our war is not with flesh and blood but with Satan himself. Call him by name. Rip off his mask. When the urge to sin rears its ugly head, look him squarely in the eye and call his bluff. "Get behind me, Satan!"

Second, *accept God's forgiveness.* Romans chapter 7 is the Emancipation Proclamation for those of us who have a tendency to tumble.

"Thanks be to God, who delivers me through Jesus Christ our Lord! . . . Therefore, there is now no condemnation for those who are in Christ Jesus" (Romans 7:25–8:1 NIV).

Amen. There it is. For those *in* Christ there is *no* condemnation. Absolutely none. Claim the promise. Accept the cleansing. Throw out the guilt. Praise the Lord. And . . . watch out for open manholes.

–*On the Anvil*

AUGUST 18

The Inspired Word

You must remain faithful to the things you have been taught. . . . You have been taught the holy Scriptures from childhood, and they have given you the wisdom to receive the salvation that comes by trusting in Christ Jesus.

2 TIMOTHY 3:14–15 NLT

Can we believe that "all Scripture is inspired by God" (2 Timothy 3:16 NASB)? Here is why I think we can.

It is remarkable in composition. Composed over sixteen centuries by forty authors. Begun by Moses in Arabia and finished by John on Patmos. Penned by kings in palaces, shepherds in tents, and prisoners in prisons. Would it be possible for forty writers, writing in three different languages and several different countries, separated by as much as sixteen hundred years, to produce a book of singular theme unless behind them there was one mind and one designer?

It is remarkable in durability. It is the single most published book in history. Translated into at least twelve hundred languages.[2] Bibles have been burned by governments and banished from courtrooms, but God's Word endures. The death knell has been sounded a hundred times, but God's Word continues.

It is remarkable in prophecy. More than three hundred fulfilled prophecies about the life of Christ[3] were all written at least four hundred years before he was born. Imagine if something similar occurred today. If we found a book written in 1900 that prophesied two world wars, a depression, an atomic bomb, and the assassinations of a president and a civil rights leader, wouldn't we trust it?

–Glory Days

UNENDING INTERCESSION

Though we were spiritually dead because of the things we did against God, he gave us new life with Christ. You have been saved by God's grace. And he raised us up with Christ and gave us a seat with him in the heavens. . . . You did not save yourselves; it was a gift from God.

EPHESIANS 2:5–8 NCV

Jesus "is in the presence of God at this very moment sticking up for us" (Romans 8:34 MSG). Let this sink in for a moment. In the presence of God, in defiance of Satan, Jesus Christ rises to your defense. He takes on the role of a priest. "Since we have a great priest over God's house, let us come near to God with a sincere heart and a sure faith, because we have been made free from a guilty conscience" (Hebrews 10:21–22 NCV).

A clean conscience. A clean record. A clean heart. Free from accusation. Free from condemnation. Not just for our past mistakes but also for our future ones.

"Since he will live forever, he will always be there to remind God that he has paid for [our] sins with his blood" (Hebrews 7:25 TLB). Christ offers unending intercession on your behalf.

Jesus trumps the Devil's guilt with words of grace.

–Grace

AUGUST 20

A Prayer . . . to Let Others In

When they continued asking Him, [Jesus] raised Himself up and said to them, "He who is without sin among you, let him throw a stone at her first."

JOHN 8:7

Gracious Lord, in the Bible you are called "the One who sees me," and I know that your eyes are always upon me to guide and protect and bless and correct. You have given me eyes too. Grant me the power to use them to truly see. Help me see those you put in my path—really see them, with all their hurts, their desires, their longings, their needs, their joys, and their challenges. As you open my eyes, prompt me to open wide my arms to offer whatever help and encouragement I have to give. In Jesus' name I pray, amen.

–*Outlive Your Life*

AUGUST 21

Get Out of Your Shell

God has not given us a spirit of fear, but of power and of love and of a sound mind.
2 TIMOTHY 1:7

Clamshells. We all wear them. They're better than body armor, thick as an army tank. Think of them as bunkers for the soul. Inside there is no hunger or orphans, poverty or injustice.

We come by our shells honestly. We don't intend to stick our heads in a hole. We want to help. But the problems are immense, complex, and intense.

Let God unshell you. And when he does, "make a careful exploration of who you are and the work you have been given, and then sink yourself into that" (Galatians 6:4 MSG). Try starting with two questions:

> *With whom do you feel most fluent?* Teenagers? Drug addicts? The elderly? You may be tongue-tied around children but eloquent with executives. This is how God designed you. "God has given us different gifts for doing certain things well" (Romans 12:6 NLT).
>
> *For whom do you feel most compassion?* God doesn't burden us equally.[4] He fashions our hearts individually (Psalm 33:15). When does your heart break and pulse race? When you spot the homeless? When you travel to the inner city?

It's amazing what happens when we get out of our shells . . . and go to work for God.

—*Outlive Your Life*

AUGUST 22

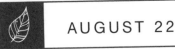

Opening Closed Doors

"God will always give what is right to his people who cry to him night and day, and he will not be slow to answer them."
LUKE 18:7 NCV

When God locks a door, it needs to be locked. When he blocks a path, it needs to be blocked. When he stuck Paul and Silas in prison, God had a plan for the prison jailer. As Paul and Silas sang, God shook the prison. "At once all the prison doors flew open, and everyone's chains came loose" (Acts 16:26 NIV).

There God goes again, blasting open the most secure doors in town. When the jailer realized what had happened, he assumed all the prisoners had escaped. He drew his sword to take his life.

When Paul told him otherwise, the jailer brought the two missionaries out and asked, "What must I do to be saved?" (v. 30 NIV). Paul told him to believe. He did, and he and all his family were baptized. The jailer washed their wounds, and Jesus washed his sins. God shut the door of the jail cell so that he could open the heart of the jailer.

So might that closed door you're facing be God's way of opening someone's heart?

–*God's Story, Your Story*

AUGUST 23

CHOSEN VESSELS

Ananias answered, "Lord, I have heard from many about this man, how much harm he has done to Your saints in Jerusalem." . . . But the Lord said to him, "Go, for he is a chosen vessel of Mine."

ACTS 9:13, 15

God's chosen vessels aren't always gleaming and golden. They may be tarnished or cracked, broken or even discarded. They may be a Saul, driven by anger, motivated to hurt. Saul was. Eager to root out and persecute the early Christians.

But God saw possibilities in Saul and sent Ananias to teach and minister to him. What will you do when God sends you to salvage one of his chosen vessels? What will you do when God shows you your Saul? The Saul that everyone else has written off.

"He's too far gone." "She's too hard . . . too addicted . . . too old . . . too cold." No one gives your Saul a prayer. But you are beginning to realize that maybe God is at work behind the scenes. You begin to believe.

Don't resist these thoughts.

Of course, no one believed in people more than Jesus did. He saw something in Peter worth developing, in the adulterous woman worth forgiving, and in John worth harnessing.

Don't give up on your Saul. When others write him off, give him another chance. Tell your Saul about Jesus, and pray. And remember this: God never sends you where he hasn't already been. By the time you reach your Saul, who knows what you'll find.

–*Outlive Your Life*

AUGUST 24

Our Battle Strategy

Though we live in the world, we do not wage war as the world does. The weapons we fight with are not the weapons of the world. On the contrary, they have divine power to demolish strongholds.

2 CORINTHIANS 10:3–4 NIV

Today's problem is not necessarily tomorrow's problem. Don't incarcerate yourself by assuming it is. Resist self-labeling. "I'm just a worrier." "Gossip is my weakness." "My dad was a drinker, and I guess I'll carry on the tradition."

Stop that! These words create alliances with the Devil. They grant him access to your spirit. It is not God's will that you live a defeated, marginalized, unhappy, and weary life. Turn a deaf ear to the old voices and make new choices. "The lines have fallen to me in pleasant places; yes, I have a good inheritance" (Psalm 16:6). Live out of your inheritance, not your circumstance.

God has already promised a victory. And he has provided weapons for the fight.

Every battle, ultimately, is a spiritual battle. Every conflict is a contest with Satan and his forces. Paul urged us to stand "against the wiles of the devil" (Ephesians 6:11). Satan is not passive or fair. He is active and deceptive. He has designs and strategies. Consequently, we need a strategy as well. And God gives us one: let him do the fighting for us.

–*Glory Days*

AUGUST 25

God Doesn't Let Go

I am persuaded that neither death nor life, nor angels nor principalities nor powers, nor things present nor things to come, nor height nor depth, nor any other created thing, shall be able to separate us from the love of God which is in Christ Jesus our Lord.

ROMANS 8:38–39

Many Christians live with a deep-seated anxiety about eternity. They *think* they are saved, *hope* they are saved, but still they doubt, wondering, *Am I* really *saved?*

Our behavior gives us reason to wonder. We are strong one day, weak the next. Devoted one hour, flagging the next. Believing, then unbelieving.

Conventional wisdom draws a line through the middle of these fluctuations. Perform above this line, and enjoy God's acceptance. But dip below it, and expect a pink slip from heaven. In this paradigm a person is lost and saved multiple times a day. Salvation becomes a matter of timing. You just hope you die on an upswing. No security, stability, or confidence.

This is not God's plan. He draws the line, for sure. But he draws it beneath our ups and downs. Jesus' language couldn't be stronger: "And I give them eternal life, and they shall never lose it or perish throughout the ages. . . . And no one is able to snatch them out of My hand" (John 10:28 AMPC).

God doesn't let go.

–Grace

AUGUST 26

Flip the Switch

"You will call upon Me and go and pray to Me, and I will listen to you."
JEREMIAH 29:12

One of our Brazilian church leaders taught me something about earnest prayer. He met Christ during a yearlong stay in a drug-rehab center. His therapy included three one-hour sessions of prayer a day.

I expressed amazement and confessed that my prayers were short and formal. He invited (dared?) me to meet him for prayer. We knelt on the concrete floor of our small church and began to talk to God. Change that. I talked; he cried, wailed, begged, cajoled, and pleaded. He prayed like Moses.

When God determined to destroy the Israelites for their golden calf stunt, "Moses begged the Lord his God and said, 'Lord, don't let your anger destroy your people, whom you brought out of Egypt. . . . Remember the men who served you—Abraham, Isaac, and Israel. You promised with an oath to them'" (Exodus 32:11–13 NCV).

Moses on Mount Sinai is not calm and quiet, with folded hands and a serene expression. He's on his knees, lifting his hands, shedding tears.

And God heard him! "So the Lord changed his mind and did not destroy the people as he had said he might" (v. 14 NCV).

Our passionate prayers move the heart of God. Prayer does not change God's nature. Prayer does, however, impact the flow of history. God has wired his world for power, but he calls on us to flip the switch.

–*Outlive Your Life*

A Prayer . . . to Seek God

"You will seek Me and find Me, when you search for Me with all your heart."
JEREMIAH 29:13

Father, I want to be among the searchers who are always seeking Jesus. That you have prepared an eternal home for me and want me to be with you is the best news I've ever heard. Ready my heart to find you. In Jesus' name, amen.

—*In the Manger*

AUGUST 28

Ready to March?

I pray that the eyes of your heart may be enlightened in order that you may know the hope to which he has called you, the riches of his glorious inheritance.

EPHESIANS 1:18 NIV

Think about the Christian you want to be. What qualities do you want to have? More compassion? More conviction? More courage? What attitudes do you want to discontinue? Greed? Guilt? Endless negativity? A critical spirit?

Here is the good news. You can. With God's help you can close the gap between the person you are and the person you want to be, indeed, the person God made you to be. You can live "from glory to glory" (2 Corinthians 3:18).

Joshua and his men did this. They went from dry land to the Promised Land, from manna to feasts, from arid deserts to fertile fields. They inherited their inheritance (Joshua 21:43–45).

To inherit your inheritance is God's vision for your life too. Imagine the thought. You at full throttle. You as you were intended. You as victor over the Jerichos and giants.

It's a life that is yours for the taking.

Expect to be challenged. The enemy won't go down without a fight. But God's promises outweigh personal problems. Victory becomes, dare we imagine, a way of life. Isn't it time for you to change your mailing address from the wilderness to the Promised Land?

Are you ready to march?

–*Glory Days*

Will You Be Someone?

In the day of my trouble I sought the Lord.
PSALM 77:2

When disasters strike, the human spirit responds by reaching out to help those affected. People stand in line to give blood. Millions of dollars are donated to aid victims and their families. Rescue teams work for endless hours. But the most essential effort is accomplished by another valiant team. Their task? To guard and gird the world with prayer. Those who pray keep alive the watch fires of faith. For the most part, we don't even know their names. Such is the case of someone who prayed on a day long ago.

His name is not important. His looks are immaterial. His gender is of no concern. His title is irrelevant. He is important not because of who he was, but because of what he did.

He went to Jesus on behalf of a friend. His friend was sick, and Jesus could help, and someone needed to go to Jesus, so someone went. Others cared for the sick man in other ways. Some brought food; others provided treatment; still others comforted the family. Each role was crucial. Each person was helpful, but no one was more vital than the one who went to Jesus.

John wrote, "So Mary and Martha sent *someone* to tell Jesus, 'Lord, the one you love is sick'" (John 11:3 NCV, emphasis mine).

Someone carried the request. Someone walked the trail. Someone went to Jesus on behalf of Lazarus. And because someone went, Jesus responded.

–*For the Tough Times*

AUGUST 30

Put God's Plan in Place

> I am not perfect. But Christ has taken hold of me. So I keep on running and struggling to take hold of the prize. . . . I forget what is behind, and I struggle for what is ahead.
>
> PHILIPPIANS 3:12–13 CEV

My wife and I spent five years on a missionary team in Rio de Janeiro, Brazil. Our first two years felt fruitless and futile. We gringos typically outnumbered the Brazilians in the worship service. More often than not I went home frustrated.

So we asked God for another plan. We prayed and reread the Epistles. We especially focused on Galatians. It occurred to me that I was preaching a limited grace. When I compared our gospel message with Paul's, I saw a difference. His was high-octane good news. Mine was soured legalism. So as a team we resolved to focus on the gospel. In my teaching I did my best to proclaim forgiveness of sins and resurrection from the dead.

We saw an immediate change. We baptized forty people in twelve months! Quite a few for a church of sixty members. God wasn't finished with us. We just needed to put the past in the past and God's plan in place.

Don't spend another minute in the past. Ask God for his plan.

–*Glory Days*

Why Not?

Jesus went about all Galilee, teaching in their synagogues, preaching the gospel of the kingdom, and healing all kinds of sickness and all kinds of disease among the people.

MATTHEW 4:23

Christ stunned people with his authority and clarity. His was not the mind of a deranged wild man. Demented fool? No. Deceiving fraud? Some have said so.

Some believe that Jesus masterminded the greatest scheme in the history of humanity. If that were true, billions of humans have been fleeced into following a first-century pied piper over the edge of a cliff.

Should we crown Christ as the foremost fraud in the world?

Not too quickly. Look at the miracles Jesus performed. The four Gospels detail approximately thirty-six miracles and reference many more. He multiplied bread and fish, changed water into wine, calmed more than one storm, restored sight to more than one blind man. Yet, in doing so, Jesus never grandstanded his miraculous powers. Never went for fame or profit. Jesus performed miracles for two reasons: to prove his identity and to help his people.

Had Jesus been a fraud or trickster, people would have denounced the miracles of Christ. But they did just the opposite. Can you imagine the testimonies? "If you were a part of the crowd he fed, one of the dead he raised, or one of the sick he healed, speak up and tell your story."

And speak they did. The church exploded like a fire on a West Texas prairie. Why? Because Jesus healed people.

Why not let him heal you?

–*God's Story, Your Story*

SEPTEMBER

SEPTEMBER 1 

The Monumental Offer of God

Christ also suffered once for sins, the just for the unjust, that He might bring us to God.

1 PETER 3:18

God dressed Christ in our sins. *Our* sins, each and every one.

I cheated my friends.
I lied to my wife.
I abused my children.
I cursed my God.

As if Jesus deserved them, he wore them. Our sins were put on Christ. "The LORD has laid on him the iniquity of us all" (Isaiah 53:6 NIV). "He bore the sin of many" (v. 12 NIV). Paul proclaimed that God made Christ "to be sin" (2 Corinthians 5:21 NIV) and become "a curse for us" (Galatians 3:13 NIV). Peter agreed: "'[Jesus] himself bore our sins' in his body on the cross" (1 Peter 2:24 NIV).

This is the monumental offer of God. What does God say to the woman who wants to work and offset her guilt? To the man who wants to earn his way out of sin? Simple: the work has been done. My Son wore your sin on himself, and I punished it there.

–*God's Story, Your Story*

SEPTEMBER 2

A Covenant-Keeping God

Every word of God is pure;
He is a shield to those who put their trust in Him.
PROVERBS 30:5

We live in a world of falling words. Broken promises. Empty vows. Pledges made only to be retracted. Assurances given, then ignored. They were spoken with great fanfare. "I'll always love you." "Count on us to recognize good work." "Till death do us part."

But words tend to tumble. They are autumn leaves in November's wind. You've heard your share.

But you'll never hear them from God. In a world of falling words, his remain. In a life of broken promises, he keeps his. "The Lord's promise is sure. He speaks no careless word; all he says is purest truth, like silver seven times refined" (Psalm 12:6 TLB).

God is a covenant-keeping God.

–*Glory Days*

A Prayer . . . for Help and Grace

There is born to you this day in the city of David
a Savior, who is Christ the Lord.
LUKE 2:11

Everlasting Father, you are the mighty God. You sent your Son and performed the final sacrifice, and you deserve all of our praise.

I need your help today. I am a sinner and am feeling the weight of my sin. Show me what your Son's birth means for me in this moment.

Give grace to those who have not accepted your Son and do not know the freedom he gives. Let them see that you are their loving Father.

Thank you for loving me not just yesterday or today but always, no matter the depth of my sin. I am grateful.

In your Son's precious name, amen.

–*Pocket Prayers*

SEPTEMBER 4

Who You Are

He makes everything work out according to his plan.

EPHESIANS 1:11 NLT

What is the text of our lives?

The question is not a new one. Self-help gurus, talk-show hosts, and magazine headlines urge you to find your narrative. But they send you in the wrong direction. "Look inside yourself," they say. But the promise of self-discovery falls short. Can you find the plot of a book in one paragraph or hear the flow of a symphony in one measure? By no means. You are so much more than a few days between the womb and the tomb.

Your story indwells God's. This is the great promise of the Bible and the hope of this book. "It's in Christ that we find out who we are and what we are living for. Long before we first heard of Christ and got our hopes up, he had his eye on us, had designs on us for glorious living, part of the overall purpose he is working out in everything and everyone" (Ephesians 1:11–12 MSG).

Above and around us God directs a grander saga, written by his hand, orchestrated by his will, unveiled according to his calendar. And you are a part of it. Your life emerges from the greatest mind and the kindest heart in the history of the universe: the mind and heart of God.

–*God's Story, Your Story*

Risk Believing

We have seen and testify that the Father has sent his Son to be the Savior of the world.
1 JOHN 4:14 NIV

God's people risk believing. When forced to stand at the crossroads of belief and unbelief, they choose belief. They place one determined step after the other on the pathway of faith. Seldom with a skip, usually with a limp. They make a conscious decision to step toward God, to lean into hope, to heed the call of heaven. They press into the promises of God.

Joshua's story urges us to do likewise. In fact, one might argue that the central message of the book of Joshua is this headline: "God keeps his promises. Trust him."

The three verses of Joshua 21:43–45 are the theological heart of the book. The writer pounds the point in triplicate. Three times in three verses he declares: *God did what he said he would do.*

1. "The Lord gave . . . all . . . He had sworn to give" (v. 43).
2. "The Lord gave . . . rest . . . according to all that He had sworn to their fathers" (v. 44).
3. "Not a word failed of any good thing which the Lord had spoken. . . . All came to pass" (v. 45).

Learn from Joshua. Take a risk. Believe God. He will do what he has said he will do.

–*Glory Days*

SEPTEMBER 6

Live with Gratitude

Let the message about Christ, in all its richness, fill your lives. Teach and counsel each other with all the wisdom he gives. Sing psalms and hymns and spiritual songs to God with thankful hearts.

COLOSSIANS 3:16 NLT

God's solution to any challenge is simply this: a grateful spirit. No mist is so thick that the sunlight of appreciation cannot burn it away. Case in point? Jack Ryan.

Pastors aren't supposed to have favorites, I know. But Jack has always been one of mine. He's a seventy-year-old, silver-haired saint, quick to smile and encourage.

He'd been absent for some time. Heart disease had sucked the strength out of his body. I went to visit him.

"Jack," I asked, "I hear you aren't doing well?"

"Oh, Max," he corrected with a weak smile. "Never better."

"They say you can't sleep."

"No, I can't. But I can pray."

His eyes danced as he tilted his head. "I just talk to Jesus, Max. I tell him I love him. I tell him, 'Thanks.' These are good times for me. I'm just talking to Jesus."

Poor circulation took Jack's color. Disease sapped his vigor. His hands trembled. Yet you'd have thought he was a kid on Christmas Eve.

In a sense he was. Early the next morning he went home to Jesus. Who is the real victor in life? Is it not the person who dies with a thankful and hope-filled spirit? How do we die with gratitude? We live with it.

–*Before Amen*

The Woes of Beachfront Property

"Everyone who hears these sayings of Mine, and does not do them, will be like a foolish man who built his house on the sand: and the rain descended, the floods came, and the winds blew and beat on that house; and it fell. And great was its fall."

MATTHEW 7:26–27

Obedience leads to blessing. Disobedience leads to trouble.

Remember Jesus' parable about the two builders who each built a house? One built on cheap, easy-to-access sand. The other built on costly, difficult-to-reach rock. The second construction project demanded more time and expense, but when the spring rains turned the creek into a gulley washer . . . guess which builder enjoyed a blessing and which experienced trouble? Beachfront property doesn't make for much if it can't withstand the storm.

According to Jesus the wise builder is "whoever hears these sayings of Mine, and does them" (Matthew 7:24). Both builders heard the teachings. The difference between the two was not knowledge and ignorance but obedience and disobedience. Security comes as we put God's precepts into practice. We're only as strong as our obedience.

Ignore the lure of beachfront property; build your house on the Rock.

–*Glory Days*

SEPTEMBER 8

Whatever Does This Mean?

Jesus was lifted up to heaven and is now at God's right side. The Father has given the Holy Spirit to Jesus as he promised. So Jesus has poured out that Spirit, and this is what you now see and hear.

ACTS 2:33 NCV

"Whatever could this mean?" (Acts 2:12) the people asked. The sound of rushing wind, the images of fire, the sudden linguistic skills of the disciples . . . whatever could these occurrences mean? Jerusalemites had surely heard of Jesus. But did they *know* Jesus? In rapid succession Peter fired a trio of God-given endorsements of Christ.

1. "God proved that he sent Jesus to you by having him work miracles, wonders, and signs" (v. 22 CEV). Jesus' miracles were proof of his divinity.
2. Then God delivered him to death. "[He] had already planned and decided that Jesus would be handed over to you. So you took him and had evil men put him to death on a cross" (v. 23 CEV). God deemed Christ worthy of God's most important mission—to serve as a sacrifice for humankind. But God did not leave Jesus in the tomb.
3. "God set him free from death and raised him to life. Death could not hold him in its power" (v. 24 CEV).

"Whatever did this mean?" It means that death was no match for the Son of God . . . and it is no match for those who belong to him.

–*Outlive Your Life*

Fit for a King

"See, I have removed your iniquity from you,
and I will clothe you with rich robes."
ZECHARIAH 3:4

When you make God's story yours, he covers you in Christ. You wear him like a vest. Old labels no longer apply—only labels that would be appropriately worn by Jesus Christ. Can you think of a few phrases for your new vest? How about

- royal priest (1 Peter 2:9 NIV)
- complete (Colossians 2:10)
- free from condemnation (Romans 8:1 NIV)
- secure (John 10:28 NIV)
- established and anointed one (2 Corinthians 1:21)
- God's coworker (2 Corinthians 6:1 NIV)
- God's temple (1 Corinthians 3:16–17 NIV)
- God's workmanship (Ephesians 2:10)

How do you like that outfit?

–*God's Story, Your Story*

SEPTEMBER 10

A Prayer . . . to Slow Down and See

He was in the world, and the world was made through Him, and the world did not know Him. He came to His own, and His own did not receive Him.

JOHN 1:10–11

Gracious Father, I am caught in the busyness of everyday life, and it is easy to miss what you are doing in my life today. Slow me down and open my eyes, Lord. Make your presence known that I may behold you doing the impossible. In Jesus' name, amen.

–*In the Manger*

Stop at the Gate

Peter said, "Silver and gold I do not have, but what I do have I give you: In the name of Jesus Christ of Nazareth, rise up and walk."
ACTS 3:6–8

The thick, meaty hand of the fisherman reached for the frail, thin one of the beggar. The cripple swayed like a newborn calf finding its balance. And as he stood, he began to shout, and passersby began to stop.

The crowd thickened around the trio. Other beggars pressed toward the scene in their ragged coverings and tattered robes and cried out for their portion of a miracle.

So Peter complied. He escorted them to the clinic of the Great Physician and invited them to take a seat. "Faith in His name . . . has made this man strong. . . . Repent therefore and be converted, that your sins may be blotted out, so that times of refreshing may come from the presence of the Lord" (Acts 3:16, 19).

An honest look led to a helping hand that led to a conversation about eternity. Works done in God's name long outlive our earthly lives.

Let's be the people who stop at the gate. Let's look at the hurting until we hurt with them. No hurrying past, turning away, or shifting of eyes. No pretending or glossing over. Let's look at the face until we see the person.

–*Outlive Your Life*

SEPTEMBER 12

Nothing to Prove

The devil took him to the holy city and had him stand on the highest point of the temple. "If you are the Son of God," he said, "throw yourself down."

MATTHEW 4:5–6 NIV

Satan came to Jesus in the desert to test him, to tempt him, to trick him. But testing isn't limited to the desert; it also occurs in the sanctuary. The two—Satan and the Son of God—stood on the southeastern wall of the temple, more than a hundred feet above the Kidron Valley, and Satan told Jesus to jump into the arms of God. Jesus refused, not because he couldn't, not because God wouldn't catch him. He refused because he didn't have to prove anything to anyone, much less the Devil.

Neither do you. Satan is going to tell you otherwise. In church, of all places, he will urge you to do tricks: impress others with your service, make a show of your faith, call attention to your good deeds. He loves to turn church assemblies into Las Vegas presentations where people show off their abilities rather than boast in God's.

Don't be suckered. Showing off in the sanctuary is just another of Satan's schemes.

–*God's Story, Your Story*

SEPTEMBER 13 

Don't Stroll Through the Swamp

"Accept my teachings and learn from me, because I am gentle and humble in spirit, and you will find rest for your lives."
MATTHEW 11:29 NCV

"You're gonna regret it." I waved away the warning without turning around. What was to regret? Everyone else was taking the long way; I took the short-cut. Let the others walk around the water; I would wade through it. After all, it was just the Everglades. But water is water, right?

"Wrong," my newfound Florida friends tried to tell me. They were taking me to a picnic. The tables sat on the other side of a marsh. The parks department had kindly constructed a bridge by which pedestrians could pass over the marsh. But who needed a bridge?

"I'll wade across."

Someone pointed at the sign. "Swamp water not recommended for recreation."

I couldn't be slowed by a warning, so I ventured in. The mud swallowed my feet. The brine was home to a million mosquitoes. Squiggly things swam past me. I think I saw a set of eyeballs peering in my direction.

I backpedaled. Both flip-flops were sucked into the abyss, never to be seen again. I exited, mud covered, mosquito bitten, and red faced. I walked over the bridge and took my seat at the picnic table.

Made for a miserable picnic.

Makes for an apt proverb.

Life comes with voices. Voices lead to choices.

Choices have consequences.

–*Glory Days*

SEPTEMBER 14

Faith Is a Choice

"Let not your heart be troubled; you believe
in God, believe also in Me."
JOHN 14:1

I was on a plane when a fellow tapped me on the shoulder. He'd scribbled a message on a napkin and handed it to me.

> Six summers ago Lynne and I buried our twenty-four-year-old daughter who was two weeks on life support. . . .
>
> Friends rallied around our family. A country lawyer with his encouraging message that "God means you good, not harm" was one of those encouraging voices. . . .
>
> To unplug our daughter from life support was very hard. Although the decision was painful, we were confident that we were doing the right thing in laying her in the arms of a mighty God.
>
> His best work may not have been restoring Erin to this life but his assistance for Lynne and me to let him have her. He made our daughter better than new. He restored my Erin to his eternal presence. That is his best work! . . .
>
> Our faith is getting us through this.
>
> Faith is a choice.[1]

How does a dad bury a daughter and believe, so deeply believe, that God meant him good not harm?

Simple. This grieving dad believes God's promises. "Faith is a choice." It is.

–*Glory Days*

Jesus Heals Us All

Jesus stood still and called them, and said,
"What do you want Me to do for you?"
MATTHEW 20:32

Are you waiting for Jesus to heal you? Take hope from Jesus' response to the blind men of Matthew 20:29–34.

"Have mercy on us, O Lord," they cried.

"Jesus stood still." He stopped dead in his tracks. Everyone else kept going, but Jesus froze. Something caught his attention. What did Jesus hear?

A prayer. An unembellished appeal for help, floating across the path on the winds of faith and landing against his ear. Jesus heard the words and stopped.

He still does. And he still asks, "What do you want me to do for you?"

The duo in Jericho told him. "Lord, that our eyes may be opened," they said.

And you? What in your life needs healing?

Jesus' heart went out to the blind men. He "had compassion and touched their eyes." He healed them.

He will heal you, my friend. I pray he heals you instantly. He may choose to heal you gradually. But this much is sure: Jesus will heal us all ultimately. Wheelchairs, ointments, treatments, and bandages are confiscated at the gateway to heaven. God's children will once again be whole.

Because ultimately Jesus heals us all.

–Before Amen

SEPTEMBER 16

Be Still

Be still, and know that I am God;
I will be exalted among the nations,
I will be exalted in the earth!
PSALM 46:10

Jesus taught us to pray with reverence when he modeled for us "Hallowed be Your name" (Matthew 6:9). This phrase is a petition, not a proclamation. A request, not an announcement. "Be hallowed, Lord." Do whatever it takes to be holy in my life. Take your rightful place on the throne. Exalt yourself. Magnify yourself. Glorify yourself. You be Lord, and I'll be quiet.

"Be still, and know that I am God" (Psalm 46:10 NIV). This verse contains a command with a promise.

The command? *Be still. Cover your mouth. Bend your knees.*

The promise? *You will know that I am God.*

The vessel of faith journeys on soft waters. Belief rides on the wings of waiting.

In the midst of your daily storms, and in this storm that has swept over our country and even the entire world, make it a point to be still and set your sights on him. Let God be God. Let him bathe you in his glory so that both your breath and your troubles are sucked from your soul. Be still. Be quiet. Be open and willing. Take a moment to be still, and know that he is God.

Be still and allow God to be hallowed in your life.

–For the Tough Times

A Prayer . . . for Washing with Mercy

"Now that I, your Lord and Teacher, have washed your feet, you also should wash one another's feet. I have set you an example that you should do as I have done for you. Very truly I tell you, no servant is greater than his master, nor is a messenger greater than the one who sent him."

JOHN 13:14–16 NIV

King of the universe, I'd like to think I would have washed your feet and done better than the other disciples, but I know that's not true. Thank you for loving me and washing my feet and offering me mercy when I deserve none. In Jesus' name, amen.

–*On Calvary's Hill*

SEPTEMBER 18

Give Grace

"Now that you know these things, you will be blessed if you do them."

JOHN 13:17 NIV

L*ord, you expect me to wash his feet and let him go?*

Most people don't want to. They use the villain's photo as a dart target. Their Vesuvius blows up every now and again, sending hate airborne, polluting and stinking the world. Most people keep a pot of anger on low boil.

But you aren't "most people." Grace has happened to you. Look at your feet. They are wet, grace soaked. Your toes and arches and heels have felt the cool basin of God's grace. Jesus has washed the grimiest parts of your life. He didn't bypass you and carry the basin toward someone else. If grace were a wheat field, he's bequeathed you the state of Kansas. Can't you share your grace with others?

"Since I, the Lord and Teacher, have washed your feet, you ought to wash each other's feet. I have given you an example to follow. Do as I have done to you" (John 13:14–15 NLT).

To accept grace is to accept the vow to give it.

–*Grace*

How Much Is Enough?

"If you forgive other people when they sin against you, your heavenly Father will also forgive you. But if you do not forgive others their sins, your Father will not forgive your sins."

MATTHEW 6:14–15 NIV

How much justice is enough? Picture your enemy for a moment. Picture him tied to the whipping post. The strong-armed man with the whip turns to you and asks, "How many lashes?" And you give a number. The whip cracks and the blood flows and the punishment is inflicted. Your foe slumps to the ground, and you walk away.

Are you happy now? Do you feel better? Are you at peace? Perhaps for a while, but soon another memory will surface, and another lash will be needed, and . . . when does it all stop?

It stops when you take seriously the words of Jesus: "For if you forgive men when they sin against you, your heavenly Father will also forgive you. But if you do not forgive men their sins, your Father will not forgive your sins" (Matthew 6:14–15 NIV).

"Treat me as I treat my neighbor." Are you aware that this is what you are saying to your Father? "Give me what I give them. Grant me the same peace I grant others. Let me enjoy the same tolerance I offer." God will treat you the way you treat others.

Would you like some peace? Then quit giving your neighbor such a hassle. Want to enjoy God's generosity? Then let others enjoy yours. Would you like assurance that God forgives you? I think you know what you need to do.

–*For the Tough Times*

SEPTEMBER 20

Bringing Everyone In

As Scripture says, "Anyone who believes in him will never be put to shame." For there is no difference between Jew and Gentile—the same Lord is Lord of all and richly blesses all who call on him.

ROMANS 10:11–12 NIV

People are prone to pecking orders. We love the high horse. The boy over the girl or girl over boy. The affluent over the destitute. The educated over the dropout. The old-timer over the newcomer. The Jew over the Gentile.

An impassable gulf yawned between Jews and Gentiles in the days of the early church. A Jew could not drink milk drawn by Gentiles or eat their food. Jews could not aid a Gentile mother in her hour of need. Jewish physicians could not attend to non-Jewish patients.[2]

No Jew would have anything to do with a Gentile. They were unclean.

Unless that Jew, of course, was Jesus. Suspicions of a new order began to surface because of his curious conversation with the Canaanite woman. Her daughter was dying, and her prayer was urgent. Yet her ancestry was Gentile. "I was sent only to help God's lost sheep—the people of Israel," Jesus told her. "That's true, Lord," she replied, "but even dogs are allowed to eat the scraps that fall beneath their masters' table" (Matthew 15:24, 27 NLT).

Jesus healed the woman's daughter and made his position clear. He was more concerned about bringing everyone in than shutting certain people out.

–*Outlive Your Life*

The Sigh

Then, looking up to heaven, He sighed, and said to him, "Ephphatha," that is, "Be opened."
MARK 7:34

As God's story becomes your story, you make this wonderful discovery: you will graduate from this life into heaven. Jesus' plan is to "gather together in one all things in Christ" (Ephesians 1:10). "All things" includes your body. Your blood-pumping heart, arm-hinging elbow, weight-supporting torso. God will reunite your body with your soul and create something unlike anything you have seen: an eternal body.

You will finally be healthy. You never have been. Even on the days you felt fine, you weren't. You were a sitting duck for disease, infections, airborne bacteria, and microbes.

I hate disease. I'm sick of it.

So is Christ. Consider his response to the suffering of a deaf mute. "He took him aside from the multitude, and put His fingers in his ears, and He spat and touched his tongue. Then, looking up to heaven, He sighed, and said to him, 'Ephphatha,' that is, 'Be opened'" (Mark 7:33–34).

Everything about this healing stands out. The way Jesus separates the man from the crowd. The tongue and ear touching. But it's the sigh that we notice. Jesus looked up to heaven and sighed. This is a sigh of sadness, a deep breath, and a heavenly glance that resolves, "It won't be this way for long."

–*God's Story, Your Story*

SEPTEMBER 22

Grace for the Mess

For the sin of this one man, Adam, caused death to rule over many. But even greater is God's wonderful grace and his gift of righteousness, for all who receive it will live in triumph over sin and death through this one man, Jesus Christ.

ROMANS 5:17 NLT

The meaning of life. The wasted years of life. The poor choices of life. God answers the mess of life with one word: *grace.*

We talk as though we understand the term. The bank gives us a *grace* period. The seedy politician falls from *grace.* Musicians speak of a *grace* note. At church *grace* graces the songs we sing and the Bible verses we read. *Grace* shares the church parsonage with its cousins: *forgiveness, faith,* and *fellowship.* Preachers explain it. Hymns proclaim it. Seminaries teach it.

But do we really understand it?

Here's my hunch: we've settled for wimpy grace. It politely occupies a phrase in a hymn, fits nicely on a church sign. Never causes trouble or demands a response. When asked, "Do you believe in grace?" who could say no?

Have you been changed by grace? Shaped by grace? Strengthened by grace? Softened by grace? God's grace has a drenching about it. A wildness about it. A white-water, riptide, turn-you-upside-downness about it. Grace comes after you. It rewires you. From insecure to God secure. From regret-riddled to better-because-of-it. From afraid-to-die to ready-to-fly. Grace is the voice that calls us to change and then gives us the power to pull it off.[3]

–*Grace*

Pray Boldly

Pray to the Father. He loves to help. You'll get his help, and won't be condescended to when you ask for it. Ask boldly, believingly, without a second thought.
JAMES 1:5–6 MSG

When Martin Luther's coworker became ill, the reformer prayed boldly for healing. "I besought the Almighty with great vigor," he wrote. "I attacked him with his own weapons, quoting from Scripture all the promises I could remember, that prayers should be granted, and said that he must grant my prayer, if I was henceforth to put faith in his promises."[4]

As John Wesley was crossing the Atlantic Ocean, contrary winds came up. When he learned that the winds were knocking the ship off course, he responded in prayer.

> Almighty and everlasting God, . . . thou holdest the winds in thy fists and sittest upon the water floods, and reignest a king for ever. Command these winds and these waves that they obey thee, and take us speedily and safely to the haven whither we would go.[5]

Boldness in prayer is an uncomfortable thought for many. Agonizing before God? Storming heaven with prayers? Isn't such prayer irreverent? Presumptuous? It would be had God not invited us to pray as such. "So let us come boldly to the very throne of God and stay there to receive his mercy" (Hebrews 4:16 TLB).

Dare to pray boldly.

–Glory Days

SEPTEMBER 24

A Prayer . . . to the One, True God

"I am God, and there is no other; I am God, and there is none like Me, declaring the end from the beginning, and from ancient times things that are not yet done, saying, 'My counsel shall stand, and I will do all My pleasure.'"

ISAIAH 46:9–10

God above, there is no one like you. You are the one, true God. The only God that I worship, the Alpha and Omega.

I need to know that you have gone before me. I see no solution for the problems I'm facing. Remind me that you are not perplexed by the struggles I face so that I may be comforted by your all-knowing power.

Be near to my family and friends who are suffering. Their pain is paralyzing, but you are greater than anything they face.

Thank you for your perfect will. May it be done in my life as I seek you.

In your name alone, amen.

–*Pocket Prayers*

God Does What We Cannot

"Most assuredly, I say to you, he who hears My word and believes in Him who sent Me has everlasting life, and shall not come into judgment, but has passed from death into life."
JOHN 5:24

God's people trust his hold on them more than their hold on God. They place their trust in the finished work of Christ. They deeply believe that they are "delivered . . . from the power of darkness and conveyed . . . into the kingdom of the Son" (Colossians 1:13).

They point to Calvary as *prima facie* evidence of God's commitment to them.

The followers of Joshua did something similar. They looked not to a hill but to a river. Not to Calvary but to the Jordan. The miraculous crossing convinced them that God was in their presence. As their leader had promised, "By this [crossing] you shall know that the living God is among you" (Joshua 3:10).

And cross they did! "All Israel crossed over on dry ground, until all the people had crossed completely over the Jordan" (v. 17).

"*All Israel* crossed over on dry ground." The men. The women. Old. Young. Believers and doubters. The faithful and the murmurers.

"All Israel crossed over *on dry ground*." Might as well have been concrete. No wagon wheels got stuck. No feet got damp.

God did for them what they could not do. And God does for us what we cannot do. In Christ, he allows us to cross over from the mud of sin and death to the dry ground of life eternal.

–*Glory Days*

SEPTEMBER 26

But, God, You Can

"So I tell you, keep on asking, and you will receive what you ask for. Keep on seeking, and you will find. Keep on knocking, and the door will be opened to you."

LUKE 11:9 NLT

When you feel helpless and impotent, where can you turn? I suggest you turn to Luke 11:5–10 and to one of Jesus' most intriguing teachings about prayer. It's the story of a persistent neighbor looking to borrow bread at midnight.

Imagine that neighbor is you. That's you ringing the doorbell at midnight. That's you waking up his Chihuahua. The porch light comes on. The door opens. Boy, does he look like a mess. Boxer shorts. T-shirt. Bed hair.

"What are you doing here?" he asks.

"A friend of mine has just arrived for a visit, and I have nothing for him to eat," you answer.

The home owner grumbles and complains, but you insist. "Come on, Hank, please." Finally Hank takes you to his pantry. And your surprise guest doesn't have to go to bed hungry. All because you spoke up on behalf of someone else.

This is intercessory prayer at its purest. *Father, you are good. They need help. I can't, but you can.*

This prayer gets God's attention. After all, if Hank, a cranky, disgruntled friend, will help out, how much more will God do?

–*Before Amen*

SEPTEMBER 27

Rahab!

Now Joshua the son of Nun sent out two men from Acacia Grove to spy secretly, saying, "Go, view the land, especially Jericho." So they went, and came to the house of a harlot named Rahab, and lodged there.

JOSHUA 2:1

Much could be said about Rahab without mentioning her profession. She was a Canaanite. She provided cover for the spies of Joshua. She came to believe in the God of Abraham before she ever met the children of Abraham. She was spared in the destruction of her city. She was grafted into the Hebrew culture. She married a contemporary of Joshua's, bore a son named Boaz, had a grandson named Jesse, a great-grandson named David, and a descendant named Jesus. Yes, Rahab's name appears on the family tree of the Son of God.

Yet in five of the eight appearances of her name in Scripture, she is presented as a "harlot."[6] Five! Wouldn't one suffice? And couldn't that one reference be nuanced in a euphemism such as "Rahab, the best *hostess* in Jericho"? Put a little concealer on this biblical blemish.

But the Bible doesn't. It points a neon sign at it. It's even attached to her name in the Hebrews Hall of Fame. The list includes Abel, Noah, Abraham, Isaac, Jacob, Joseph, Moses . . . and then, all of a sudden, "the harlot Rahab" (Hebrews 11:31). Her history of harlotry is part of her testimony.

Now, you may or may not sell your body, but you've sold your allegiance, affection, attention, and talents. You've sold out. We all have. We've all thought, *I am too . . . soiled, dirty, afflicted.*

God's one-word reply for such doubt? *Rahab!*

–*Glory Days*

SEPTEMBER 28

Forgiveness Can Happen

Bear with each other, and forgive each other. If someone does wrong to you, forgive that person because the Lord forgave you.

COLOSSIANS 3:13 NCV

Sequence matters. Jesus washes first; we wash next. He demonstrates; we follow. He uses the towel, then extends it to us, saying, "Now you do it. Walk across the floor of your Upper Room, and wash the feet of your Judas."

So go ahead. Get your feet wet. Remove your socks and shoes, and set your feet in the basin. First one, then the other. Let the hands of God wipe away every dirty part of your life—your dishonesty, adultery, angry outbursts, hypocrisy, pornography. Let him touch them all. As his hands do their work, look across the room.

Forgiveness may not happen all at once. But it can happen with you. After all, you have wet feet.

–*Grace*

Strength to Overcome

Those who hope in the Lord
will renew their strength.
They will soar on wings like eagles;
they will run and not grow weary,
they will walk and not be faint.
ISAIAH 40:31 NIV

God's word to Joshua is God's word to us: "Be strong and of good courage" (Joshua 1:6). Do not heed your fear. Do not cower before your woes. Take the land God has given you to possess.

"And the Lord said to Joshua: 'See! I have given Jericho into your hand, its king, and the mighty men of valor'" (6:2).

God did not say, "Joshua, take the city."

God said, "Joshua, receive the city I have taken."

Joshua did not go forth hoping to win. He knew that God had already won.

The same can be said about you and your challenge. God does not say, "Bob, break your bad habit."

He says, "Bob, I have broken the bad habits of your life. Receive the blessing of my victory."

Remember, you are a coheir with Christ. Every attribute of Jesus is at your disposal. Was Jesus victorious? Did he overcome sin and death? Yes! Will you be victorious? Can you overcome sin and death? Yes! The question is not, will you overcome? It is, *when* will you overcome? Life will always bring challenges. But God will always give strength to face them.

–*Glory Days*

SEPTEMBER 30

Keep the Power Supply Open

The Holy Spirit helps us in our weakness.

ROMANS 8:26 NLT

The Holy Spirit is not enthusiasm, compassion, or bravado. He might stimulate such emotions, but he himself is a person. He determines itineraries (Acts 16:6), distributes spiritual gifts (1 Corinthians 12:7–11), and selects church leaders (Acts 13:2). He teaches (John 14:26), guides (John 16:13), and comforts (John 16:7 KJV).

"He dwells with you and will be in you" (John 14:17). Occasional guest? No sir. The Holy Spirit is a year-round resident in the hearts of his children. As God's story becomes our story, his power becomes our power. Then why do we suffer from power failures?

We're prone to depend on God's Spirit to save us but not sustain us. We are like the Galatians whom Paul asked, "After beginning by means of the Spirit, are you now trying to finish by means of the flesh?" (Galatians 3:3 NIV). We turn to him to get us started, and then continue in our own strength.

The same hand that pushed the rock from the tomb can shove away your doubt. The same power that stirred the still heart of Christ can stir your flagging faith. The same strength that put Satan on his heels can, and will, defeat Satan in your life. Just keep the power supply open.

–*God's Story, Your Story*

OCTOBER

OCTOBER 1

A Prayer . . . for the Nearness of God

What marvelous love the Father has extended to us! Just look at it—we're called children of God! That's who we really are.

1 JOHN 3:1 MSG

Gracious Father, I thank you that there are no limits to when you will come to us. You still come near, every day, when we come and behold you. Help me to focus the eyes of my heart on you today and take your presence with me wherever I go. In Jesus' name, amen.

–*In the Manger*

What You Need Most

"For God so loved the world that He gave His only begotten Son, that whoever believes in Him should not perish but have everlasting life."
JOHN 3:16

God is enough. Isn't this the message of Moses and Joshua and the journey to the Promised Land? Who opened the Jordan River? Who led the people across on dry ground? Who appeared to encourage Joshua? Who brought down the Jericho walls? Who has fought for and delivered the people?

God!

He cared for his people. Even in the wilderness they never went without provision. They may have grown weary of manna-nut bread, but they were never hungry.

He gave them not just food but clothing and good health. Moses once reminded the Hebrews, "Your clothes did not wear out and your feet did not swell during these forty years" (Deuteronomy 8:4 NIV).

The following phrases were never heard in the wilderness:

"I need to soak my feet in Epsom salts."

"Oh, bummer, my robe has another rip in it."

"Hey, new sandals. Where did you get them?"

No want for food. No need for clothing. Never a blister or a bunion. God provided for them. And God promised to provide you more. He promised you a Savior.

–*Glory Days*

OCTOBER 3

Invoke His Name

I will pray to the LORD,
and he will answer me from his holy mountain.
PSALM 3:4 NCV

Prayer slaps handcuffs on Satan. Prayer takes problems out of the domain of the Devil and into the presence of God. Prayer confesses, "God can handle it. Since he can, I have hope!"

When we pray in the name of Jesus, we come to God on the basis of Jesus' accomplishment. "Since we have a great high priest [Jesus] over the house of God, let us draw near with a true heart in full assurance of faith" (Hebrews 10:21–22 HCSB). As our high priest, Jesus offers our prayers to God. His prayers are always heard. "Truly, truly, I say to you, if you ask the Father for anything in My name, He will give it to you" (John 16:23 NASB).

There are those who say, "Prayer changes things because it changes us." I agree but only in part. Prayer changes things because prayer appeals to the top power in the universe. Prayer is not a magical formula or a mystical chant. It is the yes to God's invitation to invoke his name.

–*Before Amen*

OCTOBER 4

Come to Me

"Come to me, all you who are weary and burdened."
MATTHEW 11:28 NIV

In August 1930, forty-five-year-old Joseph Crater waved good-bye to friends after an evening meal in a New York restaurant, flagged down a taxi, and rode off. He was never seen or heard from again.

Fifty years of research has offered countless theories but no conclusions. A search of his apartment revealed one clue. It was a note attached to a check, and both were left for his wife. The check was for a sizable amount, and the note simply read, "I am very weary. Love, Joe."

The note could have been nothing more than a thought at the end of a hard day. Or it could have meant a great deal more—the epitaph of a despairing man.

Weariness is tough. I don't mean physical weariness that comes from mowing the lawn or the mental weariness that follows a hard day of decisions and thinking. No, the weariness that attacked Joseph Crater is much worse. It's the weariness that comes just before you give up. That feeling of honest desperation. It's that stage in life when motivation disappears: the children grow up, a job is lost, a spouse dies. The result is weariness—deep, lonely, frustrated weariness.

Only one man in history has claimed to have an answer for it. He stands before all the Joseph Craters of the world with the same promise: "Come to me, all you who are weary . . . and I will give you rest" (Matthew 11:28 NIV).

–On the Anvil

OCTOBER 5

Where the Healing Begins

Great crowds came to him, bringing the lame, the blind, the crippled, the mute and many others, and laid them at his feet; and he healed them.

MATTHEW 15:30 NIV

Jesus never refused an intercessory request. Ever! Peter brought concerns for his sick mother-in-law. The centurion brought a request for his sick servant. Jairus had a sick daughter. A woman from Canaan had a demon-possessed daughter. From sunrise to sunset Jesus heard one appeal after another. He heard so many requests that at times the disciples attempted to turn people away (Matthew 15:22–23). Yet Jesus would not let them.

He never grew impatient at the requests. But he did grow impatient at the lack of one.

A father once brought his demon-possessed son to the disciples of Jesus. They attempted to help the boy but failed. When Jesus learned of their failure, he erupted in frustration. "O faithless and perverse generation, how long shall I be with you? How long shall I bear with you? Bring him here to Me" (Matthew 17:17).

Such an outburst! What was the oversight of the disciples? Simple. They attempted to heal the boy without calling on Christ. He had to command them: "Bring him here to Me."

Jesus' command to you today is the same: "Bring them here to Me." Those that you love, those that you worry about, even those that you struggle with—bring them to Jesus first. Prayerfully lay them at his feet. That's where the healing begins.

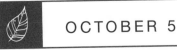

–Before Amen

OCTOBER 6

But God Said . . .

Because of his glory and excellence, he has given us great and precious promises. These are the promises that enable you to share his divine nature and escape the world's corruption caused by human desires.

2 PETER 1:4 NLT

Nothing deserves your attention more than God's covenants. No words written on paper will ever sustain you like the promises of God. Do you know them?

To the bereaved: "Weeping may stay for the night, but rejoicing comes in the morning" (Psalm 30:5 NIV).

To the besieged: "The righteous person may have many troubles, but the LORD delivers him from them all" (Psalm 34:19 NIV).

To the sick: "The LORD sustains them on their sickbed and restores them from their bed of illness" (Psalm 41:3 NIV).

To the lonely: "When you pass through the waters, I will be with you" (Isaiah 43:2 NIV).

To the dying: "In my Father's house are many rooms. . . . I go to prepare a place for you" (John 14:2 ESV).

To the sinner: "My grace is sufficient for you" (2 Corinthians 12:9).

Press into God's promises. When fears surface, respond with this thought: *But God said* . . . When doubts arise, *But God said* . . . When guilt overwhelms you, *But God said* . . .

Search the Scriptures like a miner digging for gold. Once you find a nugget, grasp it. Trust it. Take it to the bank. There is no greater treasure.

–*Glory Days*

OCTOBER 7

The Lord of Heaven

When I consider Your heavens, the work of Your fingers,
The moon and the stars, which You have ordained,
What is man that You are mindful of him,
And the son of man that You visit him?
PSALM 8:3–4

When tragedy strikes, people wonder how God could allow such things to happen. Can we trust him to run the universe if he would allow *this*?

It is important to recognize that God dwells in a different realm. He occupies another dimension. "Just as the heavens are higher than the earth, so are my ways higher than your ways and my thoughts higher than your thoughts" (Isaiah 55:9 NCV).

How vital that we pray, armed with the knowledge that God is in heaven. Pray with any lesser conviction, and our prayers are hollow. Look up at the heavens and see what God has done, and watch how your prayers are energized.

This knowledge gives us confidence as we face the uncertain future. We know that he is in control of the universe, and so we can rest secure. But also important is the knowledge that this God in heaven has chosen to bend near toward earth to see our sorrow and hear our prayers. He is not so far above us that he is not touched by our tears.

Though we may not be able to see his purpose or his plan, the Lord of heaven is on his throne and in firm control of the universe and our lives.

–*For the Tough Times*

A Prayer . . . to Bless Others

The Lord God formed man of the dust of the ground, and breathed into his nostrils the breath of life; and man became a living being.

GENESIS 2:7

Loving Father, you made me, so you know very well that I am but dust. Yet you have called me into your kingdom to serve you at this specific place, at this specific time, for a very specific purpose. Despite my ordinariness, I belong to you—and you are anything but ordinary! Help me pour out your grace and compassion upon others that they, too, may experience the richness of your love. Through me, my Father, show others how you can use an ordinary life to bring extraordinary blessing into the world. In Jesus' name I pray, amen.

–*Outlive Your Life*

OCTOBER 9

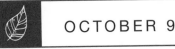

Is Your Cause Too Small?

"Truly I tell you, if anyone says to this mountain, 'Go, throw yourself into the sea,' and does not doubt in their heart but believes that what they say will happen, it will be done for them."

MARK 11:23 NIV

If your problems are great, then your cause is too small. When your cause is great, the problems begin to shrink.

Do you have a holy cause? A faith worth preserving? A mission worth living for? Ask God to give you a cause to claim to his glory. An orphanage to serve. A neighbor to encourage. A needy family to feed. A class to teach. Some senior citizens to encourage. It really is better to give than receive. In the kingdom of Christ we gain by giving, not taking. We grow by helping, not hurting. We advance by serving, not demanding. Want to see your troubles evaporate? Help others with theirs.

You'll always face problems. But you don't have to face them in the same way. Instead:

Immerse your mind in God-thoughts.

Turn a deaf ear to doubters.

Set your mind on a holy cause.

Once you find your mountain, no giant will stop you, no age will disqualify you, no problems will defeat you.

–*Glory Days*

OCTOBER 10

Who's Coming to Dinner?

Cheerfully share your home with those who need a meal or a place to stay. God has given each of you a gift from his great variety of spiritual gifts. Use them well to serve one another.

1 PETER 4:9–10 NLT

The Greek word for *hospitality* compounds two terms: *love* and *stranger.* The word literally means to love a stranger. All of us can welcome a guest we know and love. But can we welcome a stranger?

In one of Jesus' resurrection appearances, he accompanies two disciples as they walk from Jerusalem to their village of Emmaus.

As they near their village, Jesus acts as if he is going to continue on his journey.

It had been a long day. The two pilgrims had much on their minds. Certainly they had obligations and people in their lives. But their fellow traveler stirred a fire in their hearts. So they welcomed him in. Still not knowing that their guest was Jesus, they pulled out an extra chair, poured some water in the soup, and offered bread. Jesus blessed the bread, and when he did, "their eyes were opened and they recognized him" (Luke 24:31 NIV).

We still encounter people on the road. And sometimes we sense a peculiar warmth, an affection. We detect an urge to open our doors to them. In these moments let's heed the inner voice. We never know whom we may be hosting for dinner.

–*Outlive Your Life*

OCTOBER 11

What Would Happen . . . ?

While Peter was in prison, the church prayed very earnestly for him.

ACTS 12:5 NLT

King Herod jailed Peter and resolved to behead him on the anniversary of Jesus' death. And what could the church do about it? They had no recourse: no clout, no political chips to cash. So our Jerusalem ancestors left us a strategy. When the problem is bigger than we are—we pray!

Our passionate prayers move the heart of God. "The effective, fervent prayer of a righteous man avails much" (James 5:16). Prayer does not change God's nature; who he is will never be altered. Prayer does, however, impact the flow of history. God has wired his world for power, but he calls on us to flip the switch.

And the Jerusalem church did just that.

> The night before Peter was to be placed on trial, he was asleep, fastened with two chains between two soldiers. Others stood guard at the prison gate. Suddenly, there was a bright light in the cell, and an angel of the Lord stood before Peter. The angel struck him on the side to awaken him and said, "Quick! Get up!" And the chains fell off his wrists. (Acts 12:6–7 NLT)

The church earnestly prayed, and what happened? An angel appeared, chains fell away, gates opened, and Peter walked free.

Imagine the possibilities if the church today did the same. Imagine what could happen to hunger, violence, greed, despair. Just imagine. And pray.

–*Outlive Your Life*

OCTOBER 12

A Short-Term Condition

Do not love the world or the things in the world. If anyone loves the world, the love of the Father is not in him.

1 JOHN 2:15

Perhaps you need the reminder that I need? It can all come crashing down. In a moment. In a fire. In an economic free fall. In a job crisis. Don't put your trust in stuff.

Paul told Timothy, "Command those who are rich in this present world not to be arrogant nor to put their hope in wealth, which is so uncertain, but to put their hope in God, who richly provides us with everything for our enjoyment" (1 Timothy 6:17 NIV).

The "rich in this . . . world." That is you. That is me. If you have enough education to read this page, enough resources to own this book, you likely qualify as a prosperous person. And that is okay. Prosperity is a common consequence of faithfulness (Proverbs 22:4). Paul didn't tell the rich to feel guilty about being rich; he just urged caution.

Nothing breeds failure like success.

Money is just a short-term condition. The abundance or lack of money will only be felt for one life . . . so don't get tangled up in it.

–Glory Days

OCTOBER 13

A Deposit of Power

When you believed, you were marked in him with a seal, the promised Holy Spirit, who is a deposit guaranteeing our inheritance until the redemption of those who are God's possession—to the praise of his glory.

EPHESIANS 1:13–14 NIV

The word *inheritance* is to Joshua's book what delis are to Manhattan: everywhere. The word appears nearly sixty times. The command to possess the land is seen five times. The great accomplishment of the Hebrew people came down to this: "So Joshua let the people depart, each to his own inheritance" (Joshua 24:28).

Is it time for you to receive yours?

You have one. If you have given your heart to Christ, God has given Canaan to you. He "has blessed [you] with every spiritual blessing in the heavenly places in Christ" (Ephesians 1:3).[1]

Note the tense: "he *has* blessed." Not "he *will* bless, *might* bless, or *someday could possibly* bless." You already have everything you need to be everything God desires. You have access to "every spiritual blessing in the heavenly places."

This well may be the best-kept secret in Christendom. We underestimate what happened to us upon conversion. Because conversion is more than a removal of sin. It is a deposit of power. He embedded within you the essence of Christ. "Therefore, if anyone is in Christ, he is a new creation; old things have passed away; behold, all things have become new" (2 Corinthians 5:17).

Claim your inheritance.

–*Glory Days*

OCTOBER 14

Wave the White Flag

Don't keep looking at my sins.
Remove the stain of my guilt.
Create in me a clean heart, O God.
PSALM 51:9–10 NLT

Don't make this inward journey to free yourself from the stabbing pain of sin and guilt without God. Many voices urge you to look deep within and find an invisible strength or hidden power. A dangerous exercise. Self-assessment without God's guidance leads to denial or shame. We can either justify our misbehavior with a thousand and one excuses or design and indwell a torture chamber. Justification or humiliation? We need neither.

We need a prayer of grace-based confession, like David's. After a year of denial and a cover-up, he finally prayed, "God, be merciful to me because you are loving. Because you are always ready to be merciful, wipe out all my wrongs. Wash away all my guilt and make me clean again. I know about my wrongs, and I can't forget my sin. You are the only one I have sinned against; I have done what you say is wrong. You are right when you speak and fair when you judge" (Psalm 51:1–4 NCV).

David waved the white flag. No more combat. No more arguing with heaven. He came clean with God. And you? Are you ready to wave the white flag, throw down your weapons, and admit your arguments are futile? Are you ready to come clean with God?

–*Grace*

OCTOBER 15

A Prayer . . . to Offer Everyone Grace

Now there was a certain disciple at Damascus named Ananias; and to him the Lord said in a vision, "Ananias." And he said, "Here I am, Lord."

ACTS 9:10

O Lord, nobody lies beyond the grasp of your grace. Who in my life do I see as hopeless? What man or woman who currently seems far from you do you want to bring into your family, in part through me? What Saul is out there to whom I could become an Ananias? Father, I pray that you would show your greatness and your power by using me in some way to introduce an "unlikely candidate" to your son. Help me triumph over my fears and obliterate my misconceptions as you work through me to bring someone else, through faith, into the circle of your love. In Jesus' name I pray, amen.

–*Outlive Your Life*

OCTOBER 16 

Your Saul

I was shown mercy so that in me, the worst of sinners, Christ Jesus might display his immense patience as an example for those who would believe in him and receive eternal life.

1 TIMOTHY 1:16 NIV

Ananias enters and sits on the stone floor. He takes the hand of Saul, the had-been terrorist, and feels it tremble. He observes Saul's quivering lip. Ananias realizes Christ has already done the work. All that remains is for Ananias to show Saul the next step. "Brother Saul . . ." (How sweet those words must have sounded. Saul surely wept upon hearing them.)

"Brother Saul, the Lord Jesus, who appeared to you on the road as you came, has sent me that you may receive your sight and be filled with the Holy Spirit" (Acts 9:17).

Tears rush like a tide against the crusts on Saul's eyes. The scaly covering loosens and falls away. He blinks and sees the face of his new friend.

Within the hour he's stepping out of the waters of baptism. Within a few days he's preaching in a synagogue. Saul soon becomes Paul, and Paul preaches from the hills of Athens, pens letters from the bowels of prisons, and ultimately sires a genealogy of theologians, including Aquinas, Luther, and Calvin.

God used Paul to touch the world. But he first used Ananias to touch Paul. Has God given you a similar assignment? Has God given you a Saul?

–*Outlive Your Life*

OCTOBER 17

A Flame of Fire

The tongue is a flame of fire. It is a whole world of wickedness, corrupting your entire body. It can set your whole life on fire.

JAMES 3:6 NLT

I once knew an extremely courageous lady. For one thing, she was waging an uphill battle against alcoholism. For another, she was doing all she could to restore her relationship with God.

She chose a small church to attend, a church where she knew many members. On Sunday, as she walked toward the front door, she overheard two ladies talking.

"How long is that alcoholic going to hang around here?"

She turned and went back to the car. She never entered another church building until she died. Those ladies meant no harm, yet seemingly painless gossip did irreparable damage.

These five ideas will help us control our tongues:

1. Never say anything about someone that you wouldn't say to his face.
2. Never say anything about someone unless she is there to respond.
3. Refuse to listen to someone else's gossip.
4. Initiate positive statements about people whom you're discussing.
5. Remember, "the tongue is a fire" (James 3:6).

–On the Anvil

OCTOBER 18 

An Entirely Different Approach

God has shown me that he doesn't think anyone is unclean or unfit.

ACTS 10:28 CEV

As long as we can call people common or unfit, we can go our separate ways. Labels relieve us of responsibility. Pigeonholing permits us to wash our hands and leave.

"Oh, I know John. He is an alcoholic." (Translation: "Why can't he control himself?")

"Oh, I know her. She's divorced." (Translation: "She has a lot of baggage.")

Categorizing others creates distance and gives us a convenient exit strategy for avoiding involvement.

Jesus took an entirely different approach. He was all about including people, not excluding them. "The Word became flesh and blood, and moved into the neighborhood" (John 1:14 MSG). Jesus touched lepers and loved foreigners and spent so much time with partygoers that people called him a "lush, a friend of the riffraff" (Matthew 11:19 MSG).

His Facebook page included the likes of Zacchaeus the Ponzi-meister, Matthew the IRS agent, and some floozy he met at Simon's house. Jesus spent thirty-three years walking in the mess of this world. "He had equal status with God but didn't think so much of himself that he had to cling to the advantages of that status no matter what. Not at all. When the time came, he set aside the privileges of deity and took on the status of a slave, became *human*!" (Philippians 2:6–7 MSG).

His example sends this message: "Don't call any person unfit."

–*Outlive Your Life*

OCTOBER 19

YOUR ADVOCATE

If anyone sins, we have an Advocate with the Father, Jesus Christ the righteous. And He Himself is the propitiation for our sins.

1 JOHN 2:1–2

Not all guilt is bad. God uses appropriate doses of guilt to awaken us to sin. We know guilt is God-given when it causes "indignation . . . alarm . . . longing . . . concern . . . readiness to see justice done" (2 Corinthians 7:11 NIV). God's guilt brings enough regret to change us.

Satan's guilt, on the other hand, brings enough regret to enslave us. Don't let him lock his shackles on you.

Remember, "your life is hidden with Christ in God" (Colossians 3:3). When he looks at you, he sees Jesus first. In the Chinese language the word for *righteousness* is a combination of two characters, the figure of a lamb and a person. The lamb is on top, covering the person. Whenever God looks down at you, this is what he sees: the perfect Lamb of God covering you. It boils down to this choice: Do you trust your Advocate or your Accuser?

–Grace

To Outwit the Devil

I will call upon the LORD, who is worthy to be praised;
So shall I be saved from my enemies.
PSALM 18:3

God will help us stand against the Devil. He will disclose the craftiness of Satan. But we must regularly consult him. In everything. His word is a "lamp unto [our] feet" (Psalm 119:105 KJV), not a spotlight into the future. He gives enough light to take the next step.

Our best days come when we learn to hear God's voice telling us to turn this way or that way. "Your own ears will hear him. Right behind you a voice will say, 'This is the way you should go,' whether to the right or to the left" (Isaiah 30:21 NLT).

Refer every decision to the tribunal of heaven. Like David you can ask God to "bend low and hear my whispered plea" (Psalm 31:2 TLB). Wait until God speaks before you act. Be patient. Monitor your impulse. "I will instruct you and teach you in the way you should go; I will guide you with My eye" (Psalm 32:8). If you feel a check in your heart, heed it and ask God again. To ask God is the only way to outwit the Devil's deceit.

–Glory Days

OCTOBER 21

Remember Jesus

Humble yourselves, therefore, under God's mighty hand, that he may lift you up in due time.
1 PETER 5:6 NIV

Moses served as the prince of Egypt and emancipator of the slaves, yet "Moses was . . . more humble than anyone else" (Numbers 12:3 NIV). The apostle Paul knew to go low and not high. He was saved through a personal visit from Jesus, granted a vision of the heavens and the ability to raise the dead. But when he introduced himself, he simply stated, "I, Paul, am God's slave" (Titus 1:1 MSG). John the Baptist was a blood relative of Jesus and one of the most famous evangelists in history. But he is remembered in Scripture as the one who resolved: "He must increase, but I must decrease" (John 3:30).

We can rise too high but can never stoop too low. What gift are you giving that he did not first give? What truth are you teaching that he didn't first teach? You love. But who loved you first? You serve. But who served the most? What are you doing for God that he could not do alone?

How kind of him to use us. How wise of us to remember.

Stephen remembered. And since he remembered Jesus, Jesus remembered him. As Stephen's accusers reached for their rocks, "Stephen, full of the Holy Spirit, gazed steadily into heaven and saw the glory of God, and he saw Jesus standing in the place of honor at God's right hand" (Acts 7:55 NLT).

Stephen stood on behalf of Christ, and Christ returned the favor. Remember Jesus, and he will remember you.

–*Outlive Your Life*

A Prayer . . . to Talk to the Lord

Now then, we are ambassadors for Christ, as though God were pleading through us: we implore you on Christ's behalf, be reconciled to God. For He made Him who knew no sin to be sin for us, that we might become the righteousness of God in Him.

2 CORINTHIANS 5:20–21

God above, you have torn the veil. You have conquered death and made a way for me to have a relationship with you.

I forget so quickly that I can talk to you anytime. Allow me to turn to you today with each step, question, and difficulty.

Surround my friends and family with your forgiveness today. Remind them that you are eager to forgive them. Help them let go of any guilt they cling to.

Thank you for making us your ambassadors on this earth.

In the name of Jesus, the One who knew no sin, amen.

–*Pocket Prayers*

OCTOBER 23

Stop Talking and Listen

"Oh, that My people would listen to Me."
PSALM 81:13

When we're hurting, sometimes we find healing by talking about it—with a friend, a counselor, to God. But eventually, the time comes to stop talking and listen.

There are times when silence represents the highest respect. The word for such times is *reverence.*

This was a lesson Job learned—the man in the Bible most touched by tragedy and despair. If Job had a fault, it was his tongue. He talked too much.

Not that anyone could blame him. Calamity had pounced on the man like a lioness on a herd of gazelles, and by the time the rampage passed, there was hardly a wall standing or a loved one living. His wife told him to "curse God and die!" (Job 2:9). His four friends came with the bedside manner of drill sergeants, telling him that God is fair, and pain is the result of evil, and as sure as two plus two equals four, Job must have some criminal record in his past to suffer so.

Each had his own interpretation of God and who God is and why God had done what he had done. They weren't the only ones talking about God. When his accusers paused, Job spends six chapters giving his opinions on God.

We are thirty-seven chapters into the book before God clears his throat to speak. Chapter 38 begins with these words: "Then the Lord answered Job."

When the Lord speaks, it's wise to stop talking and listen.

–For the Tough Times

Reverence

Where were you when I made the earth's foundation? . . .
Who marked off how big it should be? Surely you know!
Who stretched a ruler across it?
What were the earth's foundations set on,
or who put its cornerstone in place
while the morning stars sang together
and all the angels shouted with joy?
JOB 38:4–7 NCV

When God speaks to Job, he floods the sky with queries, and Job cannot help but get the point: only God defines God. You've got to know the alphabet before you can read, and God tells Job, "You don't even know the ABCs of heaven, much less the vocabulary." For the first time, Job is quiet.

The Father's implication is clear: "As soon as you are able to handle these simple matters of storing stars and stretching the neck of the ostrich, then we'll have a talk about pain and suffering. But until then, we can do without your commentary."

Does Job get the message? I think so. Listen to his response: "I am not worthy; I cannot answer you anything, so I will put my hand over my mouth" (Job 40:4 NCV).

Notice the change. Before he heard God, Job couldn't speak enough. After he heard God, he couldn't speak at all.

Silence was the only proper response. The word for such moments is *reverence*.

–*For the Tough Times*

OCTOBER 25

Whose Voice Do You Heed?

Your statutes have been my songs.

PSALM 119:54

Are you fully trusting in God's Word? The day-in/day-out, sunshine-and-storm kind of trusting? Getting to our own Promised Land life requires an ongoing trust in God's Word. Wilderness people trust Scripture just enough to escape Egypt. Canaan dwellers, on the other hand, make the Bible their go-to book for life.

As God told Joshua, "Meditate in it day and night" (Joshua 1:8). The image is one of a person reciting, rehearsing, reconsidering God's Word over and over again.[2] Canaan is loud with enemy voices. The Devil megaphones doubt and death into our ears. Take heed to the voice you heed.

"Let the word of Christ dwell in you richly in all wisdom, teaching and admonishing one another" (Colossians 3:16). Chew it. Swallow it. Speak it. Heed it.

–*Glory Days*

The Dinner Table

"When you give a banquet, invite the poor, the crippled, the lame, the blind, and you will be blessed."

LUKE 14:13–14 NIV

It's no accident that *hospitality* and *hospital* come from the same Latin word, for they both lead to the same result: healing. When you open your door to someone, you are sending this message: "You matter to me and to God."

Do you know people who need this message? Singles who eat alone? Young couples who are far from home? Teens who feel left out? Seniors who no longer drive? Some people pass an entire day with no meaningful contact with anyone else. Your hospitality can be their hospital. All you need are a few basic practices.

Issue a genuine invitation.
Make a big deal of their arrival.
Address the needs of your guests.
Send them out with a blessing.

The event need not be elaborate to be significant. Don't listen to the voice that says the house, the meal, and the after-dinner mints must be perfect. Simply open your table, and open your heart.

–*Outlive Your Life*

OCTOBER 27

Go Ahead . . . Ask

So the Lord changed his mind and did not destroy the people as he had said he might.

EXODUS 32:14 NCV

This is the promise of prayer! We can change God's mind! His ultimate will is inflexible, but the implementation of his will is not. He does not change in his character and purpose, but he does alter his strategy because of the appeals of his children. We do not change his intention, but we can influence his actions.

After all, we are ambassadors for Christ (2 Corinthians 5:20). Ambassadors represent the king. They speak with the authority of the throne. They carry with them the imprimatur of the one who sent them. If an ambassador sends a request to the king, will the king listen? If you, God's ambassador in this world, come to your King with a request, will he listen? By all means.

Be bold. Audacious. Confident. The Lord of all heaven promises that if you ask anything according to His will, He hears you (1 John 5:14).

–*Before Amen*

It's Not About Location

"When you pray, do not be like the hypocrites, for they love to pray standing in the synagogues and on the street corners to be seen by others. Truly I tell you, they have received their reward in full."

MATTHEW 6:5 NIV

Religious leaders loved (and still love) to make theater out of their prayers. They perched themselves at intersections and practiced public piety. The show nauseated Jesus. "When you pray, you should go into your room and close the door and pray to your Father who cannot be seen. Your Father can see what is done in secret, and he will reward you" (Matthew 6:6 NCV).

The words surely stunned Jesus' audience. Prayer, they likely assumed, was reserved for special people in a special place. God met with the priest in the temple, behind the curtain, in the Holy of Holies. The people were simple farmers and stonemasons. Folks of the land and earth. They couldn't enter the temple. But they could enter their closets.

"Go into your room and close the door . . ." In the Palestinian culture the room most likely to have a door was the storage closet. It held tools, seed, and farming supplies. A chicken might even wander in. There was nothing holy in it. Nothing holy about it.[3]

The point? God's low on fancy, high on accessibility. Prayers offered at home carry as much weight as prayers offered in Rome. Travel to the Wailing Wall if you want. But prayer at your backyard fence is just as effective. The One who hears your prayers is your Daddy. You needn't woo him with location.

–Before Amen

OCTOBER 29

A Prayer . . . to the One Who Gives All You Need

Therefore God also has highly exalted Him and given Him the name which is above every name, that at the name of Jesus every knee should bow, of those in heaven, and of those on earth, and of those under the earth.

PHILIPPIANS 2:9–10

Father, your name is above all other names. You deserve my worship and my praise.

Help me to remember that the same power that conquered the grave also lives in me. So often I take for granted what Christ did for me. Teach me the truths of Jesus as if I am hearing them for the first time.

Please help my friends and family to see that your way is righteous and true.

Thank you, God, that you give us what we need when we need it.

In Christ's name, amen.

–*Pocket Prayers*

OCTOBER 30

A Better Perspective

As water reflects the face,
so one's life reflects the heart.
PROVERBS 27:19 NIV

It made sense, after someone explained it to me, why our high school football coach would always disappear in the middle of the third quarter. I remember during my first game on the varsity squad, I looked up from the sidelines and noticed that he was gone. So I asked a senior "sideliner."

"Where's the coach?" I asked.

"In the press box," he answered.

"Getting coffee?" I asked.

"No, getting perspective."

Now that makes sense, doesn't it? There's no way a coach can really keep up with the game from the sidelines. Everyone yelling advice. Parents complaining. Players screaming. Sometimes you've got to get away from the game to see it.

Occasionally we need to try that on ourselves too. How vital it is that we keep a finger on the pulse of our own lives. Yet it's hard to evaluate ourselves while we're in the middle of the game: schedules pressing, phones ringing, children crying.

I've got a suggestion. Take some time and get away from everything and everyone. Spend time in prayer. Meditate on God's Word. Be quiet. Recommit your heart to your Maker.

Getting some press-box perspective could change the whole ball game.

–*On the Anvil*

OCTOBER 31

Qualifying the Called

Now may the God of peace—
who brought up from the dead our Lord Jesus,
the great Shepherd of the sheep,
and ratified an eternal covenant with his blood—
may he equip you with all you need
for doing his will.
HEBREWS 13:20–21 NLT

God doesn't call the qualified. He qualifies the called.

Don't let Satan convince you otherwise. He will try. He will tell you that God has an IQ requirement or an entry fee. That he employs only specialists and experts, governments and high-powered personalities. When Satan whispers such lies, dismiss him with this truth: God stampeded the first-century society with swaybacks, not thoroughbreds.

Their collars were blue, and their hands were calloused, and there is no evidence that Jesus chose them because they were smarter or nicer than the guy next door. The one thing they had going for them was a willingness to take a step when Jesus said, "Follow me."

Are you more dinghy than cruise ship? More stand-in than movie star? More plumber than executive? More blue jeans than blue blood? Congratulations. God changes the world with folks like you.

—*Outlive Your Life*

NOVEMBER

NOVEMBER 1

Obedience Opens the Door

"If you love Me, keep My commandments."

JOHN 14:15

Heeding God's Word is more critical than fighting God's war. Indeed, heeding God's Word *is* fighting God's war. Conquest happens as the covenant is honored.

Do you want the abundant life that Jesus promised (John 10:10)?

Obey God's commands.

What's that? You expected something more mystical, exotic, intriguing? You thought that the abundant life was birthed from ecstatic utterances or angelic visions, mountaintop moments or midnight messages from heaven?

Sorry to disappoint you. "Obedience," wrote C. S. Lewis, "is the key to all doors."[1] Don't think for a second that you can heed the wrong voice, make the wrong choice, and escape the consequences.

At the same time, obedience leads to a waterfall of goodness not just for you but for your children, children's children, great-grandchildren, and the children of a thousand generations in the future. God promises to show "love to a thousand generations of those who love me and keep my commandments" (Exodus 20:6 NIV).

As we obey God's commands, we open the door for abundant life.

–Glory Days

NOVEMBER 2

It's Your Choice

"Whoever rebels against your [Joshua's] word and does not obey it, whatever you may command them, will be put to death."

JOSHUA 1:18 NIV

Joshua 1:18 is a solemn warning to us. Obedience or death. God is jealous for our trust. He doesn't request it, suggest it, or recommend it; he demands it. His unvarnished message is clear: "Trust me and me alone."

We can see the consequences of not trusting, not obeying in the lives of one New Testament couple. The church had begun its own era of Glory Days. Miracles, sermons, baptisms, and growth. The book of Acts is all good fruit and fanfare, until chapter 5. Until Ananias and Sapphira. This couple stole what belonged to God. They pledged to sell some property and give the money to the church. When they changed their minds about the gift, they acted as if they hadn't.

They lied. They died. Their bodies were carried out, and "great fear gripped the entire church" (Acts 5:11 NLT). On the topic of faith God is serious. Dead serious.

Romans 6:23 declares that "the wages of sin is death," but it also promises "eternal life" to those who choose obedience to Christ instead. It's your choice. Which do you choose?

–Glory Days

NOVEMBER 3

Struggles

He went a little farther and fell on His face, and prayed, saying, "O My Father, if it is possible, let this cup pass from Me; nevertheless, not as I will, but as You will."
MATTHEW 26:39

We all struggle. But did you ever think that perhaps God may be using your struggles to change you? To shape you? Even to heal you?

For two years I have been asking God to remove the pain in my writing hand. Even as I write these words, I feel stiffness in my thumb, fingers, forearm, and shoulder. The doctors chalk it up to thirty-plus books written in longhand. Over the decades the repeated motion has restricted my movement, rendering the simplest of tasks—writing a sentence on a sheet of paper—difficult.

So I do my part. I stretch my fingers. A therapist massages the muscles. I avoid the golf course. I even go to yoga! But most of all I pray.

Better said, I argue. Shouldn't God heal my hand? My pen is my tool. Writing is my assignment. So far he hasn't healed me.

Or has he? These days I pray more as I write. Not eloquent prayers but honest ones. *Lord, I need help . . . Father, my hand is stiff.* The discomfort humbles me. I'm not Max, the author. I am Max, the guy whose hand is wearing out. I want God to heal my hand. Thus far he has used my hand to heal my heart.

So that thing you're struggling with, that you've prayed about over and over and over again . . . could it be that God is using it to heal your heart?

–*Before Amen*

Still Part of the Team

We are surrounded by a great cloud of people whose lives tell us what faith means. So let us run the race that is before us and never give up.

HEBREWS 12:1 NCV

Scott Norwood played for the Buffalo Bills. Buffalo hadn't won a major sports championship since 1965. But one night in Tampa Bay it appeared the ball would finally bounce the Bills' way. There was time for only one more play. They turned to their kicker, Scott Norwood. All-Pro. Leading scorer. As predictable as snow in Buffalo.

The world watched as Norwood kicked the ball and . . . missed.

Norwood walked off the football field with his head down. He was still upset when the team returned to Buffalo. In spite of the loss the city hosted an event to honor the team. Norwood took his place on the platform with the other players. The fans began to chant.

"We want Scott."

The chant grew in volume until Norwood's teammates pushed him to the front. The fans gave him a rousing ovation. He missed the kick, but they made sure he knew he was still a part of their community.[2]

The Bible says that we are surrounded by a great cloud of witnesses (Hebrews 12:1). Thousands of saved saints are looking down on us. Abraham. Peter. David. Paul . . . and Joshua. Your grandma, uncle, neighbor, coach. They've seen God's great grace, and they are all pulling for you.

Do you hear them? They are chanting your name. They are pulling for you to keep going.

You may have missed a goal, but you're still a part of God's team.

–*Glory Days*

NOVEMBER 5

A Prayer . . . to Be Humble

God, who made the world and everything in it, since He is Lord of heaven and earth, does not dwell in temples made with hands.

ACTS 17:24

My Father, I desire that the attitude of John the Baptist might be my own—that Jesus would increase even as I decrease. Give me an ever-larger picture of you so I might see myself with ever-increasing clarity and revel each day in your amazing grace. Keep foolish pride far from me, and give me the sense to humble myself in healthy ways that bring strength and joy to everyone around me. Remind me constantly, Lord, that you hold my life and breath and eternal future in your loving hands and that every good thing I have comes from you. Never let me forget that although without you I can do nothing, in Christ I can do all things. The difference is you. In Jesus' name I pray, amen.

–*Outlive Your Life*

NOVEMBER 6

Still Worth Reshaping

You, O God, have tested us; You have refined us as silver is refined. You brought us into the net; You laid affliction on our backs. . . . We went through fire and through water; but You brought us out to rich fulfillment.

PSALM 66:10–12

On God's anvil. Perhaps you've been there. Melted down. Formless. Undone. Placed on the anvil for . . . reshaping? (A few rough edges too many.) Discipline? (A good father disciplines.) Testing? (But why so hard?)

I know. I've been on it. It's rough. It's a spiritual slump, a famine.

It can be caused by a death, a breakup, going broke, going prayerless. The light switch is flipped off and the room darkens.

Pound, pound, pound.

Anvil time is not to be avoided; it's to be experienced. Anvil time reminds us of who we are and who God is. We shouldn't try to escape it. To escape it could be to escape God.

God sees our life from beginning to end. He may lead us through a storm at age thirty so we can endure a hurricane at age sixty. An instrument is useful only if it's in the right shape. A dull ax or a bent screwdriver needs attention, and so do we. A good blacksmith keeps his tools in shape. So does God.

Should God place you on his anvil, be thankful. It means he thinks you're still worth reshaping.

–*On the Anvil*

NOVEMBER 7

DEFEATING THE DIVIDER

Then Jesus was led up by the Spirit into the wilderness to be tempted by the devil.
MATTHEW 4:1

Jesus was fresh out of the Jordan River. At his baptism he had been affirmed by God with a dove and a voice: "You are my Son, whom I love; with you I am well pleased" (Luke 3:22 NIV). He stepped out of the waters buoyed by God's blessing. Yet he began his public ministry, not by healing the sick or preaching a sermon, but by exposing the scheme of Satan. A perfect place to begin.

How do we explain our badness? Our stubborn hearts and hurtful hands and conniving ways? How do we explain Auschwitz, human trafficking, abuse?

If I were the Devil, I'd blame evil on a broken political system. A crippled economy. The Wicked Witch of the West. I'd want you to feel attacked by an indefinable, nebulous force. After all, if you can't diagnose the source of your ills, how can you treat them? If I were the Devil, I'd keep my name out of it.

But God tells us the Devil's name. The Greek word for devil is *diabolos*, which means "to split." The Devil is a splitter, a divider, a wedge driver. He divided Adam and Eve from God in the garden, and has every intent of doing the same to you. Blame all unrest on him. Plunging economies and raging dictators are simply tools in Satan's tool kit.

But the One who defeated the Devil offers to take him on and defeat him for you.

–*God's Story, Your Story*

NOVEMBER 8

Chaos

Cast all your anxiety on him because he cares for you.

1 PETER 5:7 NIV

Imagine this scene. It is breakfast time, and the family is in chaos. The daughters are complaining about their brother who took too much time in the bathroom. As a result their hair isn't brushed and makeup isn't applied. Mom is doing her best to manage the conflict, but she woke up with a headache and a long list of things to do. The clock is ticking like a time bomb, ever closer to that moment when, *boom!* It's time to go. Dad stops at the kitchen entryway and surveys the pandemonium. He weighs his options:

- Command everyone to shape up and behave.
- Berate his son for dominating the bathroom, his daughters for poor planning, and his wife for not taking control.
- Sneak out before anyone notices.

Or he could turn to God with a simple prayer: *Father, you are good. I need help. Reduce the frenzy in my house, please.* Will the prayer change everything? It may. Or it may take another prayer, or two, or ten. But at least the problem will be in the hands of the One who can solve it.

–*Before Amen*

NOVEMBER 9

The Pigpen

"While the son was still a long way off, his father saw him and felt sorry for his son. So the father ran to him and hugged and kissed him."

LUKE 15:20 NCV

Like the prodigal son of old, don't we do our best to make this mess a home? Do up and doll up our own little pigpens. Revamp and redecorate. We face-lift this. Overhaul that. New throw rug over the mud. A La-Z-Boy recliner next to the trough. Salt on the slop and whitewash for the posts. Ribbons for her and tattoos for him. And, in time, the place ain't half bad.

We actually feel at home.

But then the flies come out. People die, earthquakes rumble, and nations rage. Families collapse, and children die of hunger. Dictators snort and treat people like, well, like pigs. And this world stinks . . . like a pigpen.

And we have a choice. We can pretend this life is all God intended. Or . . .

We can come to our senses. We can follow the example of the prodigal son. "I will set out and go back to my father" (Luke 15:18 NIV).

We can choose to go to our Father.

–*God's Story, Your Story*

What God Does

You intended to harm me, but God intended it for good to accomplish what is now being done, the saving of many lives.
GENESIS 50:20 NIV

Look at Joseph in the Egyptian prison. His brothers have sold him out; Potiphar's wife has turned him in. If ever a world has caved in, Joseph's has.

Or consider Moses, watching flocks in the wilderness. Is this what he intended to do with his life? Hardly. His heart beats with Jewish blood. His passion is to lead the slaves, so why does God have him leading sheep?

And Daniel. What about Daniel? He was among the brightest and best young men of Israel, the equivalent of a West Point cadet or an Ivy Leaguer. But he and his entire generation are being marched out of Jerusalem. The city is destroyed. The temple is in ruins.

Joseph in prison. Moses in the desert. Daniel in chains. These were dark moments. Who could have seen any good in them? Who could have known that Joseph the prisoner was just one promotion from becoming Joseph the prime minister? Who would have thought that God was giving Moses forty years of wilderness training in the very desert through which he would lead the people? And who could have imagined that Daniel the captive would soon be Daniel the king's counselor?

God does things like that. He did with Joseph, with Moses, with Daniel, and, most of all, he did with Jesus.

He will do it with you.

–*For the Tough Times*

NOVEMBER 11

A Pocket Prayer

He said to them, "When you pray, say:
'Father,
hallowed be your name,
your kingdom come.
Give us each day our daily bread.
Forgive us our sins,
for we also forgive everyone who sins against us.
And lead us not into temptation.'"

LUKE 11:2–4 NIV

When the disciples asked Jesus to teach them to pray, he gave them a prayer. Not a lecture on prayer. Not the doctrine of prayer. He gave them a quotable, repeatable, portable prayer (Luke 11:1–4).

Could you use the same? It seems to me that the prayers of the Bible can be distilled into one. The result is a simple, easy-to-remember, pocket-size prayer:

Father, you are good.
I need help. Heal me and forgive me.
They need help. Thank you.
In Jesus' name, amen.

Let this prayer punctuate your day. As you begin your morning, *Father, you are good*. As you commute to work or walk the hallways at school, *I need help*. As you wait in the grocery line, *They need help*. Keep this prayer in your pocket as you pass through the day.

–*Before Amen*

A Prayer . . . of Thanks for the Son

He took the cup, and when He had given thanks He gave it to them, and they all drank from it. And He said to them, "This is My blood of the new covenant, which is shed for many."
MARK 14:23–24

Father, you are good. You sent your Son for us and you are merciful to us daily, moment by moment, even to the final cost.

Remind me today of your sacrifice; keep it close to my heart. Make me not only thankful for but a vessel of your grace. Don't let your grace stop with me, but show it to others through me.

Be with all those who do not believe in you and have hard hearts. Let them know the promise of your good news.

Thank you for the depth of your love. You sent your Son to die a sinner's death so that I could be redeemed. Thank you that you want to have a relationship with me through Jesus Christ.

In his precious name, amen.

–*Pocket Prayers*

NOVEMBER 13

Remember Who Holds You

For of Him and through Him and to Him are all things, to whom be glory forever. Amen.
ROMANS 11:36

Frightening thing, pride. It would rather kill the truth than consider it. Doesn't it sneak up on us? We begin spiritual journeys as small people. The act of conversion is a humbling one. We confess sins, beg for mercy, bend our knees. Timid children who extend muddy hands to our sinless God.

We come to God humbly. No swagger, no boasts, no "all by myself" declarations. And he immerses us in mercy. He stitches together our shredded souls. He deposits his Spirit and implants heavenly gifts. Our big God blesses our small faith.

We understand the roles. He is the Milky Way galaxy. We are the sand flea. We need a big God because we've made a big mess of our lives.

Gradually our big God changes us. And, gratefully, we lust less, love more, lash out less, look heavenward more. People notice the difference. They applaud us. Promote us. Admire us. We don't feel so small anymore. People talk to us as if we are something special.

Feels nice. Kudos become ladder rungs, and we begin to elevate ourselves. We forget who brought us here.

Take time to remember. "Look at what you were when God called you" (1 Corinthians 1:26 NCV). Remember who held you in the beginning. Remember who holds you today.

–*Outlive Your Life*

NOVEMBER 14 

A Cure for Snakebites and Ingratitude

Since we are receiving a Kingdom that is unshakable, let us be thankful and please God by worshiping him with holy fear and awe.

HEBREWS 12:28 NLT

Nothing silences grumps like gratitude.

Consider the grumbling Israelites. "They began to speak against God and Moses. 'Why have you brought us out of Egypt to die here in the wilderness? . . . And we hate this horrible manna!'" (Numbers 21:5 NLT).

Had they forgotten God's deliverance? The Red Sea became the red carpet. Manna fell like silver dollars. They danced the Jubilee jig and carried Moses on their shoulders. They were grateful at first.

But with the passage of time, ingratitude took over. So they bellyached. They complained. They turned sour and dour.

God responded with an object lesson for the ages. He unleashed snakes into their camp. Toxic fangs everywhere. Shades of Eden. The symbolism is inescapable. Ingratitude is a devil's brew. It will kill you.

Many were bitten and died. The people cried out, "We have sinned by speaking against the LORD and against you. Pray that the LORD will take away the snakes" (v. 7 NLT). So Moses prayed for the people.

Then the Lord told him, "Make a replica of a poisonous snake and attach it to a pole. All who are bitten will live if they simply look at it!" (v. 8 NLT).

The cure for ingratitude? Look up! Lift up your eyes! Look what God has done!

–Before Amen

NOVEMBER 15

A Good Pilot

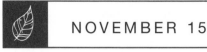

You are good, Lord.
PSALM 25:7 NCV

As I boarded a plane, the pilot called my name. He was standing in the cockpit entrance, greeting passengers. "Well, hello, Max." I looked up. It was my friend Joe. My *old* friend. He is the Methuselah of the airways. He's been flying forever. He's faced every flight crisis from electrical storms to empty fuel tanks. He is a good pilot.

And he is a friend, a *good* friend—good in skill and good in heart.

We chatted for a few minutes, and I went to my seat with a sense of assurance. *What more could I request?* I thought. *The pilot is experienced and proven. Even more, he is my tried-and-true friend. I am in good hands.*

The knowledge came in handy. An hour into the flight we hit a wall of winds. People gasped and dentures rattled. I've had smoother roller coaster rides. Unlike the other passengers, I stayed calm. I knew the pilot. I knew his heart and trusted his skill. *Joe can handle this,* I told myself. The storm was bad, but the pilot was good. So as much as one can relax in a squall, I did.

Friend, it's a stormy world out there. The question during these troubling times is this: Do we have a good pilot?

The resounding response of the Bible is yes!

–*Before Amen*

Satan's Deadliest Trick

Because you are lukewarm, and neither hot nor cold, I will spit you out of my mouth.
REVELATION 3:16 ESV

He's a deadly snake. Satan's snake. Be on your guard.

He strikes with abandon. The old, the rich, the poor, the young—all are his prey.

Who is this snake? Greed? Lust? Egotism? No, I'm unmasking the vilest of hell's vipers—complacence.

We're complacent to hope. Many people settle for a stale, vanilla lifestyle that peaks at age seventeen. Hope? What's to hope for? Life is a paycheck and a weekend. Nothing more.

We're complacent to death. Masked faces at a funeral endure the procession; weep at the burial; and then, a few hours later, giggle at the television comic.

We're complacent to God. Churchgoers pack the pews and sing to the back of someone's head. Fellowship is lost in formality. One, two, three times a week people pay their dues, endure a ritual, and walk out.

We're complacent to purpose. Never asking "Why am I here?" Or, worse yet, asking why and being content with no answer.

Sometimes I want to stand at the corner of the street and yell, "Doesn't anyone want to know why? Why lonely evenings? Why broken hearts? Why fatherless babies?" But I never yell it. I just stick my hands in my pockets and stare . . . and wonder.

The most deadly trick of Satan is not to rob us of answers. It's to steal our questions.

–*On the Anvil*

NOVEMBER 17

A Fait Accompli

The Lord your God, who goes before you, He will fight for you.
DEUTERONOMY 1:30

Time to declare war on the pestilence that goes by the name "I can't." It attacks our self-control: "I can't resist the bottle." Careers: "I can't keep a job." Marriages: "I can't forgive." Our faith: "I can't believe God cares for me."

"I can't." The phrase loiters on the corner of Discouragement and Despair. Had Joshua mumbled those words, who would have blamed him? Joshua had reason to say "I can't."

Excuse #1: "Moses is dead." Excuse #2: "My people are battlefield tender-feet." Excuse #3: "Canaanites eat folks like us for breakfast."

But Joshua never declared defeat. Before he could assemble any fears, God gave him reason for faith. "Arise, go over this Jordan, you and all this people, to the land which I am giving to them" (Joshua 1:2).

Not "the land *I might* give them."

Not "the land you must conquer."

Not "the land of which you must prove worthy."

Not "the land you must earn, confiscate, or purchase."

But "the land which I *am* giving to them."

The transaction had already happened. The land had already been transferred. The conquest was *a fait accompli*. Joshua wasn't sent to take the land but to receive the land God had taken. Victory was certain because the victory was God's.

Hmmm.

–*Glory Days*

NOVEMBER 18

The Kindness of God

When the kindness and love of God our Savior appeared, he saved us, not because of righteous things we had done, but because of his mercy.

TITUS 3:4–5 NIV

How then can I do this great wickedness, and sin against God?" (Genesis 39:9).

God's kindness stirred Joseph's holiness. The temptation Potiphar's wife so freely offered was likely strong. Joseph was, after all, a young man, all alone in a distant land. But Joseph had seen the kindness of God, the grace and mercy that rescued him from the bottom of a well. And Joseph simply could not sin against God's kindness.

God's grace does the same in us. "For the grace of God . . . teaches us to say 'No' to ungodliness and worldly passions, and to live self-controlled, upright and godly lives in this present age" (Titus 2:11–12 NIV). A robust grace this is, that both convicts and comforts! Let it convict you. If you ever catch yourself thinking, *I can do whatever I want because God will forgive me*, then grace is not happening to you. Selfishness, perhaps. Arrogance, for sure. But grace? No. Grace creates a resolve to do good, not permission to do bad.

And let grace comfort you. Look to Christ for your beginning and ending. He is Alpha *and* Omega. He will hold you. And he will hold on to the ones you love. Do you have a prodigal? Do you long for your spouse to return to God? Do you have a friend whose faith has grown cold? God wants them back more than you do. Keep praying, and don't give up.

–*Grace*

NOVEMBER 19

A Prayer . . . to Transform My Life

Now there were in the same country shepherds living out in the fields, keeping watch over their flock by night. And behold, an angel of the Lord stood before them, and the glory of the Lord shone around them, and they were greatly afraid.

LUKE 2:8–9

O Lord, I rejoice that you are the uncommon God who comes to ordinary people like me. As the shepherds did, I simply welcome you to transform my life into the extraordinary by your grace and love. Come and dance with me. In Jesus' name, amen.

–*In the Manger*

Simple Folks Like Us

God is able to make all grace abound toward you,
that you, always having all sufficiency in all things,
may have an abundance for every good work.
2 CORINTHIANS 9:8

Does God still use simple folks like us to change the world? We suffer from such ordinariness. The fellow to my right snoozes with his mouth open. The gray-haired woman next to him wears earphones and bobs her head from side to side. (I think I hear Frank Sinatra.) They don't wear halos or wings. And excluding the reflection off the man's bald spot, they don't emit any light.

Most of us don't. We are Joe Pot Roast. Common folk. We sit in the bleachers, eat at diners, change diapers, and wear our favorite team's ball cap. Fans don't wave when we pass. Servants don't scurry when we come home. Chauffeurs don't drive our cars; butlers don't open our doors or draw our baths. Doormen don't greet us, and security doesn't protect us. We, like the Jerusalem disciples, are regular folk.

Does God use the common Joe?

Look at some of the Joes and Josephines God has used. A common fisherman who became the rock of his church. A shepherd boy God chose for a king. And that whispered-about woman at the well. She brought the whole town to Jesus. Yes, God still uses simple folks—just like you and me.

–*Outlive Your Life*

NOVEMBER 21

Get Ready

Yours, Lord, is the greatness and the power
and the glory and the majesty and the splendor,
for everything in heaven and earth is yours.
Yours, Lord, is the kingdom;
you are exalted as head over all.
1 CHRONICLES 29:11 NIV

Imagine what would happen if a generation of Christians lived out of their inheritance. Men and women would turn off Internet porn. The lonely would find comfort in God, not the arms of strangers. Struggling couples would spend more time in prayer, less time in anger. Children would consider it a blessing to care for their aging parents.

A generation of Christians would vacate the wilderness.

"God's power is very great for us who believe. That power is the same as the great strength God used to raise Christ from the dead" (Ephesians 1:19–20 NCV).

The same steely, burly force that raised Christ from the dead will turn every "I can't" into "I can." "I can do all things through Christ, because he gives me strength" (Philippians 4:13 NCV).

A new day awaits you, my friend. A new season of accomplishment, discovery, and strength. Leave every "I can't" behind you. Set your "God can" ahead of you. Get ready to witness the power of God unleashed in your life.

–*Glory Days*

Lingering in the Presence

Now as they [Peter and John] spoke to the people, the priests, the captain of the temple, and the Sadducees came upon them, being greatly disturbed that they taught the people and preached in Jesus the resurrection from the dead.

ACTS 4:1–2

Persecution happens. Peter and John can tell you. They healed the cripple one minute and faced harassment the next.

A brawny soldier presses through the crowd. Priests follow him.

> Peter, filled with the Holy Spirit, said to them, . . . "Let it be known to you all, and to all the people of Israel, that by the name of Jesus Christ of Nazareth, whom you crucified, whom God raised from the dead, by Him this man stands here before you whole." (Acts 4:8–10)

No backdown in those words.

Peter and John don't budge an inch. What's gotten into them?

Luke gives us the answer in verse 13: Peter and John had been with Jesus. The resurrected Jesus. They had lingered long and delightfully in the presence of the resurrected King. Awakening with him, walking with him. And because they had, silence was no longer an option. "We cannot but speak the things which we have seen and heard" (v. 20).

–*Outlive Your Life*

NOVEMBER 23

The Great Healer

You were bought at a price; therefore glorify God in your body and in your spirit, which are God's.
1 CORINTHIANS 6:20

Jesus treated our sickness in the same way he treated our sin. He took it away. He bore it in himself on the cross. When Matthew saw the large number of healings in Galilee, he remembered the prophecy of Isaiah: "[Jesus] fulfilled Isaiah's well-known sermon: He took our illnesses, He carried our diseases" (Matthew 8:17 MSG).

Did Jesus die for your sins? Yes. Did Jesus die for your sicknesses? Yes! It is inconsistent to say that Jesus saved your soul but not your body. When Jesus took our sins to the cross, he took our cancers, disfigurements, and depression as well.

So talk to him about your stomach, your skin, your moles. After all, he owns you. Your body was "bought at a price."

Jesus is the Great Healer.

–*Before Amen*

Commander of Angels

Jesus Christ is the same yesterday, today, and forever.
HEBREWS 13:8

Is it difficult to imagine Jesus as an active being before his birth on earth? If so, let me challenge you to widen your imagination. Remember, "He was chosen before the creation of the world" (1 Peter 1:20 NIV). The normal restrictions of time and place do not apply to him. We would be wrong to limit his corporal ministry to thirty-three years in Palestine. Long before Jesus ate with Zacchaeus in Jericho, he shared a moment with Joshua near Jericho.

And what a moment it was. "I am the commander of the army of the LORD," Jesus declared (Joshua 5:14 ESV). The human eye saw two armies: the Canaanites and the Israelites. Actually, there was a third. The Lord's army, God's angels. Dismiss the notion of angels with chiffon wings and rosy cheeks. God's angels were strong enough to close the mouths of lions for Daniel. According to the book of Revelation, just one angel can dispense with the Devil.

Imagine what thousands of angels can do! This many exist. When John was given a glimpse into the heavens, he saw too many angels to count: "The number of them was ten thousand times ten thousand, and thousands of thousands" (Revelation 5:11).

Angels are "ministering spirits sent forth to minister for those who will inherit salvation" (Hebrews 1:14). All God's children can be sure of God's angels. They are mighty in power. They are many in number. And Jesus is the commander of them all.

–*Glory Days*

NOVEMBER 25

Welcome, Stranger

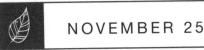

Do not forget to show hospitality to strangers, for by so doing some people have shown hospitality to angels without knowing it.

HEBREWS 13:2 NIV

Not everyone can serve in a foreign land, lead a relief effort, or volunteer at the downtown soup kitchen. But who can't be hospitable? Do you have a front door? A table? Chairs? Bread and meat for sandwiches? Congratulations! You just qualified to serve in the most ancient of ministries: hospitality. You can join the ranks of people such as . . .

Abraham. He fed, not just angels, but the Lord of angels (Genesis 18).

Rahab, the harlot. She received and protected the spies (Joshua 6:22–23).

Martha and Mary. They opened their home for Jesus (John 11:1–45).

Zacchaeus. He welcomed Jesus to his table (Luke 19:1–10).

And what about the greatest example of all—the "certain man" of Matthew 26:18? On the day before his death, Jesus told his followers, "Go into the city to a certain man and tell him, 'The Teacher says: "The chosen time is near. I will have the Passover with my followers at your house"'" (NCV).

How would you have liked to be the one who opened his home for Jesus? You can be. "Whatever you did for one of the least of these brothers and sisters of mine, you did for me" (Matthew 25:40 NIV). As you welcome strangers to your table, you are welcoming God himself.

–*Outlive Your Life*

A Prayer . . . Because Jesus Is Lord!

At the name of Jesus every knee should bow, of those in heaven, and of those on earth, and of those under the earth, and that every tongue should confess that Jesus Christ is Lord, to the glory of God the Father.

PHILIPPIANS 2:10–11

Dear Lord, the day is coming when at the name of Jesus every knee will bow and every tongue will confess that you are Lord. I bow my knee today and make my confession that you are my Lord. Help me to honor your great name above all else. In Jesus' name, amen.

–*In the Manger*

NOVEMBER 27

Where You Came From

"The Son of Man came to seek and to save the lost."

LUKE 19:10 NIV

We *need* to know where we came from. Knowing connects us, links us, bonds us to something greater than we are. Knowing reminds us that we aren't floating on isolated ponds but on a grand river.

That's why God wants you to know his story. Framed photos hang in his house. Lively talks await you at his table. A scrapbook sits in his living room, brimming with stories. Stories about Bethlehem beginnings and manger miracles. Enemy warfare in the wilderness and fishermen friends in Galilee. The stumbles of Peter, the stubbornness of Paul. All a part of the story.

But they are all subplots to the central message: "For God so loved the world that he gave his one and only Son, that whoever believes in him shall not perish but have eternal life" (John 3:16 NIV). This is the headline of the story: God saves his people! He casts his net over cities and individuals, princes and paupers, the Pontius Pilates of power and the Peters, Jameses, and Johns of the fishing villages. God takes on the whole mess of us and cleans us up.

This quest is God's story. And you are a part of it!

–*God's Story, Your Story*

NOVEMBER 28

YOUR STRENGTH

The LORD is my rock and my fortress and my deliverer;
My God, my strength, in whom I will trust;
My shield and the horn of my salvation, my stronghold.
PSALM 18:2

Look to Jesus to comfort you. Turn your gaze away from your wall of Jericho. You've looked at it long enough. No need to memorize its circumference or itemize its stones. Healing happens as we look to the Commander of heaven's armies. Lift up your eyes and bow your knees. "Joshua fell on his face to the earth and worshiped" (Joshua 5:14).

Joshua was a five-star general. Forty thousand soldiers saluted as he passed. His tent was the Oval Office. Two million people looked up to him. Yet in the presence of God, he fell on his face, removed his sandals, and worshiped.

We are never so strong or mighty that we do not need to worship. Worship-less people have no power greater than themselves to call on. The worship-less heart faces Jericho all alone.

Don't go to your Jericho without first going to your Commander. Let him remind you of the ever-present angels. Let him assure you of his all-encompassing power. He has given you this promise: "I will never fail you. I will never abandon you" (Hebrews 13:5 NLT).

Jericho may be strong. But Jesus is stronger. Let him be your strength.

–*Glory Days*

NOVEMBER 29

It All Began with a Prayer

When they had prayed, the place where they were assembled together was shaken; and they were all filled with the Holy Spirit, and they spoke the word of God with boldness.

ACTS 4:31

Ernstena is a pastor's wife. Clara is a businesswoman. Jo Anne had just started a small relief organization. They traveled to Cambodia to encourage Jim-Lo, a missionary friend. He led them to a section of his city where the modern sex trade runs rampant. An estimated fifteen thousand girls were on sale. At the time more than a hundred thousand young women in Cambodia had been sold into forced prostitution. Jo Anne, Clara, Ernstena, and Jim-Lo looked into the faces of teen girls, even preteens, and could see a devastating story in each. The Christians had no idea what to do but pray.

Lord, what do you want us to do? It's so overwhelming. They wept.

God heard their prayer and gave them their tools. Upon returning to the United States, Jo Anne wrote an article about the experience, which prompted a reader to send a great deal of money. With this gift the women formed an anti-trafficking ministry of World Hope International. In just three years, four hundred children were rescued.

When the U.S. State Department sponsored an event called "The Salute to the 21st Century Abolitionists," they honored World Hope. The prayer that began on a Cambodian street continued in front of some of the most influential government officials in the world.[3]

And it all began with a prayer.

What can God—through you—begin with a prayer?

–*Outlive Your Life*

The Pure Water of Grace

Many of the believers began to confess openly and tell all the evil things they had done. . . . So in a powerful way the word of the Lord kept spreading and growing.

ACTS 19:18, 20 NCV

People are attracted to honesty.

Find a congregation that believes in confession. Avoid a fellowship of perfect people (you won't fit in), but seek one where members confess their sins and show humility, where the price of admission is simply an admission of guilt. Healing happens in a church like this. Followers of Christ have been given authority to hear confession and proclaim grace. "If you forgive the sins of any, they are forgiven them" (John 20:23).

Confessors find a freedom that deniers don't.

"If we say we have no sin, we are fooling ourselves, and the truth is not in us. But if we confess our sins, he will forgive our sins, because we can trust God to do what is right. He will cleanse us from all the wrongs we have done" (1 John 1:8–9 NCV).

Oh, the sweet certainty of these words. "He *will* cleanse us." Not he *might*, *could*, *would*, or *has been known to*. He *will* cleanse you. Tell God what you did. Again, it's not that he doesn't already know, but the two of you need to agree. Spend as much time as you need. Share all the details you can. Then let the pure water of grace flow over your mistakes.

–*Grace*

DECEMBER

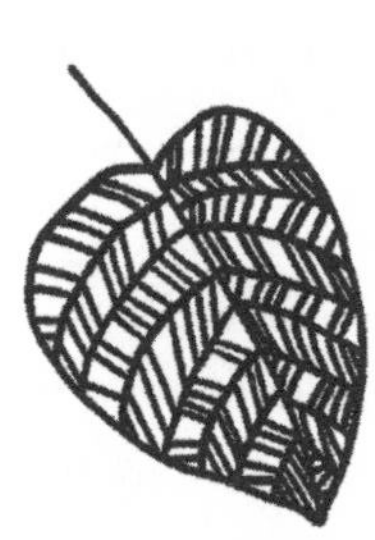

Already Victorious

"I have told you these things, so that in me you may have peace. In this world you will have trouble. But take heart! I have overcome the world."

JOHN 16:33 NIV

Here is what you need to know about Joshua. He didn't bring Jericho's walls down. Joshua's soldiers never swung a hammer. His men never dislodged a brick. The shaking, quaking, rumbling, and tumbling of the thick, impervious walls? God did that for them.

God will do that for you. Your Jericho is your fear. Your Jericho is your anger, bitterness, or prejudice. Your insecurity about the future. Your guilt about the past. Your negativity, anxiety, and proclivity to criticize, overanalyze, or compartmentalize. Your Jericho is any attitude or mind-set that keeps you from joy, peace, or rest.

To live a Promised Land life, you must face your Jericho.

It's not always easy. Every level of inheritance requires a disinheritance from the Devil. Satan must be moved off before the saint can move in. Joshua told his people to "go in to possess the land which the LORD your God is giving you to possess" (Joshua 1:11).

Satan won't leave without a fight. He will resist. He will push back. But he will not win. Why? Because God has already declared that you are the victor. Satan, defanged and defeated at Calvary, has no authority over you.

–*Glory Days*

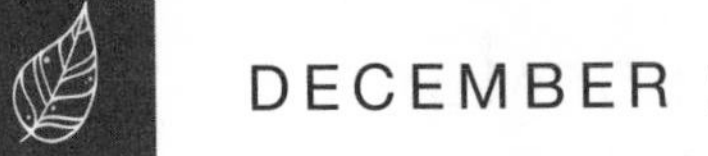

DECEMBER 2

The Best Is Yet to Come

Since you have been raised to new life with Christ, set your sights on the realities of heaven, where Christ sits in the place of honor at God's right hand. Think about the things of heaven, not the things of earth.

COLOSSIANS 3:1–2 NLT

Do you feel as if your best years have passed you by? Hogwash. You will do your best work in heaven. Do you regret wasting seasons of life on foolish pursuits? So do I. But we can stop our laments. We have an eternity to make up for lost time. Are you puzzled by the challenges of your days? Then see yourself as an uncut jewel and God as a lapidary. He is polishing you for your place in his kingdom. Your biggest moments lie ahead, on the other side of the grave.

So "seek those things which are above, where Christ is, sitting at the right hand of God" (Colossians 3:1). Scripture uses a starchy verb here. *Zēteite* ("to seek") is to "covet earnestly, strive after, to inquire for, desire, even require."

Seek heaven the way a sailor seeks the coast or a pilot seeks the landing strip or a missile seeks heat. Head for home the way a pigeon wings to the nest or the prodigal strode to his papa. "Think only about" it (v. 2 NCV). "Keep your mind" on it (v. 2 GW). "Set your sights on the realities of heaven" (v. 1 NLT). "Pursue the things over which Christ presides" (v. 1 MSG). Obsess yourself with heaven! The best is yet to come!

–*God's Story, Your Story*

A Prayer . . . to the One Who Intercedes

Jesus said to her, "Did I not say to you that if you would believe you would see the glory of God?"
JOHN 11:40

Jesus Christ, the Righteous One, thank you for being my Advocate before the Father's throne. I am delighted to be in your hands, under the shelter of your wings. Bless and praise you for your intercession over my life. In your name, amen.

–*On Calvary's Hill*

DECEMBER 4

Rest in Redemption

It is by his great mercy that we have been born again, because God raised Jesus Christ from the dead. Now we live with great expectation.

1 PETER 1:3 NLT

Let the cross convince you. Be settled about God's faithfulness. In one of the psalms the writer described a person of faith with these words: "He is settled in his mind that Jehovah will take care of him" (Psalm 112:7 TLB). Life has many unanswered questions, but God's ability to save needn't be one of them. Let this issue be settled once and for all.

Look at you. Like the Israelites of old you have crossed the Jordan. There is no mud on your sandals, no water on your robe. There is no sin on your record, no guilt attached to your name. Let there be no doubt in your heart. If God "did not spare his own Son but gave him for us all," will he not also give you all you need for a Promised Land life (Romans 8:32 NCV)?

Join the chorus of the confident and declare, "I am convinced that nothing can ever separate us from God's love. . . . Indeed, nothing in all creation will ever be able to separate us from the love of God that is revealed in Christ Jesus our Lord" (Romans 8:38–39 NLT).

Rest in your redemption. The past is past. The future is bright. God's Word is sure. His work is finished.

A new season awaits you.

–*Glory Days*

Unnecessary Messes

For the Lord Most High is awesome;
He is a great King over all the earth.
PSALM 47:2

May I make a suggestion? Before you face the world, face your Father. Here is how it works. It's a Monday morning. The alarm clock lives up to its name. *Clang! Clang! Clang!* You groan, roll over, and sit up. In the old days you would have made the coffee and turned on the news.

But today you turn to your Father. You don't look like much: face pillow creased, hair smashed. No matter. You haven't come to look at you. You have come to look at God.

Father, my Daddy . . . The words come slowly at first. But you stay at it. *The weather is bad, the economy is bad, but, God, you are awesome.*

Don't underestimate the power of this moment. You just opened the door to God and welcomed truth to enter your heart. Faith sneaked in while despair was dozing.

Who knows, you might start to worship.

Father, you are good. You consult no clock. You keep no calendar. You report to no one. You are good!

Is your world different because you prayed? In one sense, no. Wars still rage, traffic still clogs, and heartbreakers still roam the planet. But you are different. You have peace. You've spent time with the Father. And the Father is up to the task.

–*Before Amen*

DECEMBER 6

Grace Even in the Dust

"Teacher," [the Pharisees] said to Jesus, "this woman was caught in the act of adultery. The law of Moses says to stone her. What do you say?" . . . Jesus stooped down and wrote in the dust with his finger.

JOHN 8:4–6 NLT

Let it change you. Give no heed to Satan's voice. You "have an Advocate with the Father, Jesus Christ the righteous" (1 John 2:1). As your Advocate, he defends you and says on your behalf, "There is therefore now no condemnation to those who are in Christ Jesus" (Romans 8:1). Take that, Satan!

Wasn't this the message of Jesus to the woman caught in adultery?

"Where are your accusers? Didn't even one of them condemn you?"

"No, Lord," she said.

And Jesus said, "Neither do I. Go and sin no more" (John 8:10–11 NLT).

Within a few moments the courtyard was empty. Jesus, the woman, her critics—they all left. But let's linger. Look at the rocks on the ground, abandoned and unused. And look at the scribbling in the dust. It's the only sermon Jesus ever wrote. Even though we don't know the words, I'm wondering if they read like this:

Grace happens here.

–*Grace*

I Was . . . but Now

But now that you have been set free from sin and have become slaves of God, the benefit you reap leads to holiness, and the result is eternal life.

ROMANS 6:22 NIV

Grace House is a transition home for women who are coming out of prison. They live under the same roof, eat at the same table, and seek the same Lord. They study the Bible. They learn a trade. Most of all, they learn to trust their new identity.

At a fundraiser for the ministry, one of the residents gave her testimony. She described a life of prostitution, drugs, and alcohol. She lost her marriage, her children, and ultimately her freedom. But then Christ found her. What struck me was the repeated rhythm of her story: "I was . . . but now." "I was on drugs, but now I'm clean." "I was on the streets, but now I'm on my feet."

I was . . . but now. This is the chorus of grace. And this is the work of God. It's the work he did in the life of Rahab. It's the work he can do for you.

Maybe your past is a checkered one.

Maybe your peers don't share your faith.

Maybe your pedigree is one of violence, your ancestry one of rebellion.

If so, then Rahab is your model.

We don't drop scarlet cords from our windows. But we trust the crimson thread of Christ's blood.

–*Glory Days*

DECEMBER 8

We Shall Be Like Him

There will be no more death or sorrow or crying
or pain. All these things are gone forever.
REVELATION 21:4 NLT

Jesus will heal all who seek healing in him. There are no exceptions to this promise—no nuances, fine-print conditions, or caveats. To say some will be healed beyond the grave by no means diminishes the promise. The truth is this: "When Christ appears, *we shall be like him*, for we shall see him as he is" (1 John 3:2 NIV, emphasis mine).

"We shall be like him." Let every parent of a Down syndrome or wheelchair-bound child write these words on the bedroom wall. Let the disabled, infected, bedridden, and anemic put themselves to sleep with the promise "We shall be like him." Let amputees and the atrophied take this promise to heart: "We shall be like him." We shall graduate from this version of life into his likeness.

In heaven "there shall be no more curse" (Revelation 22:3). As much as we hate carcinomas and cardiac arrests, don't we hate sin even more? Cystic fibrosis steals breath, but selfishness and stinginess steal joy. Diabetes can ruin the system of a body, but deceit, denial, and distrust are ruining society.

Heaven, however, has scheduled a graduation. Sin will no longer be at war with our flesh. Eyes won't lust, thoughts won't wander, hands won't steal, our minds won't judge, appetites won't rage, and our tongues won't lie. We will be brand-new.

We shall be like him.

–*God's Story, Your Story*

Our Sin Bearer

Christ was offered as a sacrifice one time to
take away the sins of many people.
HEBREWS 9:28 NCV

Three thousand years ago the Hebrew people were given an annual opportunity to watch their guilt being taken away. Each year as part of the Day of Atonement, thousands of Jews gathered in front of the tabernacle. The priest selected two goats. The first goat was sacrificed. The second goat was presented by the priest. He placed his hands on the head of the goat and confessed the sins of the people.

The people watched as the guide led the animal away. The pair grew smaller and smaller and eventually disappeared over the horizon. The people waited until the man reappeared, empty-handed. The object lesson was clear: God does not want guilt among his people.

You can bet your Torah that some ten-year-old boy tugged on his mother's robe and said, "Why, Mommy? Why did they send the goat away? He didn't do anything wrong." The mother would explain, "That is the point, my child. God uses the sinless to carry away the sins of the guilty."

Or, as Isaiah would write several hundred years later, "The Lord has put on him the punishment for all the evil we have done" (Isaiah 53:6 NCV).

Isaiah did not know the name of God's sin bearer. But we do. Jesus Christ. He came to "put away sin by the sacrifice of Himself" (Hebrews 9:26). He "was offered once to bear the sins of many" (v. 28). So that we could be free.

—Before Amen

DECEMBER 10

A Prayer . . . to Be Grateful

Pray without ceasing, in everything give thanks; for this is the will of God in Christ Jesus for you. Do not quench the Spirit.

1 THESSALONIANS 5:17–19

Heavenly Father, I sit here in awe of all that I should thank you for. You are so much bigger and greater than I could ever understand.

Give me reminders to be grateful today. Don't allow me to miss the small—or big—blessings around me. Fill my heart with gratitude.

For my friends who struggle to pray, would you give them a desire to know you more? Teach them to pray, as you're teaching me to.

Thank you for Jesus. Thank you for loving us. Thank you for the gift of grace.

In Christ's name, amen.

–Pocket Prayers

If You Choose Gratitude . . .

Always give thanks to God the Father for everything,
in the name of our Lord Jesus Christ.
EPHESIANS 5:20 NCV

In Scripture the idea of giving thanks is not a suggestion or recommendation; it is a command. More than a hundred times, either by imperative or example, the Bible commands us to be thankful. If quantity implies gravity, God takes thanksgiving seriously.

Here's why. Ingratitude is the original sin. Adam and Eve had a million reasons to give thanks. The waterfalls and fowl, shorelines and sunsets. They indwelt a perfect world. One with creation, one with God, one with each other.

But then Satan slithered into the garden. He raised a question about the forbidden tree. Adam and Eve could eat from all the others. But Satan focused on the single fruit they could not touch. "Eat it," he hissed, "and you will be like God" (Genesis 3:5 NLT).

Just like that, Eden was not enough. It *was* enough, mind you. "But there could be more . . . ," suggested the Devil, gesturing to the shiny, glimmering delicacy that lay just across the boundary line. And with that, discontent moved in like a bully on the block.

What if gratitude had won the day? Suppose Adam and Eve had scoffed at the snake's suggestion. "Are you kidding? Let us take you on a tour, snake. We will show you what God has given to us."

Had they chosen gratitude, would the world be different?

If you choose gratitude, will your world be different?

—*Before Amen*

DECEMBER 12

THE ABCs OF GRATITUDE

Every good gift and every perfect gift is from above,
and comes down from the Father of lights, with whom
there is no variation or shadow of turning.
JAMES 1:17

Alphabetize your blessings. Start with *A* and work your way down the alphabet, thanking God as you go.

Rather than catalog burdens, itemize benefits. The sure cure for the grumpy spirit.

A = Andy
B = bald spot
C = chocolate
D = dictionary

It dawns on me that my wife's name, Denalyn, begins with a *d*. The next time I make the list, my wife trumps *dictionary*. Which, by the way, is a lesson of the exercise. A person never runs out of reasons to say "thanks."

Thanks. Just the word lifts the spirit. To say thanks is to celebrate a gift. Something. Anything. Animals. Bald spots. Chocolate. Dictionaries and Denalyn. To say thanks is to cross the tracks from have-not to have-much, from the excluded to the recruited. *Thanks* proclaims, "I'm not disadvantaged, disabled, victimized, scandalized, forgotten, or ignored. I am blessed." Gratitude is a dialysis of sorts. It flushes the self-pity out of our systems.

Have you said your ABCs today?

–*Before Amen*

THE CON ARTIST

"I will give you a new heart and put a new spirit within you; I will take the heart of stone out of your flesh and give you a heart of flesh."
EZEKIEL 36:26

When grace happens, generosity happens. Unsquashable, eye-popping bigheartedness happens.

It certainly happened to Zacchaeus. If the New Testament has a con artist, this is the man. He never met a person he couldn't cheat or saw a dollar he couldn't hustle. He was a "chief tax collector" (Luke 19:2). First-century tax collectors fleeced anything that walked. When Jesus traveled through Jericho, half the town showed up to take a look. Zacchaeus was among them. Citizens of Jericho weren't about to let short-in-stature, long-on-enemies Zacchaeus elbow his way to the front of the crowd. He was left hopping up and down behind the wall of people, hoping to get a glimpse.

That's when he spotted the sycamore, shimmied up, and scurried out on a limb to get a good look at Christ. He never imagined that Christ would take a good look at him. "Zacchaeus, come down immediately. I must stay at your house today" (v. 5 NIV).

Zacchaeus was never quite the same. "Look, Lord! Here and now I give half of my possessions to the poor, and if I have cheated anybody out of anything, I will pay back four times the amount" (v. 8 NIV).

Grace walked in the front door, and selfishness scampered out the back. It changed his heart.

Is grace changing yours?

–Grace

DECEMBER 14

Miracles

Finally, brothers and sisters, whatever is true, whatever is noble, whatever is right, whatever is pure, whatever is lovely, whatever is admirable—if anything is excellent or praiseworthy—think about such things.

PHILIPPIANS 4:8 NIV

Miracles. Look for them and you'll find them.

Rebecca did. She has spent the last three years in pain. "On a scale of one to ten," the doctor explained, "she is a twelve every day." Rebecca's pancreas has shut down. After a dozen operations and changes in medication, no solution is in sight.

Pretty tough challenge. But Rebecca is a tough kid. She is ten years old. She has fudge-brown hair, eyes that sparkle, a weatherproof smile, and a book of miracles. She showed it to me.

It's a spiral notebook, edges weathered, adorned with crayoned flowers, stars, and an occasional clown. In the handwriting of a child, miracles:

"I slept all night last night."

"Daddy snuck a puppy into the hospital."

"Mommy is going to place a Christmas tree in the corner."

Her body is in revolt. Her parents are concerned. The doctors are confused. But Rebecca has made a decision. She is going to thank God for miracles. If Rebecca can find reasons to say thanks, can't I?

Can't you?

—Before Amen

DECEMBER 15 

Freely Given, Freely Give

My God shall supply all your need according
to His riches in glory by Christ Jesus.
PHILIPPIANS 4:19

God doesn't just love; he *lavishes* us with love (1 John 3:1 NIV). He doesn't dole out wisdom; he "gives generously to all without finding fault" (James 1:5 NIV). He is rich in "kindness, forbearance and patience" (Romans 2:4 NIV). His grace is "exceedingly abundant" (1 Timothy 1:14) and "indescribable" (2 Corinthians 9:14–15).

He overflowed the table of the prodigal with a banquet, the vats at the wedding with wine, and the boat of Peter with fish, twice. He healed all who sought health, taught all who wanted instruction, and saved all who accepted the gift of salvation.

God "supplies seed to the sower and bread for food" (2 Corinthians 9:10 NIV). The Greek verb for "supplies" (*epichoregeo*) pulls back the curtain on God's generosity. It combines "dance" (*choros*) with the verb "to lead" (*hegeomai*).[1] It literally means "to lead a dance." When God gives, he dances for joy. He strikes up the band and leads the giving parade. He loves to give.

He dispenses his goodness not with an eyedropper but with a fire hydrant. Your heart is a Dixie cup, and his grace is the Mediterranean Sea. You simply can't contain it all. So let it bubble over. Spill out. Pour forth. "Freely you have received, freely give" (Matthew 10:8 NIV).

–*Grace*

DECEMBER 16

His Grace

The Lord is my strength and my shield;
my heart trusts in him, and he helps me.
My heart leaps for joy,
and with my song I praise him.
PSALM 28:7 NIV

'Tis grace hath brought me safe thus far, and grace will lead me home."[2] When John Newton penned this promise, he did so out of personal experience. His greatest test came the day he buried his wife, Mary. He had loved her dearly and prayed his death would precede hers. But his prayer was not answered.

Yet God's grace proved sufficient. On the day she died Newton found strength to preach a Sunday sermon. The next day he visited church members, and later he officiated at his wife's funeral. He grieved but in his grief found God's provision. He later wrote, "The Lord, the all-sufficient God, speaks, and it is done. Let those who know Him, and trust Him, be of good courage. He can give them strength according to their day. He can increase their strength as their trials increase . . . and what He can do He has promised that He will do."[3]

Let God's grace dethrone your fears. Anxiety still comes, for certain. The globe still heats up; wars still flare up; the economy acts up. Disease, calamity, and trouble populate your world. But they don't control it! Grace does. God has embedded your life with a fleet of angels to meet your needs in his way at the right time. His grace will lead you home.

–Grace

A Prayer . . . of Wonder

For unto us a Child is born, unto us a Son is given; and the government will be upon His shoulder. And His name will be called Wonderful, Counselor, Mighty God, Everlasting Father, Prince of Peace.

ISAIAH 9:6

Dear Lord, it's impossible for me to fathom what it meant for you to take on human flesh and live as a man. Nevertheless, I believe in you. Help me to hope for even more—that one great day soon I'll see you and be changed forever! In Jesus' name, amen.

–In the Manger

DECEMBER 18

YOUR CHRISTMAS STORY

Now in the sixth month the angel Gabriel was sent by God to a city of Galilee named Nazareth, to a virgin betrothed to a man whose name was Joseph, of the house of David. The virgin's name was Mary.

LUKE 1:26–27

What if Joseph and Mary had shown up in furs with a chauffeur, bling-blinged and high-muckety-mucked? And what if God had decked out Bethlehem like Hollywood on Oscar night: red carpet, flashing lights, with angels interviewing the royal couple? "Mary, Mary, you look simply divine."

Had Jesus come with such whoop-de-do, we would have read the story and thought, *My, look how Jesus entered their world.*

But since he didn't, we can read the story and dream. *My, might Jesus be born in my world? My everyday world?*

Isn't that what you indwell? Not a holiday world. Or a red-letter-day world. No, you live an everyday life. You have bills to pay, beds to make, and grass to cut. Your face won't grace any magazine covers, and you aren't expecting a call from the White House. Congratulations. You qualify for a modern-day Christmas story. God enters the world through folks like you and comes on days like today.

So be alert . . . today just might be your Christmas story.

–*God's Story, Your Story*

The Gift

Thanks be to God for His indescribable gift!
2 CORINTHIANS 9:15

When a person gives a genuine gift, don't you cherish the presence of affection? The hand-knit sweater, the photo album from last summer, the personalized poem, the Lucado book. Such gifts convince you that someone planned, prepared, saved, searched. Last-minute decision? No, this gift was just for you.

Have you ever received such a gift? Yes, you have. Sorry to speak on your behalf, but I know the answer as I ask the question. You have been given a perfect personal gift. One just for you. "There has been born *for you* a Savior, who is Christ the Lord" (Luke 2:11 NASB, emphasis mine).

An angel spoke these words. Shepherds heard them first. But what the angel said to them, God says to anyone who will listen. "There has been born *for you* . . ." Jesus is the gift.

–*Grace*

DECEMBER 20

King More

"Do not store up for yourselves treasures on earth, where moths and vermin destroy, and where thieves break in and steal. But store up for yourselves treasures in heaven, where moths and vermin do not destroy, and where thieves do not break in and steal."

MATTHEW 6:19–20 NIV

Imagine you were living in the South during the Civil War and had accumulated large amounts of Confederate currency. Through a series of events you became convinced that the South was going to lose and your money would soon be worthless. What would you do? If you had any common sense, you would get rid of your Southern cents. You'd put every penny you could into the currency that is to come and prepare yourself for the end of the war.

Are you investing in the currency of heaven? The world economy is going down. Your wallet is full of soon-to-be-useless paper. The currency of this world will be worth nothing when you die or when Christ returns, both of which could happen at any moment. If you and I stockpile earthly treasures and not heavenly treasures, what does that say about where we put our trust?

Glory fills our lives to the degree that we trust God.

Whom do you trust? God or King More? King More is a rotten ruler. He never satisfies. He rusts. He rots. He loses his value. He goes out of style. For all the promises he makes, he cannot keep a single one. King More will break your heart.

But the King of kings? He will catch you every single time.

–*Glory Days*

DECEMBER 21 

A Part of You

Beloved, let us love one another, for love is of God; and everyone who loves is born of God and knows God. He who does not love does not know God, for God is love.

1 JOHN 4:7–8

Sarah sat alone. Her hands, freckled with age, rested in her lap. She wore her finest dress. Her nursing-home room spoke of springtime: daisies in the vase, a poinsettia blooming outside her window.

Sarah sat alone. "They came last Christmas," she said brightly (as if defending her family).

A thousand miles away a family played.

Sarah is not sick or ugly. She is not useless or decrepit. Sarah is simply old.

Our society has little room for the aged. People like Sarah come in scores. No one intentionally forgets them. Maybe that's why it is so painful. If there were a reason: a fight, a mistake, a dispute . . . But usually it's unintentional.

Unintentional rejection. It will kill Sarah; she'll die of loneliness. It doesn't matter how nice the convalescent home is; nurses and old folks don't replace a grandbaby's smile or a son's kiss.

Spend all your love on her now.
Forget not the hands, though spotted,
The hair, though thinning,
The eyes, though dim,
For they are a part of you.
And when they are gone, a part of you is gone.

–*On the Anvil*

DECEMBER 22

He Dwelt Among Us

The Word became flesh and dwelt among us,
and we beheld His glory, the glory as of the only
begotten of the Father, full of grace and truth.
JOHN 1:14

Astounding, this thought of heaven's fetus floating within the womb. Joseph and Mary didn't have the advantage we have: ultrasound. When Denalyn was pregnant, we took full advantage of the technology. The black-and-white image on the screen looked more like Doppler radar than a child. But with the help of the doctor, we were able to see the arms and hands and the pierced nose and prom dress . . . Wait, I'm confusing photos.

As the doctor moved the instrument around Denalyn's belly, he took inventory. "There's the head, the feet, the torso . . . Well, everything looks normal."

Mary's doctor would have made the same announcement. Jesus was an ordinary baby. There is nothing in the story to imply that he levitated over the manger or walked out of the stable. Just the opposite. He "dwelt among us" (John 1:14). John's word for *dwelt* traces its origin to *tabernacle* or *tent*. Jesus did not separate himself from his creation; he pitched his tent in the neighborhood.

The Word of God entered the world with the cry of a baby. Jesus, the Maker of the universe, the one who invented time and created breath, was born into a family too humble to swing a bed for a pregnant mom-to-be.

He dwelt among us. He longs to dwell in you.

–*God's Story, Your Story*

In the Beginning

In the beginning was the Word, and the Word was with God, and the Word was God. He was with God in the beginning.

JOHN 1:1–2 NIV

Step into the stable, and cradle in your arms the infant Jesus, still moist from the womb, just wrapped in the rags. Run a finger across his chubby cheek, and listen as one who knew him well puts lyrics to the event:

"In the beginning was the Word" (John 1:1).

The words "In the beginning" take us to the beginning. "In the beginning God created the heavens and the earth" (Genesis 1:1). The baby Mary held was connected to the dawn of time. He saw the first ray of sunlight and heard the first crash of a wave. The baby was born, but the Word never was.

"All things were made through him" (1 Corinthians 8:6 NCV). Not *by* him, but *through* him. Jesus didn't fashion the world out of raw material he found. He created all things out of nothing.

Jesus: the Genesis Word, "the firstborn over all creation" (Colossians 1:15). He is the "one Lord, Jesus Christ, through whom all things were created, and through whom we live" (1 Corinthians 8:6 NLT).

And then, what no theologian conceived, what no rabbi dared to dream, God did. "The Word became flesh" (John 1:14). The Artist became oil on his own palette. The Potter melted into the mud on his own wheel. God became an embryo in the belly of a village girl. Christ in Mary. God in Christ.

–*God's Story, Your Story*

DECEMBER 24

A Prayer . . . to Open Your Heart

"A Samaritan, as he traveled, came where the man was; and when he saw him, he took pity on him. He went to him and bandaged his wounds, pouring on oil and wine. Then he put the man on his own donkey, brought him to an inn and took care of him."

LUKE 10:33–34 NIV

Heavenly Father, every breath is a gift from your hand. Even so, I confess that sometimes my own hand remains tightly closed when I encounter the needs of others. Please open both my hand and my heart that I might learn to open my door to others. As you help me open my heart and hand, O Lord, I ask that you also prompt me to open my life to those who need a taste of your love and bounty. In Jesus' name I pray, amen.

–*Outlive Your Life*

DECEMBER 25

The Giving of Gifts

God has given each of you a gift from his great variety of spiritual gifts. Use them well to serve one another.

1 PETER 4:10 NLT

Jesus distributes gifts that are unique to each and every one of us. The apostle Paul explained it this way: "[God] has given each one of us a special gift through the generosity of Christ. That is why the Scriptures say, 'When he ascended to the heights, he led a crowd of captives and gave gifts to his people'" (Ephesians 4:7–8 NLT). The apostle was using the metaphor of a victorious king. It was common in Paul's day for the conquering monarch to return to his palace with prisoners and treasures in tow. He celebrated his conquest by giving gifts to his people.

So did Jesus. Having defeated sin and death on the cross, he ascended to heaven, took his rightful place at the right hand of God, and "gave gifts to his people."

What a delightful thought! Jesus, eternally crowned, distributing abilities and skills.

And don't think for one moment that God skipped you in the gift-giving line. "God has given *each one of us* a special gift." Thank God for your gift. And then use it to please him.

–*Glory Days*

DECEMBER 26

How Long Has It Been?

He who sows sparingly will also reap sparingly, and he who sows bountifully will also reap bountifully. So let each one give as he purposes in his heart, not grudgingly or of necessity; for God loves a cheerful giver.

2 CORINTHIANS 9:6–7

The grace-given give grace.

Is grace happening to you?

How long has it been since your generosity stunned someone? Since someone objected, "No, really, this is too generous"? If it has been a while, reconsider God's extravagant grace. "Forget not all his benefits, who forgives all your iniquity" (Psalm 103:2–3 RSV).

Let grace unscrooge your heart. "Grow in the grace and knowledge of our Lord and Savior Jesus Christ" (2 Peter 3:18). As you do, you will find that grace changes lives—your own most of all.

–Grace

Hypocrisy

"Be especially careful when you are trying to be good so that you don't make a performance out of it. It might be good theater, but the God who made you won't be applauding."

MATTHEW 6:1 MSG

H*ypocrisy.* When Jesus used that word, people ducked for cover. Consider how he lambasted the Pharisees with this blowtorch: "All their works they do to be seen by men. . . . But woe to you, scribes and Pharisees, hypocrites!" (Matthew 23:5, 13).

This is the working definition of *hypocrisy*: "to be seen by men." Jesus did not say, "Do not do good works." Nor did he instruct, "Do not let your works be seen." We must do good works, and some works, such as benevolence or teaching, must be seen in order to have an impact. So let's be clear. To do a good thing is a good thing. To do good to be seen is not. Here's why: hypocrisy turns people away from God.

When God-hungry souls walk into a congregation of wannabe superstars, what happens? When God seekers see singers strut like Las Vegas entertainers . . . when they hear the preacher play to the crowd and exclude God, don't think for a second that God approves.

Let's take hypocrisy as seriously as God does. How can we?

1. *Expect no credit for good deeds.*
2. *Give financial gifts in secret.*
3. *Don't fake spirituality.*

Bottom line: don't make a theater production out of your faith.

—*Outlive Your Life*

DECEMBER 28

Simple Deeds

Whoever is kind to the poor lends to the LORD,
and he will reward them for what they have done.
PROVERBS 19:17 NIV

There are many reasons to help people in need.

But for the Christian, none is higher than this: when we love those in need, we are loving Jesus. It is a message that Jesus made crystal clear: when we love them, we love him.

This is the theme of his final sermon. The message he saved until last. He must want this point imprinted on our conscience. The last day, the great Day of Judgment. On that day Jesus will issue an irresistible command. All will come. The whole heavenly universe will witness the event. A staggering denouement. Jesus at some point will "separate them one from another, as a shepherd divides his sheep from the goats" (Matthew 25:32).

How does Jesus separate the people?

Jesus gives the answer. The sign of the saved is their concern for those in need. Compassion does not save us. Salvation is the work of Christ. Compassion is the consequence of salvation.

The sheep will react with a sincere question: When? When did we feed, visit, clothe, or comfort you (vv. 34–39)?

Jesus will recount, one by one, all the acts of kindness. Every deed done to improve the lot of another person. Even the small ones. The works of mercy are simple deeds. And yet in these simple deeds, we serve Jesus. Astounding, this truth: we serve Christ by serving needy people.

–*Outlive Your Life*

NOT FOR SALE

My sacrifice, O God, is a broken spirit; a broken and contrite heart you, God, will not despise.
PSALM 51:17 NIV

"Lord," I said, "I want to be your man, not my own.
So to you I give my money, my car—even my home."

Then, smug and content, I relaxed with a smile
And whispered to God, "I bet it's been a while
Since anyone has given so much—so freely?"
His answer surprised me. He replied, "Not really."

"Not a day has gone by since the beginning of time,
That someone hasn't offered meager nickels and dimes,
Golden altars and crosses, contributions and penance,
Stone monuments and steeples; but why not repentance?

"Just give me a tear—a heart ready to mold.
And I'll give you a mission, a message so bold—
That a fire will be stirred where there was only death,
And your heart will be flamed by my life and my breath."

I stuck my hands in my pockets and kicked at the dirt.
It's tough to be corrected (I guess my feelings were hurt).
But it was worth the struggle to realize the thought
That the Cross isn't for sale and Christ's blood can't be bought.

–On the Anvil

DECEMBER 30

Believe

"Do not be afraid; only believe."

MARK 5:36

Take a pen and paper and get alone. Go where it's quiet, where you can think. Take your pen in your hand and—are you ready?—write down what you believe. Not what you think or hope or speculate but what you *believe*. Put on paper those bedrock convictions that are worth building a life on, that are worth giving a life for.

Now look at your list. Analyze it. What do you think? Is your foundation solid enough to stand on? If not, be patient. Give yourself some time to grow.

Don't throw that list away. Put your list someplace where you'll always have it. In your wallet, your purse . . . somewhere convenient.

The next time you're intimidated by Mr. Know-It-All or by Miss Have-It-All, the next time your self-image limps out the door, pull out your list. Take a long look at it. Have any of your undeniables been threatened? Has your foundation been attacked?

Usually not. Here's the point: If you know what you believe (I mean *really* know it), if you know what's important and what's trivial, then you won't be tied down by all the little Lilliputians in the world.

I *really* believe that.

–*On the Anvil*

DECEMBER 31

A PRAYER . . . TO TRANSFORM

Test me, LORD, and try me,
examine my heart and my mind;
for I have always been mindful of your unfailing love
and have lived in reliance on your faithfulness.
PSALM 26:2–3 NIV

O Lord, where did I see you yesterday . . . and didn't recognize you? Where will I encounter you today . . . and fail to identify you? O my Father, give me eyes to see, a heart to respond, and hands and feet to serve you wherever you encounter me! Transform me, Lord, by your Spirit into a servant of Christ, who delights to meet the needs of those around me. Make me a billboard of your grace, a living advertisement for the riches of your compassion. I long to hear you say to me one day, "Well done, good and faithful servant." And I pray that today I would be that faithful servant who does well at doing good. In Jesus' name I pray, amen.

–*Outlive Your Life*

Notes

JANUARY

1. Adapted from Joel Osteen, *Every Day a Friday: How to Be Happier 7 Days a Week* (New York: Faith Words, 2011), 131–32.

FEBRARY

1. W. E. Vine, *Vine's Expository Dictionary of New Testament Words: A Comprehensive Dictionary of the Original Greek Words with Their Precise Meanings for English Readers* (McLean, VA: MacDonald Publishing, n.d.), 554.
2. James Strong, *New Strong's Exhaustive Concordance* (Nashville: Thomas Nelson, 1996), s.v. "Compassion."
3. Todd and Tara Storch, parents of Taylor and founders of Taylor's Gift Foundation (www.TaylorsGift.org), tell the ongoing story of their journey of regifting life, renewing health, and restoring families in their book *Taylor's Gift: A Courageous Story of Life, Loss, and Unexpected Blessings* (with Jennifer Schuchmann, Grand Rapids, MI: Revell, a division of Baker Publishing Group, 2013).
4. "Conquest Confusion at Yale," Bryant G. Wood, BibleArcheology.org, November 20, 2012, www.biblearchaeology.org/post/2012/11/20/Conquest-Confusion-at-Yale.aspx#Article. Also see, Ronald B. Allen, "The Land of Israel," in *Israel: The Land and the People: An Evangelical Affirmation of God's Promises*, ed. H. Wayne House (Grand Rapids, MI: Kregel Publications, 1998), 17–18, 24.
5. Cited in Richard Mayhue, *Unmasking Satan: Understanding Satan's Battle Plan and Biblical Strategies for Fighting Back* (Grand Rapids, MI: Kregel, 2001), 22.

MARCH

1. Sam Nunn, "Intellectual Honesty, Moral and Ethical Behavior; We Must Decide What Is Important" (speech, National Prayer Breakfast, Washington, D.C., February 1, 1996).
2. Cited in John Gilmore, *Probing Heaven* (Grand Rapids: Baker, 1989), 65.

APRIL

1. Art Miller, *The Power of Uniqueness* (Grand Rapids, MI: Zondervan, 1999), 93.

MAY

1. Gene Weingarten, "Pearls before Breakfast," *Washington Post*, April 8, 2007, www.washingpost.com/wp-dyn/content/article/2007/04/04/AR2007040401721.html.

JULY

1. Greg Pruett, *Extreme Prayer: The Impossible Prayers God Promises to Answer* (Carol Stream, IL: Tyndale House, 2014), 5.
2. Ibid., 69.
3. "Price of Success: Will the Recycled Orchestra Last?" CBSNews.com, November 17, 2013, www.cbsnews.com/news/price-of-success-will-the-recycled-orchestra-last/?.
4. Joachim Jeremias, *The Prayers of Jesus* (London: SCM Press, 1967), 57.
5. Adapted from a prayer written for America Prays, a national prayer vigil on September 15, 2001.

AUGUST

1. Sean Alfano, "Teens Arrested after Posting YouTube Video of Beating 13-Year-Old Boy and Hanging Him from a Tree," *New York Daily News*, February 1, 2011, www.nydailynews.com/news/national/teens-arrested-posting-youtube-video-beating-13-year-old-boy-hanging-tree-article-1.137868. See also Rick Reilly, "Eagles over Wolves in a Rout," ESPN.com, last modified February 15, 2011, http://sports.espn.go. com/espn/news/story?id=6120346.
2. "Global Scripture Access," United Bible Societies, www.unitedbiblesocieties.org/what-we-do/translation/global-scripture-access/.
3. "353 Prophecies Fulfilled in Jesus Christ," AccordingtotheScriptures.org, www.accordingtothescriptures.org/prophecy/353prophecies.html.
4. If you want to explore in detail your "you-niqueness" and how to discern it, see my book *Cure for the Common Life: Living in Your Sweet Spot* (Nashville: Thomas Nelson, 2005).

SEPTEMBER

1. Used with permission.
2. Alfred Edersheim, *The Life and Times of Jesus the Messiah*, unabr. ed. (Peabody, MA: Hendrickson Publishers, Inc., 1993), 62–3.

3. My late friend Tim Hansel said something similar in his book *You Gotta Keep Dancin'* (Elgin, IL: David C. Cook Publishing Co., 1985), 107.
4. Donald G. Bloesch, *The Struggle of Prayer* (Colorado Springs: Helmers and Howard, 1988), 79.
5. E. M. Bounds, *The Complete Works of E. M. Bounds on Prayer* (Grand Rapids, MI: Baker Book House, 1990), 311–12.
6. Joshua 2:1; 6:17; 6:25; Hebrews 11:31; James 2:25.

OCTOBER

1. In many ways Ephesians is the New Testament counterpart to the book of Joshua.
2. Dale Ralph Davis, *Joshua: No Falling Words* (Fearn, Scotland: Christian Focus Publications, 2000), 19.
3. Frederick Dale Bruner, *Matthew: A Commentary by Frederick Dale Bruner*, vol. 1, *The Christbook: Matthew 1–12* (Dallas: Word, 1987), 234.

NOVEMBER

1. C. S. Lewis, *Yours, Jack: Spiritual Direction from C. S. Lewis* (New York: HarperCollins, 2008), 152.
2. Leigh Montville, "Wide and to the Right: The Kick That Will Forever Haunt Scott Norwood," SI.com, last modified September 21, 2011, http://sportsillustrated.cnn.com/2011/writers/painful_moments_in_sports/09/09/Scott.Norwood.Super.Bowl/.
3. Telephone interview with Jo Anne Lyon, conducted by David Drury, June 23, 2009.

DECEMBER

1. Eugene Peterson, *Traveling Light: Modern Meditations on St. Paul's Letter of Freedom* (Colorado Springs: Helmers and Howard, 1988), 91.
2. John Newton, "Amazing Grace," HymnSite.com, www.hymnsite.com/lyrics/umh378.sht.
3. Josiah Bull, *"But Now I See": The Life of John Newton* (Carlisle, PA: Banner of Truth Trust, 1998), 304, quoted in David Jeremiah, *Captured by Grace: No One Is Beyond the Reach of a Loving God* (Nashville: Thomas Nelson, 2006), 143.

Topical Index

Scripture Index

REFERENCE FOLLOWED BY PAGE NUMBER(S)

About the Author

Since entering the ministry in 1978, Max Lucado has served churches in Miami, Florida; Rio de Janeiro, Brazil; and San Antonio, Texas. He currently serves as Teaching Minister of Oak Hills Church in San Antonio. He is America's bestselling inspirational author with more than 130 million books in print.

Notes

Notes

NOTES